SOUND
the
ALARM

KELLEY ✛ VARNER

The Apocalyptic Message
from the Book of Joel

SOUND
the
ALARM

Destiny Image® Publishers, Inc.

P.O. Box 310

Shippensburg, PA 17257-0310

"We Publish the Prophets"

ISBN 0-7684-2272-8

For Worldwide Distribution

Printed in the U.S.A.

This book and all other Destiny Image, Revival Press, MercyPlace, Fresh Bread, Destiny Image Fiction, and Treasure House books are available at Christian bookstores and distributors worldwide.

1 2 3 4 5 6 7 8 9 10 / 10 09 08 07 06 05

For a U.S. bookstore nearest you, call
1-800-722-6774.

For more information on foreign distributors, call
717-532-3040.

Or reach us on the Internet:
www.destinyimage.com

DEDICATION

I dedicate this volume to all those apprehended for the "high calling" of God to stand on Mount Zion with Jesus the Lamb (Phil. 3:14; Rev. 14:1), and who have faithfully and passionately pursued that heavenly calling and vision (Acts 26:19; Heb. 3:1).

I especially salute those courageous apostles and prophets, male and female, who are fearlessly and uncompromisingly lifting up their voice like a trumpet (Isa. 58:1) to declare "all the counsel (will and purpose) of God" (Acts 20:27).

I also dedicate this book to all my sons and my grandsons, my daughters and my grand daughters, a brand new breed of young men and women who are hearing about Zion and the "high calling" for the first time. Welcome to my world!

ACKNOWLEDGMENTS

To apostle Stephen Everett, for his enduring friendship and apostolic input into my life, my family, and my local church. His classic book, *The Sound That Changed Everything*, is must reading. This scholarly treatise ably sets forth the foundational biblical theology for the current apostolic reformation.

To pastors Wendall Ward and Lottie LaBelle, part of our local apostolic team. You are my companions in tribulation and in the Kingdom and patience of Jesus Christ (Rev. 1:9). Thank you for your kind words in the Foreword of this book.

To the Holy Spirit, my Teacher, who taught me the Book of Joel.

TABLE OF CONTENTS

PREFACE

The material for this manuscript had lain dormant from the days of our Summer Conference in June of 2003 until the time I was sovereignly awakened by the Holy Spirit early Wednesday, April 7, 2004, with this God-given mandate:

"It is time to release this message to My people."

Why the delay?

I humbly ask that you forgive my candor. I am neither embarrassed nor ashamed to openly share my weaknesses with my family at large. Perhaps "we can comfort those in any trouble with the comfort we ourselves have received from God" (2 Cor. 1:4, NIV).

The three-year time period from March of 2001 until March of 2004 marked the most difficult days of my personal and ministerial life. My whole man—spirit, soul, and body—was purged with the fires of the deep dealings of our Father.

Those three years were, as the saying goes, "something else!" Doubt, despair, and depression are not usually found in my vocabulary. But the fiery trials that I, my family, and my local church went through literally drained me—spiritually, emotionally, and physically.

Come, and let us return unto the Lord: for He hath torn, and He will heal us; He hath smitten, and He will bind us up. After two days will He revive us: in the third day He will raise us up, and we shall live in His sight (Hos. 6:1-2).

Thankfully, "the Father of mercies and the God of all comfort" (2 Cor. 1:3) began to raise us up! He sent one of His prophets to encourage my heart. His servant's anointed words ministered deeply to my innermost being, seeping down through the jagged crevices of my wounded spirit like warm oil.

The Lord said to me:[1] *"I declare to you in the Name of Jesus, servant of God, this shall be the year of your resurrection...And I declare to you that the four winds of Heaven shall begin to blow upon your House, and your words shall reach the north, and the south, and the east, and the west, and even unto the nations it shall go...."*

Most leaders are afraid to preach the whole counsel of God. They draw back from the ascended life, but (as I will re-emphasize throughout this writing) there *is* a "high calling." Zion constitutes the highest place in the heavenlies and it is to be manifestly expressed as a people in the earth, as His corporate Overcomer. To His elect I boldly prophesy, "Arise, army of God. Our time has come!"

Summer Conference 2003

June is always a special month here at Praise Tabernacle. Beginning the second Wednesday of the month, God's people from several states and nations gather here for our annual Summer Conference.

The June 11-15, 2003 Summer Conference was a landmark for this ministry. God raised the bar and brought us back to the original vision. Apostle Stephen Everett was our evening speaker and he imparted the paradigm of his classic book, *The Sound That Changed Everything.*[2]

During the morning sessions, I taught the Old Testament Book of Joel, setting forth the theme, "Blow the Trumpet in Zion." Those messages ignited the original God-given commission to write this book.[3]

I had earlier prepared the congregation for the conference by preaching a series of four messages entitled, "Awake, O Zion." They now comprise Chapters Two through Five of this manuscript[4] and lay the foundation for our study of Joel.

Chapters Two and Three explain what it means for Zion to "awake." Chapters Four and Five emphasize and underscore the biblical revelation of "Zion"—the *place* and the *people* of the high calling.

My Spirit-directed purpose in that conference was simple and singular: to bring the people back to the purity and power of the real

Kingdom message (I first heard that level of "present truth" fearlessly proclaimed by apostles and prophets in the summer of 1969).

In our conference morning sessions, I boldly articulated the full apostolic weight of our "high calling" up to Zion. These truths began to be re-established in the Latter Rain Revival of 1948 and constitute the restoration of the true "apostles' doctrine" (Acts 2:42).

> *Blow ye the trumpet in Zion, and sound an alarm in My holy mountain: let all the inhabitants of the land tremble: for the day of the Lord cometh, for it is nigh at hand* (Joel 2:1).

As He did in June of 2003, may God use this in-depth exegesis of the Book of Joel to raise the standard, and to be a righteous plumb line of His proceeding Word (Matt. 4:4). I now lift my voice with the ancient prophet to bring us back to our unfeigned faith, the singleness and simplicity of a pure Christ-centered gospel.

God has awakened and stirred my spirit. I will never again go back to being "lukewarm" (Rev. 3:16). My passion is returning. Real prophets are not intimidated by controversy or the faces of men (Jer. 1:8,17). Such as I have and am, I give to you now in Jesus' name.

Those of us who have heard His voice out of Zion have *become* His corporate trumpet in the earth. For this cause this book lies before you. I am not afraid or ashamed to lift up my voice, to blow the trumpet in Zion, to "sound the alarm" in His holy mountain!

Dr. Kelley Varner
Praise Tabernacle Ministries
Richlands, North Carolina

ENDNOTES

1. The complete prophecy given to me by Pastor William Hinn, Resurrection Life Center Intl., (Phone 714-730-5555, E-mail rlcichurch@msn.com) is found in Appendix A at the end of this volume.

2. Steve and Ann Everett are two of my dearest and closest friends. Steve grew up in the Lord in Deliverance Temple in Jacksonville, N.C., under his spiritual father, the late Apostle L. O. Sanders. I have known the Everetts for over 25 years, and have traveled with Steve nationally and internationally since the 1980s. You can now order *The Sound That Changed Everything* for $12 (plus $4 postage). Contact Stephen Everett, Present Truth Ministries, 3227 SW 1st Ave,

Cape Coral, FL 33914; phone 239.541.7743 or 239.542.2488; or email: NewC
Man@aol.com

3. You will want to hear the original messages that inspired this book. The
four audio tapes of me teaching the Book of Joel, "Blow the Trumpet in Zion,"
are available for an offering of $17 (plus $4 postage). The three videos are $45
(plus $5 postage). Write to Praise Tabernacle, P.O. Box 785, Richlands, NC 28574
or call 910.324.5026 to order.

4. These four messages are also available through our church office. The
four-tape album, "Awake, O Zion" is $17 (plus $4 postage). The four videos are
$60 (plus 15% postage), or $15 each (plus $4 postage). I encourage you to order
these additional resources to fully grasp the depth of this message.

FOREWORD

Every dimension of present truth requires a trumpet: a clear prophetic voice among the people of God that articulates His heart. One such voice is Kelley Varner. His latest book, *Sound the Alarm,* presents to us a powerful apostolic plea to return to the "high calling" of God (Phil. 3:14).

In these pages you will encounter the heart of an apostolic father and the voice of a true prophet. Both aspects of this man's ministry have been tempered by the deep dealings of God and a renewed passion for the purity of the gospel of the Kingdom.

This message will be met with many reactions. However, I appeal to you at the outset: be as the noble Bereans, "for they received the message with great eagerness and examined the Scriptures every day to see if what Paul said was true" (Acts 17:11, NIV).

I am proud to count this man as my friend and myself as one of his partners in ministry. My earnest prayer for all of us who read this book is that we will "hear what the Spirit is saying to the Church," and come forth with a renewed passion for the purity of the gospel and a zealous pursuit of the "high calling" of God!

Wendall Strother Ward, Jr.
Praise Tabernacle Ministries
Richlands, North Carolina

Much of the contemporary church world has been trapped in a playpen of religious traditions, which has made the Word of God of no effect (Mk. 7:13). These manmade teachings have crippled God's people. Immature babes with no teeth cannot appropriate the Word of "present truth" (2 Pet. 1:12) that grows them up into mature sons.

I am thankful for literary prophets like Dr. Kelley Varner who dare to blow the trumpet of truth, to awaken Zion to the original purpose and call of God, "persuading them concerning Jesus" (Acts 28:23).

Sound the Alarm, a passionate word from the Book of Joel, is a clarion call to gather a mighty army, equipping them with spiritual weapons of mass destruction, and awakening them to who they have always been in Christ.

I pray that the penned words of these pages will be a light unto the path of every reader, that each of you might be drawn out of all darkness and into the marvelous light of His truth.

I count it a great honor to stand side by side with Dr. Kelley Varner as we join with the many others who are hearing Zion's trumpet and following on to know the Lord.

Lottie LaBelle
Praise Tabernacle Ministries
Richlands, North Carolina

CHAPTER ONE

INTRODUCTION: THE HIGH CALLING

The "high calling" of God has burned in my heart from early childhood. I have always sensed His sovereign hand upon my life. Though steeped in sin and religious confusion for my first 17 years, I was always different from others, and never seemed to fit in. His "high calling" harnessed me to His predetermined purpose. The abundance of His mercy and grace restrained and protected me early on from folly and harm.

This heavenly summons, this upward drawing by the Holy Spirit to the top of Mount Zion, is clearly and persuasively articulated by the apostle Paul in Philippians 3:7-11 (AMP):

> But whatever former things I had that might have been gains to me, I have come to consider as (one combined) loss for Christ's sake.

> Yes, furthermore I count everything as loss compared to the possession of the priceless privilege—the overwhelming preciousness, the surpassing worth and supreme advantage—of knowing Christ Jesus my Lord, and of progressively becoming more deeply and intimately acquainted with Him, of perceiving and recognizing and understanding Him more fully and clearly. For His sake I have lost everything and consider it all to be mere rubbish (refuse, dregs), in order that I may win (gain) Christ, the Anointed One.

> And that I may (actually) be found and known as in Him, not having any (self-achieved) righteousness that can be called my own,

based on my obedience to the Law's demands...but possessing that [genuine righteousness] which comes through faith in Christ....

[For my determined purpose is] that I may know Him—that I may progressively become more deeply and intimately acquainted with Him, perceiving and recognizing and understanding (the wonders of His Person) more strongly and more clearly. And that I in the same way come to know the power outflowing from His resurrection [which it exerts over believers]; and that I may so share His sufferings as to be continually transformed [in spirit into His likeness even] to His death, [in the hope]

That if possible I may attain to the [spiritual and moral] resurrection [that lifts me] out from among the dead [even while in the body].

The Bible prophesies about a chosen generation of overcoming men and women who will, in the words of the same apostle, "not all sleep (die)" (1 Cor. 15:51). The ultimate outworking of Christ's corporate anointing will empower the sons of Zion to put the "last enemy" of death under their feet (1 Cor. 15:26).

The Body of Christ has yet to attain this awesome foreordained purpose, yet we dare (as did the early apostles) to herald this "high calling" as a significant precept in the paradigm of "present truth" (2 Pet. 1:12). Paul continues in Philippians 3:12-14 (AMP):

Not that I have now attained [this ideal] or am already made perfect, but I press on to lay hold of (grasp) and make my own, that for which Christ Jesus, the Messiah, has laid hold of me and made me His own.

I do not consider, brethren, that I have captured and made it my own [yet]; but one thing I do[1]—it is my one aspiration: forgetting what lies behind and straining forward to what lies ahead,

I press on toward the goal to win the [supreme and heavenly] prize to which God in Christ Jesus is calling us upward.

The word for "prize" in this last verse is *brabeion* (Strong's #1017), and it means, "an award (of arbitration), (specially) a prize to the victor in the public games." It is akin to *brabeus* (umpire) and *brabeuo* (to decide, arbitrate). *Brabeion* is only used in one other reference. To all those who are called up to Zion—finish strong!

Know ye not that they which run in a race run all, but one receiveth the prize? So run, that ye may obtain (1 Cor. 9:24).

God Hates a Mixture

As Deuteronomy 22:9-11 (NIV) indicates, God hates a mixture:

Do not plant two kinds of seed in your vineyard; if you do, not only the crops you plant but also the fruit of the vineyard will be defiled.

Do not plow with an ox and a donkey yoked together.

Do not wear clothes of wool and linen woven together.

Doctrinally and politically, the holy seed, the unadulterated Word of the Kingdom, has been contaminated, jumbled and muddied by religious tradition!

Throughout America, most of what is coined and passed off as being "Kingdom" is but a dualistic, sin-conscious Pentecostal theology with a Kingdom veneer. "Third day" truths are being parroted with a "second day" application primarily geared to meeting the needs of people, rather than expressing the pure dynamics of a Christ-centered paradigm.

Moreover, real apostles are weary with the "bishop" epidemic. Too many men and women are craving titles and visibility, rather than serving and leading by example. The Scriptures reveal that foundational ministries are essentially under, not over, the people of God. Like the dew of Eden and Hermon (Gen. 2:6; Ps. 133:3), apostles and prophets are to operate with an anointing that flows from the bottom up more than it does from the top down.

Wise, fatherly master-builders are more interested in providing an inheritance for their spiritual children than they are for their sons and daughters to give them money and prestige.

Sensible young men and women refuse to play the game of "rent-a-father," the current futility of long-distance "relationships" without the reality of biblical discipleship. No relationship can be legislated; it must be birthed of and by the Holy Spirit, mediated by Jesus Himself.[2] All else is political and self-serving, just another fad that will soon pass away among those who always cry for "What's hot? What's not?"

This principle of mixture is best illustrated with one word: *Babylon!*

And they said one to another, Go to, let us make brick, and burn them throughly. And they had brick for stone, and slime had they for morter.

And they said, Go to, let us build us a city and a tower, whose top may reach unto heaven; and let us make us a name... (Gen. 11:3-4).

Babylon, the prototype of pagan idolatry, was an ancient walled city between the Tigris and Euphrates Rivers, the capital of the Babylonian Empire. Babylon means "confusion." Its root word means "mixed." "Babel" has also been translated as, "gate of Bel, court of Baal, chaos, vanity, nothingness." In the ancient language of that time, Babylon also meant "the gate of God." Thus, the word Babylon signifies *religious confusion.*

God is not the Author of "confusion" (1 Cor. 14:33). His nature is not marked by "instability, disorder, disturbance, restlessness." This word is also rendered in the King James Version as "commotion, tumult" (Lk. 21:9; 2 Cor. 6:5; 12:20). The religious systems of contemporary "Babylon" are marked by politics and power struggles. This envying and strife is the fountain of "confusion" and every evil work. In a "Babylonian" church, war is a way of life.

Like Absalom (2 Sam. 18:18), David's arrogant son, rebellious men and women love the sound of their own names. They vainly fashion their worldly political and religious monuments from the brick and slime of their own inflated egos and covert insecurities. They would rather be stamped with their own moniker than be marked by the name of the Lord (Rev. 14:1). Unfortunately, "Babylon" is ruled by men and women who value their "image" above integrity.

Tradition

But in vain they do worship Me, teaching for doctrines the commandments of men... (Matt. 15:9).

Making the word of God of none effect (deprived of force; invalid) *through your tradition, which ye have delivered...* (Mark. 7:13).

The only thing more powerful than the Word of God is tradition!

The Greek word for "tradition" is *paradosis* (Strong's #3862), and it means, "transmission, a handing down or on; giving up, a giving over which is done by word of mouth or in writing, that is, tradition by instruction, narrative, or precept."[3]

From the decline of the Early Church, throughout the gross darkness (ignorance) of the Middle Ages, and from the days of Martin Luther (1517) to the present, the Body of Christ, His righteous remnant, has been plagued with the traditions of religious mixture.

In the first chapter of the Book of Joel, an invading swarm of locusts had completely devastated the land of Judah. Their blight, accompanied by drought and famine, had withered every aspect of Judah's national existence—economically, socially, and religiously.

And I will restore to you the years that the locust hath eaten...
(Joel 2:25).

What overwhelmed and ravaged the Church, carrying her into the Babylonian captivity of the Dark Ages? What necessitated the restoration of the years of truth from the days of Luther until now? The "locusts" of tradition! These destructive hordes provide an awful picture of the idolatrous, humanistic distortion of two key dynamics:

First, man-made ideas present another image instead of the image of Christ. They present another Jesus. Second, religious tradition preaches another gospel instead of the gospel of the Kingdom.

In whom the god of this world hath blinded the minds of them which believe not, lest the light of the glorious gospel of Christ, who is the image of God, should shine unto them (2 Cor. 4:4).

But I am afraid that just as Eve was deceived by the serpent's cunning, your minds may somehow be led astray from your sincere and pure devotion to Christ. For if someone comes to you and preaches a Jesus other than the Jesus we (the apostles) *preached, or if you receive a different spirit from the one you received, or a different gospel from the one you accepted, you put up with it easily enough* (2 Cor. 11:3-4, NIV).

The teachings of men set forth another or different "image," a Jesus other than the One the apostles preached.

Many of my previous writings declare this basic truth: "Christ" is the image of God, and "antichrist" (something or someone instead of Christ) is any other image! Anything outside of the Christ nature, the new nature of the new creation man (2 Cor. 5:17), is a lying vanity.

There are only two kinds of "men" on the planet: Christ and Adam, beauty and the beast!

> *I marvel that ye are so soon removed* (to transpose or transfer, to change sides) *from Him that called you into the grace of Christ unto another* (different) *gospel:*

> *Which is not another; but there be some that trouble* (stir, agitate) *you, and would pervert* (corrupt) *the gospel of Christ.*

> *But though we, or an angel from heaven, preach any other gospel unto you than that which we* (the apostles) *have preached unto you, let him be accursed* (anathema) (Gal. 1:6-8).

Furthermore, religious Babylon preaches "another gospel" than that proclaimed by Paul and his brethren.

Brothers and sisters, it is time to sound the alarm, to repent of this scriptural negligence. We must forsake the popularity of money-making, "man-centered Christianity," and return at once to the simplicity of the "in Christ" message, the Christ-centered paradigm.

Away with the cowardice of being "politically correct," spiritually speaking! Let us burn the soft pews of seeker-sensitive comfortableness and run to the rugged Pauline altar of full surrender, of being completely crucified with Christ. The Day of the Lord has dawned. Every city and tower that men have built in His name that He did not tell them to build will be burned with fire!

The Gospel of the Kingdom

The gospel of the Kingdom is *the* gospel!

> *In those days came John the Baptist, preaching in the wilderness of Judaea, And saying, Repent ye: for the kingdom of heaven is at hand* (Matt. 3:1-2).

> *And Jesus went about all Galilee, teaching in their synagogues, and preaching the gospel of the kingdom, and healing all manner of sickness and all manner of disease among the people* (See Matthew 4:23 and compare with Matthew 9:35; 24:14; Mark 1:14-15).

The Gospel that John and Jesus preached was "the gospel (good news) of the Kingdom"!

And when they (the chief leaders of the Jews) *had appointed him* (Paul) *a day, there came many to him into his lodging; to whom he expounded* (to place out, declare, expose, set forth) *and testified* (earnestly attested and affirmed) *the kingdom of God, persuading them concerning Jesus...* (Acts 28:23).

The apostle Paul wrote half of the New Testament. We must shamelessly proclaim the gospel that he and the other early apostles preached, the gospel of the Kingdom!

This is the Kingdom message of "excellent" or "threefold things" (Prov. 22:20-21), proclaiming a complete deliverance, a full salvation. This gospel alone will "persuade" (convince) the nations "concerning Jesus," our Savior, our Baptizer, and our King (Luke 2:11; Acts 2:36).

Three times in a year shall all thy males appear before the Lord thy God in the place which he shall choose; in the feast of unleavened bread (Passover), *and in the feast of weeks* (Pentecost), *and in the feast of tabernacles...* (Deut. 16:16).

Moses' church in the wilderness (Acts 7:38) was commanded to keep all three major Feasts of Jehovah. Passover took place in the first month, Pentecost was observed in the third month, and Tabernacles was celebrated in the seventh month. The high calling of God into the Most Holy Place and up to the heights of Zion includes all three dimensions of grace. Once again we must heed the angelic admonition of the Book of Acts:

Go, stand and speak in the temple to the people all the words of this life (Acts 5:20).

The gospel of the Kingdom proclaims all three dimensions of truth, and embraces a *Third Reformation!*

The First Reformation, ushered in by Martin Luther and others during the 16th Century, was historic and life changing. Throughout Europe, many were martyred by the self-appointed guardians of worn-out religious systems for their courageous, righteous stand for the foundational truth of justification by faith, and faith alone.

The Second Reformation was experienced by a group of people led by William Seymour and Charles Parham at Azusa Street in Los Angeles at the turn of the 20th Century. They tasted the reality of a genuine Pentecostal outpouring of God's Holy Spirit, which forever changed the course of the Church. These Pentecostal pioneers paid the price of ridicule, loneliness, and disdain as they were scorned and mocked, even persecuted by a generation of evangelicals who refused the next move of God.

From the Latter Rain outpouring of 1948 to the dawning of the 21st Century, much-needed seasons of renewal and refreshing, revival and awakening, have brought us to God's time for the Third Reformation.

The apostolic and prophetic ministries, to whom God has mandated the primary stewardship of these mysteries, have been restored (Eph. 2:20; 3:1-5; 4:11-13). This Third Reformation is Hosea's "third day" of grace (2 Pet. 3:8), the fulfillment of the Feast of Tabernacles in the Church (Lev. 23:33-44), and Ezekiel's "waters to swim in" (Ezek. 47:5). Beloved, there is *more* in God for us!

Awake, O Zion

Zion is stirring. The alarm has sounded. Across America and throughout the nations, young men and women are stirring with a fresh awareness of their high calling in God.

And Adam knew his wife again; and she bare a son, and called his name Seth: For God, said she, hath appointed me another seed... (Gen. 4:25).

This new breed, an "appointed" seed, the third son for the third day, now awakes with new faith, although *it's still dark out there*—we do not have all the answers.

These called-out ones now rouse themselves with new courage, for we are *one among a thousand*—few there be that find this pathway of light and life.

Joel's army now arises with new perspective as we discover that *Zion is a place*—in Christ.

This corporate Overcomer now awakes to find new relationships, for *Zion is a people*—the brethren of whom our Elder Brother is not ashamed.

The challenge is before us. Zion must awake once again to this heavenly summons. The Lord's admonition to His remnant is heard in this prophetic song that flowed forth in a Sunday morning service here at Praise Tabernacle during my "Awake, O Zion" sermon series:

"Who Is on the Lord's Side"

I have chosen Zion, here will I dwell.
Gather the old men, gather the young men, gather the children,
Let the bridegroom come forth from his chamber,
Let the bride come out of her closet,

I plead[4] with you, O Zion, there is a controversy in Zion.
I will plead with thee, there's a controversy in Zion.
It is for the corn, the wine, and the oil.

Blow the trumpet, blow the trumpet…

I have pierced your ear so that once again you'll fear My name.
I call you to the Feast, I call you to the Harvest Feast.
I will cleanse your blood,
I will remove from you the reproach of Egypt once again,

Let the nations gather,
Let them assemble to the Valley of Jehoshaphat,
Even the Valley of Decision,
And say with your heart this day, "I choose the Lord!"

In My fury I scattered you but for a moment,
But now with My mercy I gather you again,
I plead with Zion, to a Priesthood who has wandered from Me,
"Who among you is on the Lord's side?"

There won't be another season just like this, this is serious business,
I am your Judge and jury, I plead with you.

This is the season I blow the trumpet, I blow the trumpet!

Who is on the Lord's side? Who will be My Army?

So then faith cometh by hearing, and hearing by the word of God (Rom. 10:17).

We have heard the sound of this *new day*. We are awakening with *new faith!*

ENDNOTES

1. This was Paul's "one thing." Other notables of Scripture tightly embraced "one thing"—the prophet Elisha (2 Kings 2:9-14); the psalmist David (Ps. 27:4); mighty King Solomon (1 Kings 3:5-13); Mary of Bethany (Luke 10:42); and the apostle Peter (2 Pet. 3:8).

2. This is the principle of horizontal mediation as revealed in the Scriptures (see Ps. 127:1; Matt. 16:18; 1 Cor. 3:5-11; 1 Tim. 2:5). Jesus must be King over all our horizontal, earthly relationships. He must choose those with whom we are intimately involved in real covenant.

3. Study these passages to see what the New Testament says about "tradition" (see Matt. 15:2-6; Mark 7:3-9; Gal. 1:14; Col. 2:8; and 1 Pet. 1:18).

4. The word for "plead" in Joel 3:2 (the context of Scripture from which this Song is taken) means, "to judge, to pronounce sentence, to litigate." God is the Judge, the Lawgiver, and the Arbiter. He sits in the midst of any controversy, swallows it up, and then decrees His righteous justice.

Awake, awake; put on thy strength, O Zion; put on thy beautiful garments, O Jerusalem, the holy city: for henceforth there shall no more come into thee the uncircumcised and the unclean.

Shake thyself from the dust; arise, and sit down, O Jerusalem: loose thyself from the bands of thy neck, O captive daughter of Zion.

For thus saith the Lord, Ye have sold yourselves for nought; and ye shall be redeemed without money (Isa. 52:1-3).

Wherefore he saith, Awake thou that sleepest, and arise from the dead, and Christ shall give thee light (Eph. 5:14).

CHAPTER TWO

AWAKE WITH NEW FAITH: IT'S STILL DARK OUT THERE

This chapter equips us to arise and walk with a *new faith,* despite the fact that the path before us is not always plain. *It's still dark out there,* but those apprehended for Zion follow on courageously to know the Lord in all His fullness and splendor.

God's Day Begins in the Evening

And God called the light Day, and the darkness he called Night. And the evening and the morning were the first day (Gen. 1:5).

Genesis is the seed-plot of the entire Bible. The phrase, "and the evening and the morning," are repeated five more times in this first chapter (Gen. 1:8,13,19,23,31). The principle is clear: God's day begins in the evening and ends in the morning!

And do this, understanding the present time. The hour has come for you to wake up from your slumber, because our salvation is nearer now than when we first believed.

The night is nearly over; the day is almost here. So let us put aside the deeds of darkness and put on the armor of light (Rom. 13:11-12, NIV).

The alarm is sounding. The Day of the Lord has dawned. One day with the Lord is as one thousand years. We have entered the *seventh day* from Adam and the *third day* from Jesus. All over the earth, it's a *new day*. Arise, and shine (Isa. 60:1)!

But it's still dark out there! We do not see everything clearly. Only those of us who passionately love and trust the Lord will continue to walk forward with Him, though we do not have all the answers.

The Day of the Lord is not measured by chronological time. His day and His anointing are pictured as the Golden Candlestick in the Tabernacle of Moses (Ex. 25:31-40). This glorious Lampstand had no specific measurements. Jesus, the Word made flesh, clothed Himself with time, and became the Light of the world (John 1:14; 8:12). The anointing upon the Son was "without measure" (John 3:34). His anointing is timeless (Heb. 13:8)!

The beginning of the 21st Century is critical and strategic. This era is what the Greek language calls a *kairos* moment: "a fixed or special occasion, set or proper time; a particular period or interval; a definite time or season, the time when things are brought to crisis, the decisive epoch waited for."

This *kairos* moment is a space of grace. God has all the time in the world, but we don't. It is imperative that we move at His pace. Moses' church in the wilderness followed the cloud of glory, as "the commandment of the Lord" (Num. 9:15-23). Jesus' Church is led by the Spirit of God (Rom. 8:14).

These days are serious. This is not a time to be cute, to "play church" (Ex. 32:6). Yet many in the American Church continue to toy with the popular game called, "nickels, noses, and names." Everyone craves success. But are we effective?

It's not how many of us there are, but how big a sound we are making! Only those who have power with God have any real impact upon other people (Gen. 32:24-32). The depth of our commitment to His Word and Kingdom purpose determines the breadth and scope of our influence upon others.

Ye have not passed this way heretofore.

And Joshua said unto the people, Sanctify yourselves: for tomorrow the Lord will do wonders among you (Josh. 3:4-5).

People of real faith have sanctified themselves. The old school focuses on setting themselves apart from some thing. But in this new day, we are sanctified unto *Someone!* Though the Jordan is flooded, get ready. Posture yourselves for inheritance!

There is a difference between acquiring a harvest and receiving an inheritance. To bring in a harvest, you must do something. You must sow, cultivate, and then reap. To obtain the inheritance, you must *be* someone! You must *be* a son! You don't die to receive an inheritance. The "testator" (Heb. 9:16) dies, and then gives it to you!

A Map or a Compass?

It's still dark "out there." But "in here"—in the realm of spirit—it is light. "Out there" is the realm of flesh, the natural world. "In here" is the realm of spirit, the spiritual world.

> *While we look not at the things which are seen, but at the things which are not seen: for the things which are seen are temporal; but the things which are not seen are eternal* (2 Cor. 4:18).

Our source is not in external, empirical knowledge, that which we sense. We walk by faith and not by sight, calling those things which be not as though they were (Rom. 4:17). Everything outside of Christ is darkness and death, but "in here," in Christ, all is light and life.

Light represents understanding (Eph. 1:18). Darkness speaks of ignorance. We all are still ignorant about many things. Countless people have asked, "Pastor Varner, what is the 21st Century Church going to look like?" Many are shocked by my immediate answer: "I don't know. It's going to look like Him, and right now, that's enough for me!"

The people of Zion are a company of pioneers. The story of the two spies in the Book of Joshua is a story about forerunners (See Joshua 2). Jesus Himself is called "the forerunner" in Hebrews 6:20. Most folks have not heard what these trailblazers have heard because most folks are not willing to walk into "new" things (Isa. 43:19). They refuse to grow up and change. Too many American Christians have voted for comfort, not conviction.

All our spiritual maps are old, obsolete. They show land that has been traversed and conquered. Maps point to where God used to be. But the high calling requires a compass. It directs us to where God is, and to where He is going. All we have now is a sense of direction. We have been called up into uncharted territory, the fullness of Zion, the resurrection life of the Most Holy Place. All we have in our hand is a compass. That is enough, for our compass is "Christ"!

For as many as are led by the Spirit of God, they are the sons of God (See Romans 8:14 and compare with Genesis 24:27).

By faith Abraham, when he was called to go out into a place which he should after receive for an inheritance, obeyed; and he went out, not knowing whither he went (Heb. 11:8).

Abraham, the "father" of all those called to walk by faith, pleased God (Romans 4; Galatians 3; Heb. 11:5-6). All he had was a compass.

But as it is written, Eye hath not seen, nor ear heard, neither have entered into the heart of man, the things which God hath prepared for them that love him .

But God hath revealed them unto us by his Spirit: for the Spirit searcheth all things, yea, the deep things of God (1 Cor. 2:9-10).

No man or woman has walked into all that has been prepared for us in the unexplored realms of the Spirit (Eph. 3:20). There are fresh levels of worship, service, and commitment for the corporate Man. We have never been this way before!

What's Wrong With Me?

That they should seek the Lord, if haply they might feel (grope, seek) *after Him, and find Him, though He be not far from every one of us* (See Acts 17:27 and compare with Proverbs 4:18).

The Day of the Lord begins in the evening and ends in the morning. It starts in the dark! God will sometimes throw you down what seems like a blind alley, and then tell you to find your way out. In those night seasons, you will have to "feel" after God. Folks who have come from a sin-conscious background and ministry will think that they have backslidden. In frustration and eventual desperation many cry out, "What's wrong with me?"

But God is leading His people into unprecedented things, unheard of things. God's day starts in the shadows, when and where things aren't perfectly obvious. Images are fuzzy and dim.

Years ago, in a Wednesday evening prayer service, I was sitting on the front row in the middle of our sanctuary. Suddenly, the heavens opened and I saw every aspect of our ministry finished and complete, and all was paid for. As abruptly as this vision began, the heavens closed. I sat there amazed and trembling. Once I had regained my composure, I asked the Lord, "What was that all about? Are you teasing me?" He replied, "No, son, I just want you to know that all is well and I will perform all My Word to you and your people."

The Lord will also graciously condescend to a new, young believer and show him or her the end from the beginning. He lets us taste great miracles at the first. Then it all seems to stop. Likewise, Jesus sent out His disciples without any provision (Matt. 10; Luke 10). In essence He said, "O.K., boys, now scratch it out." Later, He sent them forth again, this time with money and food (Luke 22:35-36).

Have you experienced anything during your spiritual journey that you cannot explain? Has God spoken some things to you that are still not clear? Is anything happening to you right now that you can't quite get a grip or handle on?

We sense the coming fulfillment of His promises. We hear them from a distance. We can almost smell them as we squint at cloudy things. *But it's still dark out there.* The only people who are going to walk on by faith are those who unconditionally love God. The Day of the Lord has begun in the misty evening. Morning is on the way. The Virtuous Woman of Proverbs 31 pictures the glorious Church. We are arising "while it is yet night" (Prov. 31:15).

Those who are led by their flesh and not by His Spirit will sit on their blessed assurance until they can see things clearly. They are practicing "safe church." But it soon may be too late. As in Noah's day, this *kairos* moment will end, and the door will be shut.

Which Side of the Cloud Are You Living On?

Moses' congregation was led through the wilderness by the pillar of cloud by day and the pillar of fire by night.

> [The cloud came] *between the armies of Egypt and Israel. Throughout the night the cloud brought darkness to the one side and light to the other side...* (Exod. 14:20, NIV).

The manifest Presence of Jehovah gave Israel "light by night." Egypt lay behind them. Canaan's milk and honey beckoned them onward. The back side of that cloud was a place of darkness, and it represented their past, pointing back to Egypt. The front side of that same cloud was flooded with light, and forecast their future, reaching forth to the land of overflowing abundance.

Which side of the cloud are you living on? The past or the future?

*But you are a chosen people, a royal priesthood, a holy nation,
a people belonging to God, that you may declare the praises
of him who called you out of darkness into his wonderful light*
(1 Pet. 2:9, NIV).

The darkness and death of our trespasses and sinful past lay
behind us. The tyranny of the god and prince of this world system was
overwhelmed by the blood of the Passover Lamb (Ex. 12:13,23). Our
future is bright as we ascend into Zion!

From the Negev he (Abram) *went from place to place until
he came to Bethel, to the place between Bethel and Ai...*
(Gen. 13:3, NIV).

Abraham, the father of the faith-walk, found himself between Ai
and Bethel. "Ai" means "a heap of ruins." "Bethel" means "the house of
God." We cannot return to the former things. We must press on to the
place of His holy habitation.

*Before them fire devours, behind them a flame blazes. Before them
the land is like the garden of Eden, behind them, a desert waste—
nothing escapes them* (Joel 2:3, NIV).

Joel's army, one of the many biblical descriptions of the corporate
Overcomer, the remnant of Zion, further illustrates this truth. Behind
us is a "desolate wilderness."   Before us is the Garden of Eden, the
Paradise of God, the fullness of Kingdom dominion.

God's great love for His elect has moved Him to burn up all the
stuff that we have left behind. Nothing remains for us to go back to.
Old friends, old habits, and all the familiar places have so changed that
we do not have the strength or desire to retreat. We refuse to draw back
in fear unto such destruction. We choose rather to draw near to Him
with full assurance of faith (Heb. 10:19-22,38-39).

Which side of the cloud are you living on?

*Woe unto them that call evil good, and good evil; that put dark-
ness for light, and light for darkness; that put bitter for sweet, and
sweet for bitter!* (Isa. 5:20).

*And I will bring the blind by a way that they knew not; I will lead
them in paths that they have not known: I will make darkness
light before them, and crooked things straight...* (Isa. 42:16).

The darkness of where we have been, the road of sin, was strewn with death and disorder, folly and evil. Our present pathway is marked by life and order, wisdom and goodness. The back side of the cloud that points to Egypt is crooked, distorted, and twisted. The front side of the cloud that leads to Zion is straight, just, and righteous. Paul summed up this pattern by rehearsing his apostolic commission, given by Jesus Himself on the Damascus road:

> To open their eyes, and to turn them from darkness to light, and from the power of satan unto God, that they may receive forgiveness of sins, and inheritance among them which are sanctified by faith that is in Me (Acts 26:18).

Somebody has to get up while it's still dark out there. The cloud will lead us. Three compelling stories in the Bible inspire us to arise while it is still shadowy and dusky, when everything is not always clear, and we do not have all the answers.

These three settings powerfully demonstrate how to walk while *it's still dark out there:* the four lepers of Samaria (2 Kings 6-7); the apostle Peter walking on the water (Matt. 14; Mark 6); and Mary Magdalene on resurrection morning (John 20).

They Rose Up in the Twilight

> And there was a great famine in Samaria: and, behold, they besieged it, until an ass's head was sold for fourscore pieces of silver, and the fourth part of a cab of dove's dung for five pieces of silver (2 Kings 6:25).

> And there were four leprous men at the entering in of the gate: and they said one to another, Why sit we here until we die?

> If we say, We will enter into the city, then the famine is in the city, and we shall die there: and if we sit still here, we die also. Now therefore come, and let us fall unto the host of the Syrians: if they save us alive, we shall live; and if they kill us, we shall but die.

> And they rose up in the twilight... (2 Kings 7:3-5).

There is a spiritual famine today "of hearing the words of the Lord" (Amos 8:11). Men and women have to eat "asses' head" and "doves' dung." These represent human wisdom without God, and the futile longing for yesterday's revival (all that is left of the Dove after He has flown away). In our hunger, we are crying for more than revival. We must have reformation! The young prodigal in the pigpen had nothing to eat except yesterday's leftovers—religious tradition. Stop singing songs and choruses about where the Dove of God's Spirit used to be. The cloud has moved!

The alarm has sounded. The prophets have already declared that the famine will be broken, despite the unbelief of palace pawns that cater to denominational kings (2 Kings 6:1-2). "Tomorrow" has become today!

The four lepers illustrate those who live "outside" of religion's walled cities. They were Pentecostal lepers with a dualistic mindset. Their question, "Why sit we here until we die?" reveals that they had yet to understand the truth that the old Adamic man was crucified with Christ (Rom. 6:1-14; Gal. 2:20). Nonetheless, they did what no one else had the courage to do. They "rose up in the twilight (dusk; the time of the evening breeze)" (2 Kings 7:5), while it was still dark out there!

Postured in the middle court, the Holy Place, they reasoned, "If we go back to the Outer Court, we will have to eat asses' head and doves' dung. Besides, all they do in that realm is fight, bite and devour one another (2 Kings 6:28-30 with Gal. 5:15). Let's arise while it is yet dark and walk toward the unknown. Let's dare to walk toward the Most Holy Place, toward Zion and the Feast of Tabernacles."

For the Lord had made the host of the Syrians to hear a noise of chariots, and a noise of horses, even the noise of a great host... (2 Kings 7:6).

Arise, you outcasts of Israel![1] Again, it's not how many of us there are, but how big a sound that we are making! God made the enemy to hear the "noise" (voice, sound) of chariots, horses, and a great army! The Syrians fled for their lives!

Fearless, outnumbered, hungry outsiders are arising in the twilight. The evening mist matters little to us. We have heard the Jubilee trumpet (Lev. 25 and Luke 4:18) in our hearts. That certain sound is getting louder and louder, and clearer and clearer! We have forsaken the monotonous fighting and famine of the past. We have discovered that there is no enemy in the Holy of Holies, just a table spread! We have witnessed and begun to taste the evidence of a full provision.

And when these lepers came to the uttermost part of the camp, they went into one tent, and did eat and drink, and carried thence silver, and gold, and raiment, and went and hid it...

Then they said one to another, We do not well: this day is a day of good tidings...now therefore come, that we may go and tell the king's household. (2 Kings 7:8-9).

The tendency of those who have known the message of sonship and the Kingdom (since 1948 and the Latter Rain Revival) has been to keep these treasures for themselves. Like John on resurrection morning, our understanding of the Kingdom has outrun all the others. But although we have looked into the empty tomb, we have yet to enter into the reality of what we have seen by the Spirit (John 20:1-5).

Historically, two glaring weaknesses have marked classical sonship: First, many stopped holding the Head (the Colossian error), projecting themselves more than the Lord Jesus (Col. 1:19; 2:9,19).

Second, others emphasized their sonship to be singular and not corporate, basing their "spirituality" upon their "message" and their "revelation" of the Scriptures. But God is not going to "manifest" or "unveil" us. We, corporately, are to manifest Him, Jesus the Pattern Son (Rom. 8:14-23)!

But we have learned our lessons the hard way. Our fears and insecurities have been healed. Now we run and tell the King's household the Good News! The famine is over. There is no enemy. He has fled a certain sound. Come and dine (John 21:12)!

You, too, can arise while it is yet dark. Just over the brow of the hill of Zion, in the third dimension of grace, there is plenty. There is no enemy there. Sin has been defeated. All that awaits you is a lavish banquet, the spoils of Jesus' eternal triumph in His finished work!

Lepers are getting up. Unbelief is about to be trampled in the gates of every religious city as God's people stampede out of those religious strongholds as they rush toward the Feast of the Lord.

Walk On the Word

The Bible tells about three men in a boat, and three boats in a storm. The three men are Jonah, Paul, and Jesus (Jonah 1-4; Mark 6; Acts 27). The first man, Jonah, was out of the will of God. The second man, Paul, was in the will of God. The third Man, Jesus, *was* the will of

God. The first man was overcome by the storm. The second man endured the storm. The third Man took dominion over the storm.

The story of the third Man tells of Peter, the disciple who walked on the Word, though it was still dark that night.

The sixth chapter of Mark records that John the Baptist had just been martyred, beheaded by wicked king Herod for the price of a cheap dance. The disciples besought the Master, fearing for their own lives, "Why did John have to die?" Jesus never gave them an answer.

And He said unto them, Come ye yourselves apart into a desert place, and rest a while: for there were many coming and going, and they had no leisure so much as to eat (Mark 6:31).

In other words, the Lord said to them, "Boys, let's take a vacation, and come apart before we come apart." The only problem was that everyone loved Jesus. By the time they got to their resort area, their vacation had turned into a convention (the feeding of the 5,000)! There was no time now for "leisure," which means literally, "to have a good time."

Guess who got to minister to all these people? And all with a two-piece fish dinner! Peter marveled as Jesus blessed the lad's lunch. His childlike faith ignited as he watched the Master break the first fish in half, as the head grew a tail and the tail grew a head!

After supper, the disciples were exhausted, physically and emotionally drained. It was getting dark, but Jesus did not hesitate. He gave them orders to get into the boat and go to the "other side" (Mark 6:45). Their Master purposefully sent His followers into a storm!

They rowed to the point of exhaustion through the first three watches of the night (from 6 p.m. until 3 a.m.). Meanwhile, the Master had quietly retreated to the mountain to pray, the only One who remained in the place of stability and safety.

But the ship was now in the midst of the sea, tossed with waves: for the wind was contrary.

And in the fourth watch of the night Jesus went unto them, walking on the sea.

And when the disciples saw Him walking on the sea, they were troubled, saying, It is a spirit; and they cried out for fear.

But straightway Jesus spake unto them, saying, Be of good cheer; it is I; be not afraid.

And Peter answered him and said, Lord, if it be Thou, bid me come unto Thee on the water.

And He said, Come. And when Peter was come down out of the ship, he walked on the water, to go to Jesus (Matt. 14:24-29).

After nine hours, Peter began to mutter, "Where is Jesus?" Their hearts were "hardened" and calloused. They had gathered up 12 baskets (one for each disciple) in the miracle of the loaves. Each stroke of the oars would fasten their eyes upon the evidence of His power resting at their feet, but they were blinded by their own sweat.

Men and women who focus on the darkness become that darkness. They cry, "I can't live this way. I can't give that much." But behind every excuse is a lack of desire. The Lord now brings a requirement to His people, not by the letter of the law but by the summons of the Spirit. He summons, "Arise, get out of the boat. Walk on My Word!"

During the fourth and final watch, Jesus went for a stroll on the tops of the watery billows. When He showed up that night in a form they had never seen, they first shrieked in fear. Only Peter had the courage to ask, "Lord, is that you? If so, bid me come to You."

His faith had been stirred by the revelation of who the Master really is. Jesus had said, "It is I." The Greek construction here is, *ego eimi,* literally, "I AM"! The same God who sent Moses to Pharaoh came "skipping" on the watery waves that night (Exod. 3:14-15 with Song 2:8).

At first there was an "if" in Peter's words (Matt. 14:28). After all, *it was still dark out there.* This grizzled fisherman knew the seas. He was now invited to step out of the safe place and into that which was totally unprecedented. As he began to sling one leg over the side, I can almost hear his old fishing buddies, "Oh, my God, he's going to do it! If he walks on the Word, so can we."

The Master now comes and calls for you. "But what if I sink, Lord?" He will do for you what He did for Peter—He "caught" him (Matt. 14:31). This word is a compound of *epi* (upon) and *lambano* (to take hold of, to seize). Jesus will reach down from Zion and embrace you. We are always safe when He is near!

Now unto Him that is able to keep you from falling, and to present you faultless before the presence of His glory with exceeding joy,

To the only wise God our Saviour, be glory and majesty, dominion and power, both now and ever (Jude 1:24-25).

When It Was Yet Dark

The four lepers arose in the twilight. Peter stepped out of the boat in the middle of the night. We briefly mention a third example that demonstrates Zion's awakening while *it's still dark out there.*

The first day of the week cometh Mary Magdalene early, when it was yet dark, unto the sepulchre, and seeth the stone taken away from the sepulcher... (John 20:1).

Mary Magdalene came to the tomb "when it was yet dark."

This ardent follower of the Master was not a prostitute. That is assumed by some, but the Bible does not say that.[2] She had been delivered from "seven devils" (Luke 8:2), but then, every one of us has been delivered from the devil! We were completely under the dominion of the evil one (Eph. 2:1-3). Yet Mary Magdalene was the woman who loved Jesus!

As He did with the disciples and Peter during the storm, the Master appears in a form that Mary could not relate to. You and I have come to that same place in God, the place of "unheard of" things (Josh. 3:4; Eph. 3:20). God is doing a "new thing" (Isa. 43:19).

Only courageous, faithful overcomers will follow after Him now. The others (even apostles) will remain cloistered, hunkered down in their houses, in their ministries, and in their networks, afraid to behold the full reality of resurrection life.

Many know Him as *Rabboni* (Rabbi) and "Master" (teacher). But only those apprehended for the Kingdom will address Him as "sir" (John 20:15). This Greek word *kurios* means, "supreme in authority; the possessor and disposer of a thing; the owner, one who has control." It simply means, "Lord." Hallelujah! Our King is alive!

The four lepers, then Peter, and then Mary Magdalene...

Each arose in the twilight, while *it was still dark out there.* These men and this woman were not afraid to venture into the unknown, the place that requires a compass, not a map.

Awake, O Zion! Our season has come. We are a bunch of crazy, outrageous, overcoming, "in love with God" kind of people...

All we have now is His Word. We are returning to the pure truth of biblical sonship (maturity), the Kingdom, and the high calling. We are pioneers and trailblazers, "the firstfruits unto God and to the Lamb" (Rev. 14:4). We are an extraordinary breed of people. Our compass is Christ. We are guided by His Word and Spirit.

Be determined. It's still dark out there. We don't have all the answers. But Zion is awakening with *new faith!* There's no other way but to go all the way. Renew your mind. Commit to the unknown.

Walk boldly. Walk courageously, for you are *one among a thousand!*

Endnotes

1. Study these verses to see what the Bible has to say about the "outcasts" (to push down or push away) of Israel (see Ps. 147:2; Isa. 11:12; 16:3-4; 27:13; 56:8; Jer. 30:17; 49:36).

2. Note the contexts of every place where Mary Magdalene is mentioned in the Scriptures (see Matt. 27:56,61; 28:1; Mark 15:40,47; 16:1,9; Luke 8:2; 24:10; and John 19:25; 20:1,18).

Awake, awake, O Zion, clothe yourself with strength. Put on your garments of splendor, O Jerusalem, the holy city. The uncircumcised and defiled will not enter you again.

Shake off your dust; rise up, sit enthroned, O Jerusalem. Free yourself from the chains on your neck, O captive Daughter of Zion.

For this is what the Lord says: "You were sold for nothing, and without money you will be redeemed" (Isa. 52:1-3, NIV).

For it is light that makes everything visible. This is why it is said: "Wake up, O sleeper, rise from the dead, and Christ will shine on you" (Eph. 5:14, NIV).

CHAPTER THREE

AWAKE WITH NEW COURAGE: ONE AMONG A THOUSAND

Zion is the glorious Church, the corporate Overcomer called in this Third Day to taste the release of His resurrection life. It's still dark out there. We do not have all the answers. Nonetheless, like the four lepers of Samaria in the time of famine, like the apostle Peter in the midst of the storm, and like Mary Magdalene on resurrection morning, we are waking up with *new faith*. Our compass is Christ.

The gospel of the Kingdom has been watered down with incredible mixture. The "sinners in Zion" (Isa. 33:14) have contaminated the truth with strange teachings. Many are "at ease in Zion" (Amos 6:1), fearing men's faces more than the Lord. Politics, power struggles, and personal agendas have compromised truth and integrity. There is no lifestyle behind those lips. For many preachers, the Kingdom of God is but another message, another level of biblical theology and semantics.

Someone must arise and declare the whole counsel of God. The New Testament in Jesus' better blood is Good News, not bad news. Our Savior and King has reconciled us back to our Father, back to His dream and original purpose for humankind. We have been forgiven. Our sin has been removed.

Someone must boldly arise and fearlessly herald the full weight of His glorious righteousness. Someone must awake with *new courage!*

One Among a Thousand

If there be a messenger with him, an interpreter, one among a thousand, to shew unto man (Adam) His uprightness (Job 33:23).

One among a thousand to show to man what is right for him
[how to be upright and in right standing with God] (Job
33:23, AMP).

The purpose of the gospel is to show unto humankind God's
righteousness. The men and women of Zion constitute His corporate
"messenger." This word means, "to dispatch as a deputy; a messenger;
specifically, of God, an angel (also a prophet, priest or teacher), repre-
sentative," and is rendered in the King James Version as, "ambassador,
angel, king, messenger."

We are His ambassadors. The local church is a Kingdom embassy.
This same word translated as "messenger" is also used to reference the
"Angel" of the Lord (a Christophany) in the Pentateuch (Num. 22); and
the "messenger" of the Covenant, a Messianic prophecy (Mal. 3:1).
Thus this word is directly linked to the Lord Himself.

"Interpreter" means, "to interpret, or (generally) intercede," and
is also translated in the King James Version as, "ambassador, teacher."

Consider the patriarch Joseph and the prophet Daniel, who inter-
preted dreams and visions from the realm of the Spirit. Prophetic
ministry must arise to shed light on these times, to give direction from
the Lord, to sound the alarm. The handwriting is on the wall, but
nobody can read it (Dan. 5). The Church in America is playing games,
but the party will stop as soon as the "interpreter" shows up. The half-
brothers won't like it when the dreamer appears to proclaim the dream
of God (Gen. 37).

This "messenger" and "interpreter" has been commissioned by
God to show unto humankind His divine "uprightness." This latter
word means, "the right; straightness, uprightness; evenness (moral
implications); what is right, what is due." It comes from a root which
means, "to be straight or even; figuratively, to be or to make right,
pleasant, prosperous," and is also rendered in the King James Version
as, "equity, meet, right, upright."

Not everybody can be right. And not everybody will pay the price
to scale the heights of Zion. Not everybody will rule and reign with
Him. This privilege is reserved for those who are "called, and chosen,
and faithful" (Rev. 17:14).

My dove, my undefiled is but one; she is the only one of her
mother, she is the choice one... (Song 6:9).

The Shulamite was His "choice" one. This word means, "beloved, pure, clean, sincere." Its root indicates that which is "purified, selected, polished, made bright, tested, and proven."[1]

We are not preaching exclusivism. One excludes himself or herself from the high calling by simply settling for the good or the better, instead of God's best. The brazen altar of Moses' Tabernacle (Ex. 27:1-8) was large enough for all the other pieces of furniture to fit into it. Every born-again believer has the potential for all things in Christ. But not everyone will develop his or her possibilities and potential.

He that overcometh shall inherit all things; and I will be His God, and he shall be My son (Rev. 21:7).

Those destined for Zion will inherit all things. The word for "son" used here is *huios* and indicates a "mature son." These sons are His righteous plumb line, sent to rectify and realign the original vision and purpose of the Kingdom. We are His ambassadors, His messengers and interpreters—"*one among a thousand.*"

Zion Is Awakening in Righteousness

As for me, I will behold Thy face in righteousness: I shall be satisfied, when I awake, with Thy likeness (Ps. 17:15).

David's heart was to "behold" (gaze at, perceive, contemplate with pleasure, have a vision of) God's face in righteousness. He knew that this desire could only be fulfilled when he became fully aware of God's "likeness" (image, similitude; manifestation of favor).[2]

This was God's original purpose (Gen. 1:26-28), the one hope of our one calling (Eph. 4:4). We are all invited into His presence to be transformed and changed into His image and likeness (Rom. 8:28-31). From thence we are sent to our particular assignments. There is no nobler calling, no higher aspiration, than to be like Jesus.

Awake to righteousness, and sin not; for some have not the knowledge of God: I speak this to your shame (1 Cor. 15:34).

Awake (from your drunken stupor and return) to sober sense and your right minds...you are utterly and willfully and disgracefully ignorant, and continue to be so, lacking the sense of God's presence and all true knowledge of Him... (1 Cor. 15:34, AMP).

This verse is key with regard to the theme of these opening chapters, "Awake, O Zion." God's alarm has sounded. But there is a right way to wake up.

Paul's apostolic admonition is for the Church to, literally, "awake righteously." That is only possible as we see ourselves in Christ. Our growth in grace is an ongoing awareness of who we already are in Him on the basis of what He has already done! The apostle's concern is that many "have not the knowledge of God." This is the revelation of the mystery now revealed—"Christ in you (plural) the hope of glory" (Col. 1:27). "Shame" (confusion) is the fruit of not knowing that God now inhabits His people by the Spirit.

The apostle continues, "and sin not." Jesus defined the essence of sin as unbelief—"because they believe not on (into) Me" (John 16:9). Thus, we righteously awake by believing His Word and promise. The call to Zion leads to the walk of faith.

Adam Is Walking and Talking in His Sleep

Follow closely as we build this truth line upon line. Paul got His revelation of the gospel of grace from Moses and the prophets (Acts 26:22). The fourteenth verse of the fifth chapter of Ephesians is a direct quote from Isaiah 60:1:

Wherefore he saith, awake thou that sleepest, and arise from the dead, and Christ shall give thee light (Eph. 5:14).

Making use of the definite article, the original language of this verse reads, "and the Christ shall shine upon you" (Compare 2 Cor. 4:6).

To be *asleep* in the darkness is to be dead in Adam, the old nature.

To be *awake* in the light is to be alive in Christ, the new nature.

For as in Adam all die, even so in Christ shall all be made alive (1 Cor. 15:22).

Therefore if any man be in Christ, he is a new creature: old things are passed away; behold, all things are become new (2 Cor. 5:17).

Moreover, Adam is talking in his sleep! Such words, expressed by preaching, teaching, or writing, are marked by sin-consciousness and foster death. Some people mention the devil more than Jesus. They talk more about the flesh than they do about the Spirit. Such words flow from the Adamic mind. These ministers of confusion are talking in their sleep!

Those who lack biblical discernment listen to and follow after such religious foolishness. These imprudent disciples end up living out of that lower nature, walking in their sleep! Those who remain in Adam are spiritually asleep. Consider these verses:

The dead praise not the Lord... (Ps. 115:17).

The dead know not anything... (See Eccles. 9:5 and compare Hos. 4:6).

The man that wandereth out of the way of understanding shall remain in the congregation of the dead (Prov. 21:16).

The seventh chapter of Proverbs describes the "strange woman" and her whorish wiles. We meet her again in Revelation 17-18, and learn that the name of this "great whore" is "...MYSTERY, BABYLON THE GREAT, THE MOTHER OF HARLOTS AND ABOMINATIONS OF THE EARTH" (Rev. 17:1,5). This is the classic biblical depiction of religious systems whose trademark is Adamic preaching and teaching. Be warned!

Do not let your heart turn to her ways or stray into her paths.

Many are the victims she has brought down; her slain are a mighty throng.

Her house is a highway to the grave, leading down to the chambers of death (See Prov. 7:25-27 and compare Prov. 9:13-18, NIV).

Asleep and Dead Drunk

Awake, O Zion! Arise with *new courage.* We are His messenger and interpreter, *one among a thousand.* Our calling is to declare the righteousness of Christ.

Adam is unrighteous. Adam is asleep, talking out of the old mindset. He is walking about, aimlessly wandering in the weakness of his own human wisdom and strength. Furthermore, Adam is not just asleep. He is drunk in the night!

Let us keep wide awake (alert, watchful, cautious and on our guard), and let us be sober (calm, collected, and circumspect) (1 Thess. 5:6, AMP).

For those who sleep, sleep at night, and those who get drunk, get drunk at night (1Thess. 5:7, NIV).

Christ is awake in the day, "sober" and vigilant. This word means, "to be free from the influence of intoxicants; to be calm and collected, temperate, circumspect" (compare with 1 Pet. 1:3; 4:7; 5:8).

But Adam is asleep, dead drunk in the night. As he sleeps, he dreams. His dream has become a nightmare, for he dreams of death. He is totally overwhelmed, persuaded by his hellish visions. Adam has faith in but one thing—death!

Take notice! I tell you a mystery—a secret truth, an event decreed by the hidden purpose or counsel of God. We shall not all fall asleep [in death], but we shall all be changed (transformed) (1 Cor. 15:51, AMP).

Adam is convinced that he must die. But one of the several mysteries (sacred secrets) of the New Testament is that there will be a generation who will not sleep. There shall arise a people who will, with corporate anointing, overcome the spirit of death!

Zion was the final stronghold for King David and his army (2 Sam. 5:7). The "last enemy" for the overcoming Church, David's seed, to conquer is death (1 Cor. 15:26)!

Awake, O Zion! It will take *new courage* to proclaim or write about such things. Do not be afraid, embarrassed, or ashamed to boldly make public the truth. God's end-time "messenger" and "interpreter" will show humankind the full promise of His righteousness.

We risk being misunderstood. We may be openly ostracized and even persecuted. We are willing to pay the price of walking alone as others choose to defend their traditions, determined to maintain kingdoms that they have built for themselves in His name.

Are you asleep or awake? Are you drunk in the night or sober in the day? Are you identified with who you were in Adam, or who you are in Christ? With the old man or the new man?

You will never lay hold of who you are in Christ until you understand what God did with who you used to be in Adam.

This is a critical moment in Church history. The intensified pressure of spiritual travail, the birth-pangs of this Third Reformation pulsate in heavenly places. Our greatest enemy is the mediocrity that creeps among us. There seems to be little love for God and the things of God. As Israel went whoring after other gods in the days of old, many today have forsaken their "first love" (Rev. 2:4).

The Drunkards of Ephraim

Adam is asleep, drunk in the night. To illustrate this, the prophet Isaiah describes the men and women who walked after the flesh in his day as the proud "drunkards of Ephraim."

Woe to the crown of pride, to the drunkards of Ephraim, whose glorious beauty is a fading flower... (Isa. 28:1).

Isaiah 28 truly pictures Adam's family,[3] though the double portion of the high calling is intimated in Ephraim's name, which means, "doubly fruitful." This key chapter is an indictment against those who have abused the spiritual wine of the Feast of Pentecost.

Drunk on their lust for having a "good time," these have made up their minds to camp in the Second Day. There, men and women consume the wine of the gifts of the Spirit to promote their own selfish agendas. Spiritual adolescents who crave to be seen by others have misused their gifts for the love of money. Comfortable and contented to live in the "First Church of Familiar Surroundings," they refuse to move on to know the Lord in the Feast of Tabernacles.

Woe to them that are at ease in Zion... (Amos 6:1).

Much of what is being passed off as Kingdom ministry is actually driven by a dualistic, classical Pentecostal mindset with a Kingdom facade. Neo-kingdom leaders are at ease in Zion, content to preach and live with mixture. The *charismata* (the gifts and manifestations of the Holy Spirit) were given by God to edify the Body of Christ (1 Cor. 12:1-10). But religious systems have used these endowments to help line their pockets and fill their pocketbooks with "filthy lucre."[4]

The "glorious beauty" of these manmade systems and concepts, these obsolete ways of having "church," are described in Isaiah 28:1 as a "fading flower." Void of His resurrection life, the old order is wilting and dying. The apostle Peter called this "fading flower" the "glory of man" that withers (dries up) and falls away (1 Pet. 1:24).

The creation waits in eager expectation for the sons of God to be revealed (Rom. 8:19, NIV).

The earth is groaning for release. We hear that *cry* in Joel 1:1-3. Deliverance for America will never come from the outer darkness of the Outer Court. The sophomoric mixture and compromise of the Holy Place will never liberate the nations. The sons of God must be revealed from the third room, the Most Holy Place. Those destined to roar out of Zion (Joel 3:16; Amos 1:2), will alone be the fire with which God answers creation's dilemma (1 Kings 18:24).

The prophet Isaiah goes on in chapter 28 to describe those who stop moving at the Feast of Pentecost. The drunkards of Ephraim have prophesied lies and falsehood.

> *But they also have erred through wine, and through strong drink are out of the way; the priest and the prophet have erred through strong drink, they are swallowed up of wine, they are out of the way through strong drink; they err in vision, they stumble in judgment.*

> *For all tables are full of vomit and filthiness, so that there is no place clean* (Isa. 28:7-8).

These leaders have staggered and strayed from the plain truth of apostolic orthodoxy and the clear Word of God (John 14:6). "Swallowed up" (engulfed, eaten up, destroyed) on account of wine, these drunkards have turned to their own way, teaching for doctrines the commandments of men. They are intoxicated with the false hope of an "any-minute" pre-tribulation rapture, and have robbed God's people of their true identity as the Seed of Abraham and the Seed of David.[5] Their "judgment" (reasoning, the ability to make wise decisions) is clouded and mixed.

The drunkards of Ephraim are Pentecostal drunkards. Their "tables," their places of fellowship, are unclean, soiled with the vomit[6] of yesterday's leftovers and the "filthiness," literally the "dung, excrement, dirt, pollution" of wasteful living. Religion's "fast lane" is overcrowded with the hyper-faith "boys' club" jostling and jockeying for position, those whom Jesus called "blind leaders leading the blind" (Matt. 15:14). Where there is no clear prophetic vision and revelation, the people cast off restraint (Prov. 29:18).

> *Therefore hear the word of the Lord, you scoffers who rule this people in Jerusalem.*

You boast, "We have entered into a covenant with death, with the grave we have made an agreement. When an overwhelming scourge sweeps by, it cannot touch us, for we have made a lie our refuge and falsehood our hiding place." (Isa. 28:14-15, NIV).

The greatest indictment against these scornful, bragging men is their agreement with death and hell. These scoffers have built their lives, their ministries, and their denominations with lies and deceit, taking refuge under the thin veil of dispensationalism, the false hope cunningly woven together by men. But the Lord has sealed their fate. He has prepared His scourging instrument to deal with their unbelief.

The Lord Has a Mighty and a Strong One

Zion is the place of the high calling, inhabited by God's messenger and interpreter, *one among a thousand* (Job 33:23). These overcomers are described as well in this 28th chapter of Isaiah as "a mighty and a strong one" (Isa. 28:2).

See, the Lord has one who is powerful and strong. Like a hailstorm and a destructive wind, like a driving rain and a flooding downpour, he will throw it forcefully to the ground.

That wreath, the pride of Ephraim's drunkards, will be trampled underfoot.

That fading flower, his glorious beauty, set on the head of a fertile valley, will be like a fig ripe before harvest—as soon as someone sees it and takes it in his hand, he swallows it (Isa. 28:2-4, NIV).

This "tempest of hail and a destroying storm" (Isa. 28:2) is a picture of the Day of the Lord and the sons of God who will execute the judgment written. Similarly, Moses and Aaron brought Jehovah's sentence upon Pharaoh and his court magicians (Ex. 7:1,7-13,22; 8:7,18; 2 Tim. 3:8). Peter and Paul brought their apostolic hands down upon the heads of Simon and Elymas (Acts 8:9-13; 13:6-12).

With "a driving rain and a flooding downpour," the patriarch Noah brought righteous judgment upon his generation. The same Flood that destroyed the wicked elevated Noah and his family to inherit the earth. So once again the order is changing. God is about to measure, and then dismantle religious and political Babylon (Rev. 17-18) with His sons, His righteous "plumbline" (Amos 7:7-8). Light has begun to overwhelm the darkness. Life will swallow up death.

This message, this book, this anointing, is not for everyone. But there is a high calling (Phil. 3:12-14)! Some of you have been apprehended for the top of the mountain, for the heights of Zion. You are the ones to whom I cry and plead.

Those called to be the best, and who settle for the good, are only fair. Those apprehended for the high calling who have sold their birthright for a mess of worldly "pottage" (Gen. 25:29-34), will one day weep as they look into the throne and see the overcomers seated with Jesus (Rev. 3:21). This was meant to have been their destiny as well, but they were not willing to pay the price.

> *And when He had made a scourge of small cords, He drove them all out of the temple, and the sheep, and the oxen; and poured out the changers' money, and overthrew the tables;*
>
> *And said unto them that sold doves, Take these things hence; make not My Father's house an house of merchandise* (John 2:15-16).

Somebody has been chosen to execute the judgment written at the Cross, His finished work (Ps. 149:5-9). This company will be His "overflowing scourge"[7] (Isa. 28:15). In the name of their Elder Brother, these will cleanse the House of the Lord from all those who sell doves (what's hot and what's not in the name of Christianity).

> *Judgment also will I lay to the line, and righteousness to the plummet: and the hail shall sweep away the refuge of lies, and the waters shall overflow the hiding place.*
>
> *And your covenant with death shall be disannulled, and your agreement with hell shall not stand; when the overflowing scourge shall pass through, then ye shall be trodden down by it* (Isa. 28:17-18).

There now arises in America and the nations a company of prophets and prophetesses who are not afraid to speak His Word. These voices are God's "plummet" (a leveling tool or weight with a line attached; compare 2 Kings 21:13; Zech. 4:10).

This heralding forth of "present truth" (2 Pet. 1:12) has begun to "sweep away (brush aside) the refuge of lies." Dispensationalism's "any-minute" pre-tribulation rapture theory is about to be blown away. Adam's covenant with death and hell shall be "disannulled" (covered and cancelled),[8] and his agreement with hell shall not stand!

After Four Days

Adam is asleep, drunk in the night. Christ is awake, sober in the day. Awake, O Zion, with *new courage*. You are *one among a thousand*.

And the Lord God caused a deep sleep to fall upon Adam and he slept... (Gen. 2:21).

Jesus said, Take ye away the stone. Martha, the sister of him that was dead, saith unto him, Lord, by this time he stinketh: for he hath been dead four days (John 11:39).

God put Adam to sleep, and we never read that he woke up! One day with the Lord is as one thousand years (2 Pet. 3:8). From Adam to Christ is four days, four thousand years. Like Lazarus, Adam had been dead for four days. And he stank! The odor of a decaying corpse vividly describes Adam's speech and lifestyle.

Your Knower, the Holy Ghost from within, will readily let you discern whenever Adam is preaching. What he is saying and the spirit with which he is saying it really stinks! Those teachings are old, dead, and dry. Those who listen to that kind of preaching every Sunday are in trouble, for Adam is corrupt and rotten.

There are thousands of young men and women being cloned in Bible schools and seminaries throughout the nations who have never studied the Bible for themselves. Sadly, the world believes that every teaching that comes out of America is ordained by God. But we have Westernized, not Christianized, the nations, raping and pillaging them with the stinking traditions of men and Adam's covenant with death.

Immortaility Is Brought to Light Through the Gospel

To those who by persistence in doing good seek glory, honor and immortality, He will give eternal life (Rom. 2:7, NIV)

But is now made manifest by the appearing of our Saviour Jesus Christ, who hath abolished death, and hath brought life and immortality to light through the gospel (2 Tim. 1:10).

Compare these verses with Paul's word to the Church at Corinth:

Now we know that if the earthly tent we live in is destroyed, we have a building from God, an eternal house in heaven, not built by human hands.

Meanwhile we groan, longing to be clothed with our heavenly dwelling,

because when we are clothed, we will not be found naked.

For while we are in this tent, we groan and are burdened, because we do not wish to be unclothed but to be clothed with our heavenly dwelling, so that what is mortal may be swallowed up by life.

Now it is God who has made us for this very purpose and has given us the Spirit as a deposit, guaranteeing what is to come (2 Cor. 5:1-5, NIV).

Now he Who has fashioned us [preparing and making us fit] for this very thing is God, Who also has given us the [Holy] Spirit as a guarantee [of the fulfillment of His promise] (2 Cor. 5:5, AMP).

Although Adam dreams of death, there will be a generation who will not sleep (1 Cor. 15:51), who will put their feet on the last enemy!

For this corruptible must put on incorruption, and this mortal must put on immortality

So when this corruptible shall have put on incorruption, and this mortal shall have put on immortality, then shall be brought to pass the saying that is written, Death is swallowed up in victory (1 Cor. 15:53-54 with Isa. 25:8).

"Mortal" means, "liable to die, subject to death." It is awesome to consider Paul's declaration that "incorruption" (unending existence, genuineness) and "immortality" (deathlessness) must be "put on"! This word in the above verses is *enduo* and it means, "to sink into a garment, invest with clothing." Compare the English word "endued" (Luke 24:49). The mystery of resurrection life revealed in Scripture has to do with God's people putting on:

1. The wedding garment (Matt. 22:11).
2. The best robe, the ring, the shoes (Luke 15:22).
3. Christ (Rom. 13:11-14; Gal. 3:27).
4. The new Man (Eph. 4:24; Col. 3:10).
5. The whole armor of God (Eph. 6:11; 1 Thess. 5:8).
6. Mercy and kindness (Col. 3:12; compare Isa. 55:3; Acts 13:34).
7. Fine linen, clean and white (Rev. 10:14).

"Where, O death, is your victory (triumph, conquest)? *Where, O death, is your sting* (as that of bees, scorpions, or locusts; poison)?"

The sting of death is sin, and the power (dunamis) *of sin is the law.*

But thanks be to God! He gives us the victory through our Lord Jesus Christ (1 Cor. 15:55-57, NIV).

God Speaks Three Times

Having come full circle, we return to Job 33 to direct our attention to Zion's overcoming company. We focus again on the "messenger" apprehended for the high calling—*"one among a thousand."*

For God speaketh once, yea twice, yet man perceiveth (discern, understand) *it not.*

In a dream, in a vision of the night, when deep sleep falleth upon men, in slumberings upon the bed;

Then he openeth the ears of men, and sealeth their instruction,

That he may withdraw (turn aside) *man from his purpose, and hide pride from man* (Job 33:14-17).

God always speaks in threes, in "excellent" things (Prov. 22:20-21). He spoke "once," the first time, in the Outer Court, in the Feast of Passover. He then spoke "twice," the second time, in the Holy Place, in the Feast of Pentecost. But we must move beyond the first and second day if we are to fully perceive His purpose and plan.

In the Outer Court, the evangelicals are dreaming about Heaven, with its pearly gates and mansions fair.

In the Holy Place, Pentecostals and Charismatics are sound asleep in Adam, having night visions and nightmares about the devil, the old man, the antichrist and the mark of the beast, the tribulation period, the end of the world, of hell, and their fear of being "left behind."

But *"then"* God speaks a *third time* in the Most Holy Place, in the Feast of Tabernacles! There alone does He fully open the ears of men and seal their instruction. From that place He now sounds the alarm. Only "third day" truth turns Adam away from his determined purpose to die. We have found a "Ransom," the One who is our righteousness!

This word in Job 33:24 means, "a cover; redemption-price; the price of a life." It is also translated as "satisfaction."[9]

> *"Yet if there is an angel on his side as a mediator, one out of a thousand, to tell a man what is right for him,*
>
> *to be gracious to him and say, 'Spare him from going down to the pit; I have found a ransom for him'—*
>
> *then his flesh is renewed like a child's; it is restored as in the days of his youth.*
>
> *He prays to God and finds favor with him, he sees God's face and shouts for joy; he is restored by God to his righteous state...*
>
> *...He redeemed my soul from going down to the pit, and I will live to enjoy the light.*
>
> *God does all these things to a man—twice, even three times—*
>
> *to turn back his soul from the pit, that the light of life may shine on him."* (Job 33:23-30, NIV).

God's Messenger and Interpreter will show the way to life.

As for me, I will behold thy face in righteousness: I shall be satisfied, when I awake, with thy likeness (Ps. 17:15).

We have come full circle from David's prayer. We all fell asleep somewhere in the Feast of Pentecost. It seems we are just now waking up in the Feast of Tabernacles!

In the Song of Solomon, "night" bespeaks His absence. The Shulamite had gone to the house of wine and received the Pentecostal experience (Song 2:4 with Acts 2:4). She then dreamed that she had lost Him (Song 3:1-4). But once she got beyond the watchmen, the preachers, she found Him, and passionately held Him in her understanding.

When she awoke, the first and only face that she beheld was His! Awake, O Zion! You never lost Him. Your nightmare was not real. All that time you were dreaming, your Beloved was carrying you! His left hand was under your head, and His right hand did embrace you (Song 2:6). Jesus was there all the time!

After all, you are the apple of His eye, His treasure. You are His choice one, destined to live and not die—*"one among a thousand."*

Endnotes

1. Consider these verses where the same Hebrew word rendered as "choice" in Song 6:9 is used (see Job 11:4; Ps. 19:8; 24:4; 73:1; Prov. 14;4; Song 6:10).

2. My teaching with regard to the "Genesis Face" from James 1:17-25 is fully elucidated in Volume One of my revised notes on the Tabernacle of Moses. There I show that the Brazen Laver reveals the face of Jesus, and the knowledge of the glory of God (2 Cor. 4:6). My "natural face" is my "genesis face," literally, "the face of my birth" (James 1:18). The Man in the Mirror is the New Man, created in righteousness and true holiness. The Man in the Mirror is Jesus. As we contemplate and behold Him in worship, we are changed into the "same image" from glory to glory (2 Cor. 3:18)—we become what we worship. The old order, marked by sin-consciousness, takes the Bible and says to all, "Behold your sinfulness." Men and women of Zion take the same Scriptures and say to all, "Behold His righteousness"!

3. Isaiah 28 should be studied alongside 2 Peter 2:9-22. Both passages vividly describe the old order, the religious systems of men, and the "drunkards of Ephraim," who stop at Pentecost.

4. "Filthy lucre" is the Greek word *aischrokerdes* which means, "shameful, sordid, base gain." It is especially mentioned with regard to elders and deacons (see 1 Tim. 3:3,8; Titus 1:7; 1 Pet. 5:2).

5. My book *Whose Right It Is* provides an in-depth look into what history and the Bible have to say about classical Scofieldian dispensationalism. Of special note is Chapter Ten, which is an exegesis of Daniel 9:24-27 (Daniel's Prophecy of Seventy Weeks), the keynote passage and the sole basis of Scofield's seven-year Tribulation Period with all its trappings.

6. To "vomit" is to "spew out, vomit up" (see Job 20:15; Prov. 23:8; 25:16; 26:11; Isa. 19:14; 28:8; and Jer. 48:26). The Greek word is *exerama* and means, "to spew, vomit, food disgorged." It is only mentioned in 2 Peter 2:22 – "But it is happened unto them according to the true proverb, The dog is turned to his own vomit again; and the sow that was washed to her wallowing in the mire" (a direct quote from Prov. 26:11).

7. The Hebrew word for "scourge" means, "a lash or a whip" (Job 5:21; 9:23; Isa. 10:26; 28:15,18). The Greek word used in John 2:15 means, "a whip; the Roman lash as a public punishment." *Vine's Dictionary* adds that the whip was in itself a sign of authority and judgment.

8. This is the Hebrew word *kaphar* (Strong's #3722), a primitive root that means, "to cover (specifically with bitumen); figuratively, to expiate or condone, to placate or cancel." It is rendered in the King James Version as "appease, make (an atonement, cleanse, disannul, forgive, be merciful, pacify, pardon, purge (away), put off, (make) reconcile (-liation)."

9. Note these cross-references for the word for "ransom" (see Gen. 6:14; Ex. 30:12; Num. 35:31-32; Ps. 49:7; and Prov. 13:8).

Wake up, wake up, Jerusalem, and clothe yourselves with strength [from God]. *Put on your beautiful clothes, O Zion, Holy City: for sinners—those who turn from God—will no longer enter your gates.*

Rise from the dust, Jerusalem; take off the slave bands from your neck, O captive daughter of Zion.

For the Lord says, When I sold you into exile I asked no fee from your oppressor; now I can take you back again and owe them not a cent! (Isa. 52:1-3, TLB).

That is why God says in the Scriptures, "Awake, O sleeper, and rise up from the dead, and Christ shall give you light." (Eph. 5:14, TLB).

CHAPTER FOUR

AWAKE WITH NEW PERSPECTIVE: ZION IS A PLACE

Chapter One introduced the theme of this writing, that there *is* a high calling, and that His overcoming sons and daughters are arising throughout the nations to answer that heavenly summons.

Chapter Two challenged the glorious Church to awake even though *it's still dark out there.* We do not have all the answers. There are times when our pathway to Zion's dominion is foggy and not always clear. Nonetheless, we push forward with fresh conviction as God's faith urges us on.

Chapter Three uniquely presented the people of His choosing— "*one among a thousand*" (Job 33:23). The righteous are as bold as a lion (Prov. 28:1). Godly courage is required of all those who press toward the mark for the prize of light and life.

This present chapter and the next zero in on "Zion." The writings of the prophet Isaiah reveal Zion to be the *place* of His presence. The Book of Psalms richly describes Zion as a *people* of praise and glory.

The Church is rousing from the slumber of compromise and cowardice. We are standing up with new faith and new courage. We now stir ourselves with *new perspective.* Zion is a *place,* the secret place of the Most High. This point of view is from the heavens, the foreordained place of our being seated with Christ.

God is searching the nations (2 Chron. 16:9) for a sold-out people with this new attitude of heart. We are waiting on the Lord

(Isa. 40:31), learning to see things from His point of view, to move at His pace, and to operate our lives and ministries under His directives.

We quiet our hearts that we may enter His peace. We sense our inadequacies, but are being empowered by His strength. We lay down our wills that we may clearly hear His calling. We are mounting up, lifted and carried by the wind of His Spirit. We steadily move ahead, ever sensitive to His timing. We confidently act, giving ourselves only to the things that He has asked us to do.

The Significance of Zion

Nevertheless David took (captured, seized, occupied) *the strong hold* (fortress, castle) *of Zion: the same is the city of David* (2 Sam. 5:7).

The meaning of "Zion" underwent a distinct progression in its usage. Its first mention above is the name of the ancient Jebusite fortress situated on the southeast hill of Jerusalem. After David captured this ancient stronghold, he called Zion "the city of David" (1 Kings 8:1; 1 Chron. 11:5; 2 Chron. 5:2).

When Solomon built the Temple on Mount Moriah (a hill distinct from Mount Zion), and moved the Ark of the Covenant there, the word "Zion" expanded in meaning to include also the Temple and the Temple area (Ps. 2:6; 48:2,11-12; 132:13). Later, "Zion" was used as a name for the city of Jerusalem, the land of Judah, and the people of Israel as a whole (Isa. 40:9; Jer. 31:12).

The Hebrew word for Zion is *Tsiyown* (Strong's #6726 and #6725), and it means, "conspicuousness; a monument, sign post, column, landmark, or a guiding pillar; sunny mountain."[1] "Zion" has also been translated as, "sunny; clear, unobstructed, or sunshine; set up, placed, or established."

There are two dominant themes associated with Zion in both Testaments. One is *political,* and the other is *religious.*

First, Zion was the city of King David, the capital city and the governing city of the nation—this reveals the *king* principle.

In Zion, King David (a type of King Jesus) ruled over the people of God. The government of God was revealed in the kingdom of David. The law went forth from Zion, and the Word of the Lord from

Jerusalem (Isa. 2:3; Mic. 4:2). Zion was the abode of the king and his family. It was the highest pinnacle of attainable glory, rulership, and power.

Second, Zion was the city of the Tabernacle of David, the sacred city, the religious capital of the nation—this reveals the *priest* principle.

In Zion, David also led the nation in a new order of worship and ministry. His Tabernacle was a simple, single tent (with no veil) which constituted the transplanting of the Most Holy Place with its Ark of the Covenant to the top of David's "holy hill." It was on this holy ground that the "sweet psalmist of Israel" (2 Sam. 23:1) composed many of his 73 psalms of praise.

The revelation of New Testament worship originated under David's tent. The use of the mouth (speaking, singing, and shouting), the hands (clapping, lifting, and playing instruments), and the whole body (bowing, kneeling, and dancing) to praise the Lord was a stark contrast to the old Mosaic order.

David changed the ministry of the priests. Instead of having to carry the heavy burden of the Mosaic Tabernacle from place to place, they now were appointed and divided into 24 courses (1 Chron. 24) to praise the God of Israel round the clock, seven days a week (24/7)! The present-day "harp and bowl" meetings (constant worship and intercession) are based upon David's pattern.

> *Yet have I set My king upon My holy hill of Zion...* (See Ps. 2:6 and compare with Ps. 15:1; 43:3).

The "holy hill" of Zion points to the New Testament priesthood after the order of Melchisedec (Heb. 5:1-8:6). This is the King-Priest ministry of the ascended Christ, His "more excellent ministry"[2] (Heb. 8:6), and His "royal priesthood" (1 Pet. 2:9). This priestly ministry is the manifestation of the ascended life, flowing out from the finished work of King Jesus who is seated and enthroned within the Most Holy Place. This is the outflowing of the indwelling Christ from the heart.

Again, Zion was the final stronghold for David and his army. The "last enemy" for the overcoming Church, David's seed, to conquer is death (1 Cor. 15:26). This truth was the major theme of the previous chapter, "One Among a Thousand."

In the New Testament, the significance of Zion is twofold.

*But ye are come unto mount Sion, and unto the city of the living
God, the heavenly Jerusalem...*

To the general assembly and church of the firstborn... (Heb. 12:22-23).

First, "Zion" designates the Church as a whole. The verses
above underscore the weakness of dispensationalism, which inter-
prets the New Testament in the light of the Old Testament, rather
than explain the Old Testament in the light of New Testament.
"Zion" is neither natural Israel nor the natural Jew only. "Zion" is
the *Church*, made up of both Jew and Greek in one Body by the
Cross (Eph. 2:11-22)!

*To him that overcometh will I grant to sit with Me in my throne,
even as I also overcame, and am set down with My Father in His
throne* (Rev. 3:21).

Second, "Zion" designates the corporate Overcomer within the
Church, "him that overcometh" (Rev. 2-3).[3]

Thus "Zion" constitutes the highest order, the "high calling"
(Phil. 3:12-14) of those who are destined to rule and reign with Jesus,
a Most Holy Place people (as emphasized in Chapter Five). "Zion"
represents the "throne" of God, typified by the Ark of the Covenant.
The Old Testament word for "throne" means, "the seat of honor" (Gen.
41:40; 1 Kings 10:18-20). The Greek word is similar, rendered as "the
seat of authority" (Heb. 4:16).

Moreover, the Book of Revelation says much about Zion's throne:

1. The Overcomer sits on Christ's throne (Rev. 3:21).

2. The ManChild Company rules (shepherds) the nation from
   the throne of God (Rev. 12:5).

3. The 144,000 reign with the Lamb from Mount Zion
   (Rev. 14:1).

*After this I beheld, and, lo, a great multitude, which no man could
number, of all nations, and kindreds, and people, and tongues,
stood before the throne, and before the Lamb...* (Rev. 7:9).

Not every Christian will rule and reign with Him in Zion (2 Tim.
2:12). Multitudes are serving the Lord with the light (understanding)
that they have. They stand *before* the throne and no man can number
them. But the overcoming company in Zion is granted the honor of
sitting with the Lamb *in* His throne (Rev. 3:21).

Could it be that some of those who weep "before the throne" (Rev. 7:17) are doing so because they were called to sit "in" the throne? Many who refused to pay the price will end up with a saved soul and a lost life as God burns up the wood, the hay, and the stubble of their unwise choices (1 Cor. 3:11-15). They won't go to hell, but it will be hellish to look at the Lamb's throne and behold where they should have been (with Him) and what they could have been (in Him).

Finally, the significance of Zion is seen in these key verses from the Book of Psalms:[4]

> *Great is the Lord, and greatly to be praised in the city of our God, in the mountain of his holiness.*

> *Beautiful for situation, the joy* (strength) *of the whole earth, is Mount Zion, on the sides of the north, the city of the great king* (who was David, and now is Jesus) (Ps. 48:1-2).

> *Thou shalt arise, and have mercy* (to love deeply with compassion) *upon Zion: for the time to favour her* (to bend or stoop in kindness to an inferior; to be gracious, pit, to bestow), *yea, the set time* (appointed, sacred season or feast), *is come* (Ps. 102:13).

> *For the Lord hath chosen Zion; He hath desired* (wish, wait longingly, crave) *it* (a place and a people) *for His habitation* (seat).

> *This is My rest* (resting-place – this pictures a finished people and a finished work) *for ever: here will I dwell; for I have desired it* (Ps. 132:13-14).

It's Time to Move On

For our conversation (community, citizenship) *is in heaven; from whence also we look* (take our perspective)... (Phil. 3:20).

The people of God are awakening with *fresh perspective* as we discover the reality of a place called Zion. We are returning to the original vision, the high calling. Our citizenship is settled in the heavenly places, from whence we view the earth.

King David and his priestly band fetched the Ark of glory from Obed-edom's house and moved it to Zion (1 Chron. 15:25; 16:1). God's people have begun to relocate from the Feast of Pentecost to the Feast of Tabernacles. Strike the tents (Num. 9:17-18). Move out from sophomoric adolescence into the full proof of our ministries. We must be borne along by the Spirit (Rom. 8:14). There is no Plan B and we don't get a vote. We are under new orders, new direction.

God has waited patiently for the precious fruit of the earth (James 5:7). He has worked on some of us for decades, pruning and processing, getting us ready for this day. The set time for Zion has come!

But many are fainting in the Day of the Lord. Some are unhappy because they have a hundredfold calling and a thirtyfold commitment. Divided hearts have pursued other lovers. Anyone or anything that we put ahead of the Lord is an idol of the heart. This is not a time to faint. Press on!

Zion Is the Place of the High Calling

Brethren, I count not myself to have apprehended: but this one thing I do, forgetting those things which are behind, and reaching forth unto those things which are before,

I press toward the mark for the prize of the high calling of God in Christ Jesus. (Phil. 3:13-14).

I press on toward the goal to win the prize for which God has called me heavenward in Christ Jesus (Phil. 3:14, NIV).

Our "high (upward) calling" into Zion was introduced in Chapter One.

The apostle Paul determined to "press" or "follow after" the deeper things of God, toward the "mark," the "distant mark looked at, the goal or end in view." His eye was fixed on the "prize," the award given to the victor in the public games (1 Cor. 9:24).

Note the apostle's attitude in Philippians 3:13. He declares that "forgetting" the past and "reaching forth" into our destiny constitute "one thing." We must not interpret anything that is happening now in the light of anything that has happened up till now. We no longer sing or preach about where we've been, but rather where we are, and where we are headed, a whole other place.

Who hath wrought and done it, calling the generations from the beginning? I the Lord, the first, and with the last; I am He (Isa. 41:4).

The primary Hebrew word for "call" or "calling" is *qara'* (Strong's #7121), and it means, "to call out to (loudly); to address by name; to choose." Its root means, "to encounter, meet." The key idea here is "to call out loudly" in order to get someone's attention.

> *For the gifts and (the) calling of God are without repentance* (Rom. 11:29).

> *Partakers of the heavenly calling...* (Heb. 3:1).

> *Wherefore the rather, brethren, give diligence to make your calling and election sure...*

(See 2 Pet. 1:10 and compare Eph. 1:18; 4:4.)

The Greek word for "calling" in all these verses is *klesis* (Strong's #2821), and it means, "an invitation (to a feast)."[5] It is taken from *kaleo* (to call aloud; to call by name); and *keleuo* (to hail or incite by word; command or order; and the primary *kello* (to urge on). The inward urgency of the Kingdom is the very voice of the King from within, as He ever and always urges us on!

The Characteristics of the Place Called Zion

Zion is a *place*, the place of the high calling! The study below is taken from the Book of Isaiah, where "Zion" is mentioned 46 times. The next chapter will show the characteristics of the *people* called Zion as revealed from the Book of Psalms.

1. Zion is the place to which the nations shall come (Isa. 2:3).
2. Zion is the place of the Lord's presence and glory (Isa. 4:5)
3. Zion is the place of signs and wonders (Isa. 8:18).
4. Zion is the place of God's greatness (Isa. 12:6).
5. Zion is the place of the sure foundation (Isa. 28:16).
6. Zion is the place of answered prayer (Isa. 30:19).
7. Zion is the place of the fiery furnace (Isa. 31:9).
8. Zion is the place of justice and righteousness (Isa. 33:5).
9. Zion is the place of peace, safety, and stability (Isa. 33:20).
10. Zion is the place of joy and gladness (Isa. 35:10).
11. Zion is the place of the righteous remnant (Isa. 37:32).
12. Zion is the place of fearlessness (Isa. 40:9).
13. Zion is the place of salvation and deliverance (Isa. 46:3).

14. Zion is the place of comfort and restoration (Isa. 51:3).

15. Zion is the place of the beauty of holiness (Isa. 52:1).

16. Zion is the place of the Good News (Isa. 52:7).

17. Zion is the place of unity and agreement (Isa. 52:8).

18. Zion is the place of redemption (Isa. 59:20).

19. Zion is the place of the Lord's recompense (Isa. 60:14).

20. Zion is the place of praise (Isa. 61:3).

21. Zion is the place of birthing the Man Child (Isa. 66:8).

The Book of Isaiah reveals Zion to be a *place*.

Zion Is the Place of Transformation

The very first mention of "Sion" in the Scriptures was given to us by the prophet Moses.

From Aroer, which is by the bank of the river Arnon, even unto mount Sion, which is Hermon (Deut. 4:48).

"Sion" was the ancient name for Mount Hermon. While some believe that Mount Tabor was the Mount of Jesus' Transfiguration, many others say that Hermon was the place where He displayed His glory. In this view, "Sion" was the place of His transformation.

And after six days Jesus taketh with him Peter, and James, and John, and leadeth them up into an high mountain apart by themselves: and He was transfigured before them.

And His raiment became shining, exceeding white as snow; so as no fuller (bleacher) on earth can white them (See Mark 9:2-3 and compare Matt. 17:1-2).

"Sion" was the "high mountain apart" (the high calling), the mountain of change! The word for "transfigured" is *metamorphoo*, and it means, "to change into another form." It is also translated as "transformed" (Rom. 12:2) and "changed" (2 Cor. 3:18).

Luke's narrative (Luke 9:29) says that the "fashion" (appearance) of His countenance was "altered." This Greek construction is *ginomai heteros*, and means that Jesus "became the other (nature, form, class, kind) in quality." The blue of Heaven swallowed up the ruddy red of earth. As with the Ark hidden behind the curtain of Moses' Tabernacle, so the glory of the Father was veiled beneath His flesh. Peter, James, and John saw Him as the Father saw Him all the time. His raiment "glistened" (to lighten forth, to be radiant, to send forth lightning, to shine) on the top of the mountain.

For precept must be upon precept, precept upon precept; line upon line, line upon line; here a little, and there a little: (Isa. 28:10).

Spiritual growth denotes change after change after change. Those called up to Zion are ever being changed "from strength to strength" (Ps. 84:7), "from faith to faith" (Rom. 1:17), and "from glory to glory" (2 Cor. 3:18). Our spiritual metamorphosis, our maturing in grace is a steady ascent into the hill of the Lord.

Moses and His friends experienced the Old Testament Mount of Transfiguration when they were called up to the place of worship. The entire setting is a picture of the Feast of Tabernacles.

Then went up Moses, and Aaron, Nadab, and Abihu, and seventy of the elders of Israel:

And they saw the God of Israel: and there was under His feet as it were a paved work of a sapphire stone, and as it were the body of heaven in His clearness.

And upon the nobles of the children of Israel he laid not His hand: also they saw God, and did eat and drink (Exod. 24:9-11).

And they saw the God of Israel [that is, a convincing manifestation of His presence]... (Exod. 24:10, AMP).

Zion is the mountain of change, the place of transformation. Jesus and His three disciples descended from the mountaintop to bring deliverance. We are called to roar out of Zion and to go into the earth to bring "a convincing manifestation of His presence."

When we preach salvation, men and women are saved, but not changed. When we teach about the Holy Ghost, men and women are filled with the Spirit, but not transformed. The only message that will transform people and change the world is the gospel of the Kingdom, the message of Zion!

Yet it is not enough to hear about Zion. We must have a meaningful relationship with the King and His brethren who live there with Him, or we will never be changed. May this be our prayer:

"Father, we rise up to the occasion in this place called Zion. With one voice and one Spirit, one heart, one mind, one body, marching in one step, side by side, shoulder to shoulder, we choose to be a force to be reckoned with in this world. We call out to the generations that are here, to the generations that are coming, and to the generations who have been here. Awake, O Zion! Rise up to be what you have always been. Amen!"

Make Your Calling and Election Sure

Brethren, be all the more solicitous and eager to make sure (to ratify, to strengthen, to make steadfast) *your calling and election: for if you do this, you will never stumble or fall* (2 Pet. 1:10, AMP).

Zion is the highest place in the Kingdom, the destiny of the most high saints of the Most Holy Place (Dan. 7:19-27). The God of Zion is *El-elyon*, the Most High God. The Hebrew word for the "burnt offering" is in the same word family. *Olah* means, "the ascending offering." In the burnt offering, God received all, the complete sacrifice. Zion's calling demands our complete surrender as a whole burnt offering.

David and his dynasty, the kings of Judah, ruled and reigned from Zion. The thrones of the kings, and the tombs of the kings were in Zion! You will die in Zion before you will live in Zion.[6]

What do you want out of life? Where are you headed? What has God asked of you? What is your assignment?

What is the will of the Lord for you and your family? What is the Word of the Lord for your ministry? What do you want for your children and your grandchildren?

And many nations shall come, and say, Come, and let us go up to the mountain of the Lord, and to the house of the God of Jacob; and He will teach us of his ways, and we will walk in His paths: for the law shall go forth of Zion, and the word of the Lord from Jerusalem (Micah 4:2).

Are you sure that you really want to identity with apostolic ministries like mine? That you want to journey with men like me? We live in a furnace. Zion's path is a baptism of fire. There is a law in Zion. We cannot be lawless and ascend his holy hill at the same time.

Lord, who may dwell in your sanctuary? Who may live on your holy hill?

He whose walk is blameless and who does what is righteous, who speaks the truth from his heart

and has no slander on his tongue, who does his neighbor no wrong and casts no slur on his fellowman,

who despises a vile man but honors those who fear the Lord, who keeps his oath even when it hurts,

who lends his money without usury and does not accept a bribe against the innocent. He who does these things will never be shaken (Ps. 15:1-5, NIV).

Zion inhabitants are a different breed. At first we felt so out of place, so strange. Each of us asked ourselves, "Am I losing my mind? No one is saying what I am hearing in my heart." This book is filled with hundreds of Scriptures; it puts chapter and verse to what many of you have sensed in your spirit. You have heard that still, small voice of the Spirit's wooing. Now, thank God, you can find "Zion" in the Bible!

Like Joel, I am jealous for Zion. As did the ancient prophet, I am sounding the alarm. I am crying out to peer ministry and a people who will ascend with me. When I preach these truths, the faces of people show everything from delight to terror. Many say in their hearts, "I wish he wouldn't talk about the overcoming life, about conquering death, and just stay out of that stuff."

I cannot. There *is* a high calling. If everyone (including this author) who reads this book dropped dead and went to Heaven today, it still remains that "we shall not all sleep" (1 Cor. 15:51).

And as it is appointed unto men once to die, but after this the judgment (Heb. 9:27).

Jesus met that appointment! He chose to "taste" (experience) death for every man (Heb. 2:9). Somebody is going to arise and walk in the fullness of His Testament, to live in all that He died for!

Verily, verily, I say unto you, Except a corn of wheat fall into the ground and die, it abideth alone: but if it die, it bringeth forth much fruit (John 12:24).

Make no mistake. Those who awake and rise to the heights of Zion will die a custom-designed death to self. We cannot sit in the presence of this caliber of anointed Word and stay the same. The Word and the Spirit will challenge and change us.

I have preached the gospel of the Kingdom and these truths about Zion since 1969. It frightens me when I see those in our home church or in other places who have been called to Zion, those who have heard the truth, and are not moved by it any more.

Make your calling and election sure. Crucify your fears. Who is on the Lord's side? Who among you is not afraid to identify with the *people* of Zion?

ENDNOTES

1. Compare *natsach* (Strong's #5329), which means, "to glitter from afar, to be eminent (as a superintendent, especially of the Temple services and its music); to be permanent; to excel, to be bright, to be preeminent, to be perpetual, to be overseer, to be enduring." This latter word is derived from *netsach* (Strong's #5331), which means, "a goal, the bright object at a distance traveled towards; eminence, victory; hence (figuratively), splendor, or (subjectively) truthfulness, or (objectively) confidence; but usually (adverbially), continually (to the most distant point of view), unto the end."

2. My book, *The More Excellent Ministry*, is an in-depth study of the priesthood after the order of Melchisedec.

3. The Greek word for "overcome" is *nikao* (Strong's #3528) and it means, "to subdue, conquer, prevail; to carry off the victory; to win the case (when one is arraigned or goes to law)." It is rendered in the King James Version as "conquer, overcome, prevail, get the victory" (see Luke 11:22; John 16:33; Rom. 3:4; 12:21; 1 John 2:13-14; 4:4; 5:4-5; and Rev. 2,11,17,26; 3:5:12;21; 5:5; 6:2; 11:7; 12:11; 13:7; 15:2; 17:14; 21:7).

4. The Book of Psalms is filled with references to Zion, as emphasized in the next chapter. For example, Zion is described in 2 Samuel 5:7 as a "strong hold" (KJV). David uses the same Hebrew word to describe His God, His "fortress" (rock, high tower, strong habitation, refuge)—see 2 Samuel 22:2 and Ps. 18:2; 31:3; 71:3; 91:2; 144:2.

5. *Klesis* is mentioned a total of 12 times (the biblical number denoting divine government) in the Greek New Testament. In addition to the six verses (including Philippians 3:14) given in the text of this chapter, consider also 1Cor. 1:26; 7:20; Eph. 4:1 ("vocation"); 2 Thess. (twice); and 2 Tim. 1:9.

6. The price for living in Zion is discussed in Chapter Eight of my book, *The More Excellent Ministry*, and is entitled, "A Groan from the Throne." It is based upon Psalms 122:3 – "Jerusalem is builded as a city that is compact together." There we discuss three mountains: Ophel, Moriah, and Zion, which speak of the Feasts of Passover, Pentecost, and Tabernacles.

Bestir yourself, bestir yourself, O Sion, robe yourself with strength! O sacred city of Jerusalem, put on your rich apparel! For pagans and profane men never more shall enter you.

Rise, shake the dust from you, captive Jerusalem, loosen your shackles now, O captive maiden Sion!

For this is what the Eternal declares: "Once you were sold for nothing, and now you shall be freed without any payment." (Isa. 52:1-3, Moffatt)

Therefore He says, Awake, O sleeper, and arise from the dead, and Christ shall shine [make day dawn] upon you and give you light (Eph. 5:14, AMP).

CHAPTER FIVE

AWAKE WITH
NEW RELATIONSHIPS:
ZION IS A PEOPLE

Zion is awakening in this Third Day of apostolic reformation. *New faith, new courage,* and a *new perspective* mark the corporate, overcoming Church. We have received fresh faith to arise in the misty dawning of this new day, fresh courage to fearlessly proclaim all that God is presently saying to His people, and fresh perspective to order our lives and ministries from our seated posture in the heavenly places, from the standpoint of the high calling.

None of these dynamics will effectively impact the next two generations and their seed without *new relationships.* Zion is more than a *place* in the heavenlies. Zion is a *people.* We are reconnecting to all those whom God has foreordained to walk with us in His one grand, prophetic purpose.

> *For we are God's [own] handiwork (His workmanship), recreated in Christ Jesus, [born anew] that we may do those good works which God predestined (planned beforehand) for us, (taking paths which he prepared ahead of time) that we should walk in them—living the good life which He prearranged and made ready for us to live* (Eph. 2:10, AMP).

The Sevenfold Promise to Him Who Overcometh

Zion is a *people.* This corporate Overcomer, "he that hath an ear," is addressed seven times in Revelation 2-3.

He that hath an ear, let him hear what the Spirit saith unto the churches; To him that overcometh will I give to eat of the tree of life, which is in the midst of the paradise of God (See Rev. 2:7 and compare Luke 23:43; 2 Cor. 12:4).

Zion, the glorioius Church, branches off from the One who is the Vine (John 15:5). Jesus, the Tree of Life, poured out His life on the tree of death. The corporate Overcomer partakes of Eden's dominion.

He that overcometh shall not be hurt (injured, damaged, or harmed) *of the second death* (Rev. 2:11).

Zion's army is protected, walking in a spiritual immunity.

To him that overcometh will I give to eat of the hidden manna (in the Ark of the Covenant, as in Heb. 9:4), *and will give him a white stone, and in the stone a new name written, which no man knoweth saving he that receiveth it* (Rev. 2:17).

Zion's people are partakers of the divine nature (2 Pet. 1:4), the "hidden manna" preserved within the Ark of the Covenant (Heb. 9:4). They are the benefactors of a "white stone," which was often used in the social life and judicial customs of the ancients to speak of light, and life, and favor.[1] Only those who live in Zion will "receive" (seize, embrace; obtain) this.

And he that overcometh, and keepeth my works unto the end, to him will I give power (authority) *over the nations. And he shall rule them with a rod of iron; as the vessels of a potter shall they be broken to shivers: even as I received of my Father* (Rev. 2:26-27).

Zion's family will "rule" or shepherd the nations (compare the ministry of the "man child" in Rev. 12:5).

He that overcometh, the same shall be clothed in white raiment; and I will not blot out (erase, wipe out) *his name out of the book of life, but I will confess his name before My Father, and before His angels* (Rev. 3:5).

Zion's sons and daughters are arrayed in "white raiment," which is "the righteousness of saints" (Rev. 19:8).

Him that overcometh will I make a pillar (column, support) *in the temple of my God, and he shall go no more out: and I will write upon him the name of My God, and the name of the city of My*

God, which is new Jerusalem, which cometh down out of heaven from My God: and I will write upon him My new name (nature) (Rev. 3:12).

Zion's people are like pillars, steadfast and upright, steady in their character and spiritual demeanor (compare Gal. 2:9 and 1 Tim. 3:15).

To him that overcometh will I grant to sit (down) *with Me in My throne, even as I also overcame, and am set down with My Father in His throne* (Rev. 3:21).

Zion's company rule with the Lord from His place and seat of authority (compare again the "man child" of Rev. 12:5).

He that overcometh shall inherit (possess) *all things; and I will be His God, and he shall be My son* (Rev. 21:7).

John sums up the sevenfold promise in the twenty-first chapter. The people of Zion are "heirs of God, and joint-heirs with Christ" (Rom. 8:17), kept and trained under "tutors and governors" (Eph. 4:11) until the adoption (son-placing), the "time appointed of the Father" (Gal. 4:1). The word for "son" in Revelation 21:7 is *huios*, the word used for the "mature son."

The Corporate Overcomer

Zion is a *people*, the corporate Overcomer. His "high calling" to us is to build a people who will walk and live in Zion, who will *be* Zion! The Hebrew word for "son" is *ben*. Its verb is *banah* and it means, "to build or re-build." God's eternal purpose in Christ is to "build a son"!

The previous chapter made clear that there are two ways in which "Zion" is presented in the Scriptures: First, to designate the Church as a whole (Heb. 12:22). Second, to specify the corporate Overcomer within the Church.

But small is the gate and narrow (compressed, contracted) *the road that leads to life, and only a few find it* (Matt. 7:14, NIV).

This narrower theme, the corporate Overcomer, is why we are blowing the trumpet in Zion. Our passion is to awaken men and women to this highest order, the high calling. We cry out to a Most Holy Place people.

That which is born of the flesh is flesh; and that which is born of the Spirit is spirit (John 3:6).

As shown earlier, the Tabernacle of David was in Zion. The Ark of the Covenant was placed under a simple, single tent without a veil in the place that David had prepared (1 Chron. 16:1). There is a price to pay for all this glory. Once you hear this message of "present truth" in your spirit, it's too late!

As seen in a later chapter, not even the locusts of tradition can move you. You are not a human being trying to have a spiritual experience; first and foremost, you are a spirit being of whom God Almighty is the Father (Heb. 12:9). Your mind is spiritual—you have the mind of Christ (1 Cor. 2:16). Your appetite is spiritual—you long for the Word of God (Job 23:12).

And if the servant shall plainly say, I love my master, my wife, and my children; I will not go out free:

Then his master shall bring him unto the judges; he shall also bring him to the door, or unto the door post; and his master shall bore his ear through with an aul; and he shall serve him for ever (Exod. 21:5-6).

Those who are hearing Zion's trumpet have pierced ears. In the seventh year,[2] the slave could go free. But the slave who loved his master and wanted to stay because of love, not duty, had his ear pierced at the door. Later in Israel's history, the people tired of Moses and his message of present truth (for that day), and divorced their ear from the voice of Jehovah and His servant (Exod. 32:1-6).

Blow the trumpet in Zion, sanctify a fast, call a solemn assembly (Joel 2:15).

Zion's trumpet is sounding, calling us to the Day of Atonement and a final commitment. As with Ruth, it beckons us to the threshing floor. Wash the dust, the fine points, off your feet (all those things that you've not allowed the Lord to touch in your life up till now), and humble yourself at the feet of your Kinsman-Redeemer. It is time for us, especially the leaders, to sanctify ourselves. Let every preacher and priest bend over the lip of the laver in intercession, fill it with our tears, and then bathe in it.

Biblical Pictures of the People of Zion

This corporate Overcomer and partaker of the high calling is revealed throughout the Bible. Below are listed the more notable scriptural examples. The *people* of Zion are revealed as:

1. The Joseph Company (Gen. 37-50).[3]
2. The Moses-Aaron (King-Priest) Ministry (Ex. 6-12).[4]
3. David's Mighty Men (2 Sam. 23; 1 Chron. 20).[5]
4. The Elijah Ministry (2 Kings 2).[6]
5. The Shulamite (Song 6:8-9).[7]
6. The Saints of the Most High (Dan. 7:18-27).[8]
7. Joel's Army (Joel 2:1-11) – See Chapter Ten.
8. The Melchisedec Priesthood (Heb. 5:1-8:6).[9]
9. The Hundredfold Company (Matt. 13:23).[10]
10. The Manchild Company (Rev. 12:1-5) – See below.
11. The 144,000, the Firstfruits Company (Rev. 14:1-5) – See below.

The Overcomer Is the Manchild Company

We will briefly examine the latter two of these examples. First, the people of Zion are the Manchild Company. A more in-depth study of Revelation 12:1-5 is set forth in Chapter Four of my book, *Moses, the Master, and the Manchild.*

> *And there appeared a great wonder in heaven; a woman clothed with the sun, and the moon under her feet, and upon her head a crown of twelve stars:*
>
> *And she being with child cried, travailing in birth, and pained to be delivered.*
>
> *And there appeared another wonder in heaven; and behold a great red dragon, having seven heads and ten horns, and seven crowns upon his heads.*
>
> *And his tail drew the third part of the stars of heaven, and did cast them to the earth: and the dragon stood before the woman which was ready to be delivered, for to devour her child as soon as it was born.*

And she brought forth a man child, who was to rule all nations with a rod of iron: and her child was caught up unto God, and to His throne (Rev. 12:1-5).

All through the Scriptures, we see a man, a maid, and a man child. The primary example of this is the story of Abraham, Sarah, and Isaac (Gen. 12-22).

Many believe the sun-clothed Woman of Revelation 12:1 to be natural Israel, but Israel was never in the heavens. This Woman is the Woman of Ephesians; this Woman is the Church, the "freewoman" of Paul's allegory (Gal. 4:21-31). She is clothed all around with Christ, the Sun of righteousness, the Light of the world (Mal. 4:2; John 8:12). The moon representing the law or the powers of darkness, is down under her feet (Rom. 16:20). On her head is a victor's wreath of 12 stars, denoting divine order and government.

This Church is crying aloud, travailing in birth and grievous pain to be delivered (See Gal. 4:19 and compare with Rom. 8:22-23).

The arch-enemy of this Woman and her Manchild is a great, fire-like dragon. He has grown from the serpent of Genesis 3 due to a steady diet of "dust" (Isa. 65:25 with 1 Cor. 15:44-49, AMP). The word "Philistine" means, "to wallow in the dust." The first man Adam was a man of dust.

The dragon stands ready before the Woman to swallow down her Child as soon as he is born. The devil hates the Seed (Gen. 3:15). This same pattern is revealed by the diabolical deeds of Pharaoh (Exod. 1:8-22) and Herod the Great (Matt. 2:13-20).

The Woman, the Church, brings forth a "man child." The Greek construction for this means, "a male, a son." The word for "child" is *huios* and means, "a mature son." This one was destined to rule (shepherd) the nations with a rod (staff scepter) of iron (authority that will not yield or bend). This Manchild was "caught up" (suddenly seized or snatched) unto God, and to His throne (seat of authority; a chair of state having a footstool).

The Overcomer Is the Firstfruits Company

And I looked, and, lo, a Lamb stood on the mount Sion, and with him an hundred forty and four thousand, having his Father's name written in their foreheads.

And I heard a voice from heaven, as the voice of many waters, and as the voice of a great thunder: and I heard the voice of harpers harping with their harps:

And they sung as it were a new song before the throne, and before the four beasts, and the elders: and no man could learn that song but the hundred and forty and four thousand, which were redeemed from the earth.

These are they which were not defiled with women; for they are virgins. These are they which follow the Lamb whithersoever he goeth. These were redeemed from among men, being the firstfruits unto God and to the Lamb.

And in their mouth was found no guile: for they are without fault before the throne of God (Rev. 14:1-5).

The Lamb standing firm on Mount Zion is Jesus (John 1:29). A governmental people (12 times 12,000) are standing "with" Him there. His Father's name (or nature) is written in their foreheads! These now have the same relationship with the Father that He had. These have the mind of Christ (1 Cor. 2:16; Phil. 2:5).

These overcomers carry the voice (sound) of "many waters"[11] and the voice of great thunder, the roar of the Lion of the tribe of Judah. The harpers speak of players and singers of praise.

The 144,000 sing a "new song"[12] before (in the face of) the throne. No one could learn (by use and practice) that new song save the Overcomer. These have been "redeemed" (away) from the earth (Gal. 3:13-14; 1 Pet. 1:18-20).

These prevailers are not soiled, polluted, contaminated, or stained with "women," the Babylonish religious systems of men (Isa. 4:1 with Prov. 7; Rev. 17-18). As virgins, they are pure, without mixture, sanctified unto the Lord alone. They follow Jesus all the way into the Most Holy Place (Heb. 6:19-20). This is the "firstfruits company" unto God and the Lamb—these mature early.

This troop carries the undefiled word and ministry of reconciliation. This is the Man in the throne (Zion) with a ministry of the creative spoken word. In them is no "guile" (lie, falsehood, untruth). The Firstfruits Company is "without fault" (unblemished; unblameable; without stain) before (in the face of) the throne of God!

Those who follow the Lamb wherever He goes know and have said in their hearts: "There's more to life than this. There's more to church than this. There's more in God than this."

Most who have grown up in the evangelical and Pentecostal realms have never heard of or read these truths before. I want to awaken in them and you the awareness of a third dimension, a Third Day.

Do you know what breaks my heart? It's when I look into the eyes of people who have been apprehended for the top of the mountain and who are still struggling within, saying, "Do I really want this?" Sadly, the Lord and I can't do a thing about that.

I have met thousands of people in the last 35 years, including hundreds of preachers, who were apprehended for Zion, but who never really understood the preciousness of their calling. Some of those folks are dead now. Others have left their wife and married another woman, looking for Zion in all the wrong places. Some thought that they heard the voice of God, and felt that they needed another church, another venue. Many have said to me, "Pastor Varner, the Lord has released me from your ministry."

People go from house to house, from church to church. Most "church growth" as we know it in America is like fish changing tanks, and then swimming in circles until the next feeding. Children act like that. I pray that folks will grow out of that kind of behavior.

Others are acting like Solomon of old (Eccl. 2:1-11). This genius had so many wives and concubines that he had three different women everyday and never repeated himself. What a man! But everything King Solomon was not internally, he built externally.

He had no fruit of the Spirit within, so he built gardens and orchards without. He had no living water within, so he built pools that he could see. He had no song within, so he gathered his choirs to hear. But none of these things satisfied the king of wisdom, who sighed, "All is vanity and vexation of spirit." This word for "vanity" means, "emptiness or vanity; figuratively, something transitory and unsatisfactory; a vapor, a breath." Solomon uses this word 38 times in the Book of Ecclesiastes to describe life "under the sun" rather than life "in the Son," in Christ.

The only thing that will satisfy is the message and truth about Zion. The woman at the well in John chapter 4 discovered this life principle. Jesus asked, "Where is your husband?" She replied, "I do not have a husband." But she had had five husbands, and was living with number six. But when she met the Seventh Man, the Perfect Man, she dropped her water pot, became a water pot, reached unto Him, and then ran into the city to tell everyone, "Come, see a Man!"

If you have been apprehended for Zion, you will never be a happy camper in this life until you pursue that calling. Nothing else is going to gratify you. Those of you who are in such a hurry to go someplace, and to do something, and to have something, need to be notified. Some of us are radical, "addicted" to Zion (1 Cor. 16:15). We are carrying a dangerous substance, the high calling.

Once you are infected, contaminated, impregnated with this living germ, the truth about Zion, you will never be the same.

The Characteristics of the High Calling, of Zion the People

In the preceding chapter, we learned that Zion is a *place,* using the Book of Isaiah, where "Zion" is mentioned 46 times. Now we turn to the Book of Psalms, where the psalmist refers to "Zion" 47 times. The Scriptures below reveal that "Zion" is a *people.*

1. The people of Zion are kings, seated and established (Ps. 2:6).

2. The people of Zion show forth all His praise (Ps. 9:14).

3. The people of Zion are called to aid and strengthen the nations (Ps. 20:2).

4. The people of Zion are the joy of the earth (Ps. 48:2).

5. The people of Zion are safe and secure in Christ (Ps. 48:12-13).

6. The people of Zion, the light of the world, radiate the image of God (Ps. 50:2).

7. The people of Zion bring salvation, joy, and gladness (Ps. 53:6).

8. The people of Zion are the heirs of God (Ps. 74:2).

9. The people of Zion dwell in peace and prosperity (Ps. 76:2).

10. The people of God move forward, growing in grace from strength to strength (Ps. 84:7).

11. The people of Zion are the corporate Man, established by El-elyon, the Most High God of the Most Holy Place (Ps. 87:5).

12. The people of Zion receive mercy, grace, and favor in the appointed time (Ps. 102:13).

13. The people of Zion are the place of His appearing (Ps. 102:16).

14. The people of Zion are a people of might and dominion (Ps. 110:2).

15. The people of Zion constitute a Kingdom that cannot be shaken or moved (Ps. 125:1).

16. The people of Zion are a company of dreamers (like the patriarch Joseph and the prophet Daniel) (Ps. 126:1).

17. The people of Zion are hated by the wicked (Ps. 129:5).

18. The people of Zion are the habitation (resting-place) of God (Ps. 132:13-14).

19. The people of Zion walk in commanded blessing, even life evermore (Ps. 133:3).

20. The people of Zion rule and reign with God (Ps. 146:10).

21. The people of Zion are ever joyful in their King (Ps. 149:2).

The Book of Psalms reveals Zion to be a *people*.

David, King of Zion

Zion is a *place*, and Zion is a *people*. But the one Bible character who outshines every example was a lover of Zion—David, the son of Jesse, the shepherd, giant-killer, and sweet psalmist of Israel.

David didn't arrive overnight in Zion. The young shepherd was minding his own business, tending a few sheep, doing his appointed task. Suddenly, the prophet Samuel walked into Bethlehem (1 Sam. 16). Amid the interruptions of life, and business as usual, the Word of the Lord cut through the misty dawn.

All at once, seven brothers were in a power struggle. Eliab, Abinadab, and Shammah were all daunting men like King Saul (a picture of human wisdom and human strength). After God had completely refused their natural charisma, and Samuel (who almost missed it) understood that God looks on the heart, God spoke, "None of these will do. We don't need another like Saul, who throws spears at everybody who disagrees with his program."

Then the prophet asked, "Is there anyone else?" Jesse replied, "Just the runt. He's got red hair, and freckles, and smells like sheep dung. I'll call him, but he's too short and too inexperienced for the job."

Samuel studied the teenager with the eyes of the Spirit. Then Jehovah whispered, "This is My anointed. Open the ram's horn of oil and baptize him with My purpose." Suddenly, the oil on David's brow weighed more than the diadem that he would wear one day as king. In the public arena, the exalted son was anointed in the midst of the brethren in the house of the father. This was David's first anointing.

The exalted son is "Christ in you" (Col. 1:27)! Our steady ascent into Zion began when we were filled with the Holy Ghost. This indwelling Spirit of the Son (Gal. 4:6) changes your life, swallowing up mundane things. This is all done in the midst of the brethren, so that others are blessed to partake of this endowment. It is done in the public arena, the house of the father, the local church.

Second, David was anointed by the tribe of Judah (2 Sam. 2:4)—he became king over "praise." The next stage of Zion's ascent takes place when we learn to rule everything that happens to us by the power of praise. You get to Zion through Judah. Quit talking about yourself and everybody else, and learn to live by the spirit of praise.

Third, the day came when all the elders in Hebron (the place of unity and fellowship) crowned David and made him Lord and king over all things (2 Sam. 5:3). They gathered with one purpose: to make David king. The day will come in our days when all that we are and all that we do will be motivated by one principle: Jesus Christ is King and Lord! All else must bow and change. He is King over our money, over our kids, over our minds, over what we look at and hear, over our conversations—He is King!

God will have a people in the earth called Zion through whom He will administrate and adjudicate every bit of His dominion. To this you are called. This is who you are. Zion is a *place*. Zion is a *people*.

Did David have any problems on the way to Zion? Three thousand men were deputized by the jealous king of the old order with one job description: we are going out to the wilderness to hunt David down like a dog, and then assassinate him. Saul's posse killed 85 priests in Israel trying to get to David (1 Sam. 22). There were many lonely nights in Adullam's dark cave when the young shepherd cried, "My God, what have I done?" The Lord replied, "You haven't done anything. When a man is marked for Zion, people get killed."

The day that David brought the Ark back to Zion (2 Sam. 6), Michal, his wife, was looking from the wrong side of the window. Once you have been raised in Saul's house, unless you have been delivered, you will be like your daddy. But David removed his outer garments, stripped himself, and put on an ephod. In that moment, the king also became a priest, and danced before the Lord with all his might. Zion's sons are a people of great passion. We do everything with all that is in us. We love what God loves, and we hate what God hates.

Michal let David have it. "You embarrassed me today. That's a fine way for a king to act. We never danced that like in daddy's church." But David "behaved himself wisely" on the way to Zion (1 Sam. 18:5,14,15,30; Ps. 101:2). This word means, "to be circumspect and hence, intelligent; prudent, to have insight; to prosper."

With godly zeal he replied, "Do you think I was a mess this Sunday? You wait until next week. I will be wilder than this. What I did offended you, but it was before the face of the Lord." David was more afraid of God than his wife. Michal had a problem the rest of her days. Because the daughter of Saul despised Zion, and hated a man who loved Zion, she was barren from that moment. Never again could she produce anything worthwhile.

The way of life is above to the wise, that he may depart from hell beneath (Prov. 15:24).

What God has prepared is "exceeding abundantly above" all we can ask or think (Eph. 3:20). The way of life is above, in Zion. Up here is Zion and life. Down there is hell and death. Seek those things which are "above" (Col. 3:1).

Awake, O Zion!

This was the message of Joel, the Pentecostal trumpeter! It is time for us to meet this ancient prophet.

ENDNOTES

1. Festal days were noted by a white stone, days of calamity by a black stone – this speaks of light and darkness. In the courts, a white stone indicated acquittal, and a black stone condemnation – this represents life or death. A host's

appreciation of a special guest was indicated by a white stone with the name or a message written on it – this shows honor (favor) or dishonor.

2. The "seventh" year (Exod. 21:2) compares to the Seventh Day from Adam and the Third Day (Hos. 6;1-3) from Jesus (2 Pet. 3:8). Note as well that Enoch, who was translated and who did not taste physical death, was "the seventh from Adam" (Jude 1:14).

3. Joseph wore the birthright coat of dominion. He was sent ahead of his brethren to preserve life in the earth. He was stripped three times: by his jealous half-brothers, and by Potiphar's wife; in the third stripping, he stripped himself. Joseph was sent out of prison to reign, and became second in command, only to the king. He fed his family and the nation in the time of famine.

4. Moses and Aaron brought the plagues of tribulation to Egypt (Exod. 7-12). The rod of Moses became the rod of God (Exod. 4:20; 17:9) that swallowed up the rods of the court magicians (Exod. 7:11-12; 2 Tim. 3:8). Moses became a "god" (elohim) unto Pharaoh (Exod. 7:1).

5. David's mighty men were the crowd that came unto him in the cave of Adullam. These were in distress, in debt, and discontented with Saul, the old order (1 Sam. 22). These who suffered with David in his exile later ruled with him in his kingship. David slew Goliath, the champion of the Philistines and a type of satan. David's mighty men killed all of Goliath's kinfolk (picturing those called to rid the earth of the influence of satan).

6. Elijah was called of God to bring judgment to Ahab and Jezebel (who picture, respectively, political and religious Babylon) (see Rev. 17-18). This unique prophet was transported physically from place to place by the Spirit (1 Kings 18:7-12,44-46). Elijah was translated, carried into Heaven by a whirlwind, and never tasted of physical death (2 Kings 2). There is an end-time, prophetic, corporate Elijah ministry of restoration that precedes the manifestation of the Corporate Son (Mal. 4:5-6 with Matt. 17:1-13).

7. Song of Solomon 6:8-9 reads: "There are threescore queens, and fourscore concubines, and virgins without number. My dove, my undefiled is but one; she is the only one of her mother, she is the choice one of her that bare her. The daughters saw her, and blessed her; yea, the queens and the concubines, and they praised her."

8. Daniel 7:18-27 states that the "saints of the most high," or the most high saints (of the Most Holy Place), shall possess the dominion and greatness of the Kingdom.

9. The Melchisedec Priesthood is the "more excellent (King-Priest) ministry" of the ascended Christ (Heb. 8:6; compare 1 Cor. 12:31; Heb. 1:4; 11:4). This is the "Zadok" priesthood (Ezek. 44) and the "royal priesthood" (1 Pet. 2:9). This priesthood is energized by the power of "an endless life" (Heb. 7:16), and operates by the creative, spoken Word, to forgive and to bless the creation. This is the living expression of the word and ministry of reconciliation (2 Cor. 5:17-21).

10. There is a thirtyfold, a sixtyfold, and a hundredfold realm (Matt. 13:23). This corresponds to the Outer Court, the Holy Place, and the Most Holy Place of Moses' Tabernacle (Exod. 25:40). It also parallels the three major Feasts of Jehovah (Lev. 23; Deut. 16)—the Feasts of Passover, Pentecost, and Tabernacles. The Hundredfold Company gives God 100%. The difference between 60 and 100 is 40—these have walked the "back forty" with God (the biblical number of testing and trial).

11. "Many waters" conveys the awesome sound of corporate praise and worship, and represents the voice of the Lord (see Num. 24:7; Ps. 29:3; 93:4; Ezek. 43:2; and Rev. 1:15; 19:6).

12. This is a "new song" for a new Day and a new realm, the Most Holy Place (see Ps. 33:3; 40:3; 96:1; 98:1; 144:9; 149:1; Isa. 42:10; and Rev. 5:9).

THE BOOK OF JOEL

PART ONE

DESOLATION

(JOEL 1:1-20)

---◆◇◆---

*"...Hath this been in your days, or
even in the days of your fathers?"*

CHAPTER SIX

DESOLATION — ITS CRY (INTRODUCTION AND JOEL 1:1-3)

I hear a cry coming from the top of the mountain. It's a plaintive groan from the throne, a lonely roar from the heights of Zion.[1] King Jesus weeps over the spiritual condition of His people. He has patiently waited for the precious fruit of the earth, but the crop is withered. Something has killed the harvest.

Introduction To Joel the Man

The word of the Lord that came to Joel the son of Pethuel (Joel 1:1).

That same Spirit of intercession gripped another man centuries ago. Nothing is known about the prophet Joel aside from the book that bears his name. He appeared during a locust plague of unprecedented severity, accompanied by a season of drought and consequent famine. With passionate earnestness he called upon the people to turn wholeheartedly to the Lord. His anointed cry gathered them, one and all, into the sanctuary for united prayer to avert, if possible, further judgment. They obeyed the prophet's entreaty, and the Lord heard their plea.

Joel the person is the Pentecostal Trumpeteer. He was a citizen of Jerusalem, and perhaps a Temple prophet. The Word of the Lord through Joel calls the House of Judah to genuine repentance, to an inward rending of the heart and not an outward rending of the garments. The Lord promises the southern nation a refreshing, a revival, and a restoration through a natural outpouring of rain, which foreshadowed the present outpouring of spiritual rain upon the Church. This promised baptism of the Holy Spirit (Joel 2:28-32) is Joel's distinctive link with the New Testament (Acts 2:14-21). Thus he is sometimes called the "Prophet of Pentecost."

Both Joel and his father Pethuel were men of *El* (strong and mighty), men of God. The name "Joel" means, "Jehovah is (his) God," and is a compound of "Jehovah" and *El*. His very name conveys a confession of faith.

The name of "Pethuel" means, "enlarged of God," and is a compound of *El* and the root *pathah* (to open; make roomy; be spacious, wide). This latter word hints at the high calling exemplified in the life of Jabez, whose coasts or borders were enlarged (1 Chron. 4:9-10).[2]

Introduction To Joel the Book

One of the 12 Minor Prophets, this is the Book of the Day of the Lord, and was written by Joel, who ministered to the city of Jerusalem and the House of Judah. Its date is debatable, and only can be discerned from the internal evidence of its three short chapters. Joel's ministry probably covered a period of about 30 years (810-780 B.C.), during the reigns of Joash, Amaziah, and Uzziah, kings of Judah. Its key phrase is "the day of the Lord," a major theme among the Minor Prophets (Joel 1:15 [twice]; 2:1,11,31; 3:14). Its key verses, as noted, are Joel 2:28-32 (fulfilled in Acts 2:14-21).

The first chapter is a stark picture of complete desolation and devastation. No area of Jewish life and society lay untouched by these calamities. Everything was withered and dying: the new wine and the vine; the meat and drink offerings; the corn, the wheat, the barley, and the harvest of the field; the pomegranate, palm, and apple trees; the joy and gladness of the Lord; the meat (food) and the seed; the garners (treasure-houses or store-houses) and the barns (granaries); the pasture (feeding-place) and the flocks of sheep; the rivers of waters—all were destroyed!

The picture of this vast devastation in chapter one could be applied present-day to the individual, the home, the local church, the community, the nation, or even the planet. The blowing of the trumpet and the sounding of the alarm in Chapter Two calls us back to Zion, the place of the high calling, which is consequently restored in Chapter Three.

The outline of the Book of Joel that is set forth in this writing is simple:

1. Desolation (Joel 1:1-20).
2. Consecration (Joel 2:1-32).
3. Restoration (Joel 3:1-21).

Two alternative outlines are suggested:

1. Ruin (Joel 1:1-2:11).
2. Repentance (Joel 2:12-17).
3. Revival (Joel 2:18-32)
4. Restoration (Joel 3:1-21).

1. Desolation (Joel 1:1-12).
2. Preparation (Joel 1:13-2:11).
3. Consecration (Joel 2:12-22).
4. Restoration (Joel 2:23-32).
5. Manifestation (Joel 3:1-21).

The Word of the Lord

The word of the Lord that came to Joel the son of Pethuel (See Joel 1:1 and compare with Isa. 2:3; Jer. 1:2; Ezek. 1:3; Hos. 1:1).

The Hebrew for "word" means, "a word, speech; by implication, a matter (as spoken of) or thing; adverbially, a cause." It is derived from a root, "to arrange; but used figuratively (of words), to speak, to declare, to converse, to command, to promise, to warn, to threaten, to sing." This noun refers, first, to what is said, to the actual "word" itself. The biblical phrase "the word of the Lord" is quite important, occurring over 240 times. The "word" of God indicates His highest thoughts and predetermined will.

Awake, awake; put on thy strength, O Zion... (Isa. 52:1).

Jehovah's "word" through Joel was addressed to Judah, which means, "praise." Judah is always prominent in Scripture, and was the first tribe to march forward toward Canaan (Num. 10:14). Messiah came from this chosen clan (Heb. 7:14). Judah points to the Firstfruits Company (Rev. 14:1-5), to those apprehended for Zion. Joel's message was straightforward and clear: "Awake, O Zion" (the theme of Chapters Two through Five of this writing)!

For ever, O Lord, Thy word is settled (stationed, established) *in heaven* (Ps. 119:89).

While all else is consumed and wasted in this first chapter, His Word remains constant and sure, steadfast! Heaven and earth shall pass away, but not His Word (Matt. 24:35).

To the average Christian, who is accustomed to living in the lower realms of the Spirit, the Church today (especially in America) seems to be prospering. But from the perspective of the third heaven (the Most Holy Place), her real spiritual condition parallels the widespread desolation described in Joel 1. Similarly, the apostolic view of John on the Isle of Patmos describes the Church of Laodicea (Rev. 3:14-22). In that context, John invites the corporate Overcomer to return to the high calling of sitting with Christ in His throne.

Hear this (listen, give heed), *ye old men, and give ear, all ye inhabitants of the land. Hath this been in your days* (grandfathers), *or even in the days of your fathers* (great-grandfathers)? (See Joel 1:2 and compare with Deut. 4:32).

For though ye have ten thousand instructors (tutor, guardian; boy-leader, schoolmaster who took the children to school) *in Christ, yet have ye not many fathers* (true apostles)... (1 Cor. 4:15).

The prophet first addresses the "old men" (Joel 2:28), the "aged, ancient; senators; elders (having authority)."[3]

Joel then speaks concerning the "fathers" (only mentioned here). Was this part of the problem (Mal. 4:5-6)? The natural condition of the nations and the spiritual state of the Church throughout the nations is one of dire need. Natural and spiritual famine are rampant (Amos 8:11). These "old men" and "fathers"[4] were wise counselors, and speak of the present apostolic company. To these my colleagues I ask, "Have you ever seen days such as these?"

The prophet then calls to "all" the inhabitants of the land. Jehovah speaks to the old men, the children, the children's children, another generation, the married and the unmarried, the drunkards, the vinedressers, the husbandmen (farmers), the priests and the people of the "land."[5] His judgments touch everyone and everything!

Tell ye your children (sons) of it, and let your children tell their children, and their children another generation (Joel 1:3).

The fathers are to tell the sons, the "children," of these things. As with the word "land" in verse two (see the endnote), the "children" are mentioned 11 times in the Book of Joel.[6] The number 11 speaks of disorganization and confusion (1 Cor. 14:3; Jas. 3:16). That the sons are mentioned four times in verse three reveals a global, universal dilemma. The children of the earth are mixed up, bewildered, and perplexed.

One of the nations that is in my heart is South Africa. Because of AIDS, the "street children" are everywhere. In America, church pews are filled with those who come from dysfunctional homes and families. The marginalized and disenfranchised are all around us.

The land is perplexed. Parents and children are confused. Preachers, pressured by their popular game of "nickels, noses, and names," have sacrificed their families on the altar of a "successful" ministry. Too many PK's (preachers' kids) have fled from the hypocrisy of mean church folks. Musicians and singers have turned to the world to express their gifts, to find the kind of love and acceptance they never found in the institutionalized Church.

The *cry* of Joel's first chapter is everywhere because it expresses the cry of the "whole creation."

For we know that the whole creation groaneth and travaileth in pain together until now (Rom. 8:22).

We know that the whole creation has been groaning as in the pains of childbirth right up to the present time (Rom. 8:22, NIV).

It is noteworthy that Joel 1:2-3 reveal four generations (compare this with the four stages of the locust in the next chapter). God's purposes are always generational (Exod. 30:31).

Thy holy cities are a wilderness, Zion is a wilderness, Jerusalem a desolation.

Our holy and our beautiful house, where our fathers praised thee,
is burned up with fire: and all our pleasant things are laid waste
(Isa. 64:10-11).

Zion is laid waste. But what has caused this crisis? In Joel's day, a horde of locusts, along with drought and famine, had destroyed the land.

What has devastated the Church?

ENDNOTES

1. "A Groan From the Throne" is the title of Chapter Eight of my book, *The More Excellent Ministry.*

2. The life of Jabez is unfolded in Chapter Seventeen, the Epilogue of this book.

3. Note these verses concerning the "old men" (see 1 Kings 12:8; 2 Chron. 10:8; Ps. 148:7,12; Prov. 17:6; 20:29; and Zech. 8:4).

4. Compare these verses concerning the fathers (see Ps. 148:7,12; Prov. 17:6; 20:29; Zech. 8:4; compare 1 Kings 12:8 and Job 12:12).

5. The word for "land" means, "to be firm; the whole earth," and is used 11 times in this first chapter of Joel (1:2,6,10,14; 2:1,3,19,20,21; 3:2,19). Eleven is the biblical number denoting confusion and disorganization. Contrast Joel 1:10; 2:21 (a different word for "land" is used).

6. The "children" are mentioned in Joel 1:3 (four times); 2:16,23; 3:6 (twice),8,16,19, for a total of 11 times.

CHAPTER SEVEN

DESOLATION — ITS CAUSE (JOEL 1:4-7)

"For a nation is come up upon my land..."

The previous chapter introduced Joel, the man and the book. His prophetic cry pierced the apathy of the nation of Judah 800 years before Jesus the Messiah preached in the same streets of Jerusalem.

Zion laid desolate, its land and its people ruined. What had caused this national calamity in Joel's day? How do those events parallel the New Testament days of Peter and Paul? What devastated the Early Church and carried her into the Babylonian captivity of the Dark Ages? How does Joel's message address the present condition of the House of the Lord?

The Plague of Swarming Locusts

What the chewing locust left, the swarming locust has eaten; what the swarming locust left, the crawling locust has eaten; and what the crawling locust left, the consuming locust has eaten (Joel 1:4, NKJV).

A horrific plague of locusts had consumed the land, compounded by drought and famine. This invading army was part of the curse of the law against disobedience and idolatry (Deut. 28:38, 42; 1 Kings 8:37-39; 1 Pet. 5:8). Locusts are mentioned several times in both Testaments.[1]

The terms grasshopper and locust are often used interchangeably. The locust has a brown-colored body two to three inches long, the thickness and length of a finger. This insect has powerful jaws and teeth like a saw. Their red legs and wings can give a beautiful, fiery appearance in the sunlight; they sound like rain when approaching. The watchman on the walls of the city or in the tower of the vineyard had to be discerning, not a "novice" (1 Tim. 3:6). That which may look or sound like a blessing from God may actually be devastation from the enemy, masqueraded as an angel of light (2 Cor. 11:13-15).

When airborne, with two sets of wings, the locust was dreaded in the ancient world because of its destructive power as a foliage-eating insect. Their massive numbers could fill the air and take away the brightness of the sun (Joel 2:10; 3:15).

The eighth plague that God sent upon the Egyptians in the days of Moses was an invasion of locusts (Exod. 10:1-20). Millions of these insects may be included in one of these swarms, which usually occur in the spring. Locusts in such numbers speedily eat every plant in sight, totally destroying the crops. A locust plague is practically unstoppable. Water does not work; for when enough locusts drown, the survivors use their bodies as a bridge. They have also been known to smother fires that had been set to destroy them.

> *Even these of them ye may eat; the locust after his kind, and the bald locust after his kind, and the beetle after his kind, and the grasshopper after his kind* (Lev. 11:22).

> *And the same John had his raiment of camel's hair, and a leathern girdle about his loins; and his meat* (food) *was locusts and wild honey* (Matt. 3:4).

Many Eastern people, including the Jews, eat locusts. These insects may be boiled, fried, or dried. Locusts were part of the wilderness diet of John the Baptist. Real prophets have the courage to swallow up the things that come against the people of God! They carry a birth certificate in one hand and a death certificate in the other. Every time we speak, we raise those things that need to be resurrected, and we tear down and destroy those things that need to die a much-needed death. Trumpets are blowing in Zion! Prophets are sounding an alarm to the nations. We are consuming religious tradition with the fire of His Word (Jer. 23:29; Heb. 12:29).

That which the palmerworm hath left hath the locust eaten; and that which the locust hath left hath the cankerworm eaten; and that which the cankerworm hath left hath the caterpiller eaten (Joel 1:4).

What the locust swarm has left[2] (overhanging in excess; the remainder) *the great locusts have eaten*[3] (devoured); *what the great locusts have left the young locusts have eaten; what the young locusts have left other locusts have eaten* (Joel 1:4, NIV).

This verse depicts the four stages or levels of the locust's growth and development. The Hebrew margin of Joel 1:4 reads: "Gnawer's remnant, swarmer eats; swarmer's remnant, devourer eats; devourer's remnant, consumer eats."

The first stage is the "palmerworm" (Joel 2:25; Amos 4:9). This is the Hebrew word *gazam* (Strong's #1501), and it means, "to devour." The larva of the locust emerges from its egg in the springtime. This wingless hopping creature is called the gnawing or chewing locust, sometimes called the shearer.

The second level is the "locust." This is the Hebrew word *'arbeh* (Strong's #697), and it means, "a locust (from its rapid increase); a locust swarm (collective). This is also rendered as "grasshopper" in the King James Version. Its root word means, "to increase, multiply." This is the pupa, still in its first skin. At this juncture it puts forth little wings, and so is called the swarming locust.

The third phase is the "cankerworm" (Joel 2:25). This is the Hebrew word *yekeq* (Strong's #3218), and it means, "to lick up; a devourer; specifically, the young locust." This is also rendered as "caterpillar" (compare Ps. 105:34; Jer. 51:14,27; Nah. 3:15-16). At this point, the locust develops small wings that enable it to leap better, but not to fly. It does a great deal of devouring and is known as the devourer or the licking locust (the lapper).

The fourth level is the full-grown "caterpillar" (Joel 2:25). This is the Hebrew word *chaciyl* (Strong's #2625), and it means, "the ravager, a locust." Its root means, "to eat off; consume, to finish off, to bring to an end." This word for "locust" is also rendered as "caterpillar" (see 1 Kings 8:37; 2 Chron. 6:28; Ps. 78:46; Isa. 33:4). This final stage (reached six to seven weeks from birth) is the full-grown creature with its full wings, about three inches long with two antennae an inch long. It has six legs, the two back legs being longer, thus enabling the locust to leap. The completely mature locust is known as the consuming locust, or the finisher.

The Plague of Religious Tradition

Historically, a plague of swarming locusts, accompanied by drought and famine, desolated the land of Judah in the days of Joel. What devastated the Early Church and carried her into the Babylonian captivity of the Dark Ages? From the days of Martin Luther and the First Reformation, what has consumed biblical truth and laid waste to the "apostles' doctrine" (Acts 2:42)?

> *For ye have heard of my* (Paul's) *conversation* (manner of life) *in time past in the Jews' religion, how that beyond measure I persecuted the church of God, and wasted it:* (Gal. 1:13).

The arch-enemies of the Gospel of the Kingdom are the "locusts" of *religious traditions,* the commandments and doctrines of men (Matt. 15:9; Col. 2:22)! These hordes of lies have swallowed up the life of God's people. Sadder still, the Church in America has ravaged and raped the nations of the earth with this same kind of corrupt seed.

The old order, with all its man-made teachings, follows after antichrist instead of Christ, arrogantly exalting itself above the knowledge of God (2 Thess. 2:3-4). Spiritual Babylon has "sodden" (watered down) the Lamb (Exod. 12:9), settling for "another gospel" that is man-centered and not Christ-centered (2 Cor. 11:1-4; Gal. 1:6-12).

> *Thus you nullify the word of God by your tradition that you have handed down…* (Mark 7:13, NIV).

> *See to it that no one takes you captive through hollow and deceptive philosophy, which depends on human tradition and the basic principles of this world rather than on Christ* (Col. 2:8, NIV).

The Greek word for "tradition" is *paradosis* (Strong's #3862), and it means, "transmission, a handing down or on; giving up, a giving over which is done by word of mouth or in writing, that is, tradition by instruction, narrative, or precept." It is used 13 times in the New Testament.[4] The word *paradidomi* conveys a similar idea; it means, "to yield up, entrust, transmit; to give into the hands of another something to keep, to use, to take care of, to manage."

What spiritual truths do we see here? How do these "locusts" come against the high calling? To begin with, the four developmental stages of the locust reveal four great sins.

First, the "palmerworm" is like self-indulgence (Gen. 3:14). The palmerworm creeps with all its body on the ground. Unbridled lust has consumed the hearts of men and women so that they, like the serpent on its belly, cannot lift their heads from the dust.

Second, the "locust" is like self-direction (Prov. 14:12). The locust flies by leaping. Vain glory exalts itself with empty presumption. If anyone thinks he is something when he is nothing, he deceives himself (Gal. 6:3).

Third, the "cankerworm" is like self-government (Phil. 3:18-19). The cankerworm has almost all of its body gathered into its belly. Gluttony and self-absorption have no care for anything or anyone outside of its own appetites.

Fourth, the full-grown "caterpillar" is like self-destruction (Heb. 12:15). The caterpillar leaves a mildew that burns what it touches, turning the green tips of the grain into the pale of death (Amos 4:9). Anger and bitterness that spring from the toxic waste of unforgiveness defiles everything in its path.

But the primary application here is that the four phases of the locust's growth reveal four *progressive* levels and layers of *religious tradition!*

Going deeper into this subject, we now compare the four steps of the locust's growth with the four parts of Daniel's famous image.

And in the days of these kings shall the God of heaven set up a kingdom, which shall never be destroyed: and the kingdom shall not be left to other people, but it shall break in pieces and consume all these kingdoms, and it shall stand for ever (Dan. 2:44).

The historical interpretation of Daniel 2:31-35 was that this image represented four successive "kingdoms." In this view, Daniel saw the head of gold (Babylon), the breast and arms of silver (Medo-Persia), the belly and thighs of brass (Greece), and the feet of iron and clay (Rome). God's Kingdom shatters these kingdoms of men.

Spiritually speaking, Daniel's image is an awesome picture of the full-grown, corporate "man of sin" that has evolved throughout the ages (growing in four stages like the locust). Consider all its humanistic trappings of tradition, along with all its "strange" ideologies and philoso-phies, both religious and political (Dan. 2:27-45; 2 Thess. 2:1-12). This is the mindset and mark of the beast nature (Rev. 13:13-18). Again, Christ is the "image of God" (2 Cor. 4:4). Antichrist is any other image! Daniel saw the mature, corporate son of hell!

Four Levels of Tradition Throughout the Church

Furthermore, there are four levels of man-made teaching that operate throughout the contemporary Church world. Tradition abounds at every level. These four stages stretch all the way across the three Feasts of the Lord—Passover, Pentecost, and Tabernacles—finding application among those who are born-again, Spirit-filled, and mature.

They worship me in vain; their teachings are but rules taught by men (Matt. 15:9, NIV).

First, the "palmerworm" emerges from its egg in the springtime. The larva is a wingless hopping creature called the gnawing locust or the shearer. This baby locust is a picture of religious traditions found in the Outer Court, the Feast of Passover, the evangelical realm.

These baby Christians can only hop in the earth. They have yet to experience the wings of Spirit-filed prayer and praise, to soar up on the wind of the Spirit. Like the Sadducees of Paul's day that refused the idea of resurrection (Acts 23:8), the besetting sin of this order is their adamant determination to preach and teach their doctrine of "cessationism."

This fundamentalist tradition insists that signs, wonders, mira-cles, tongues, the gifts of the Spirit, and the apostles and prophets ceased with the Early Church. These folks need to understand that the Book of Acts happened the day before yesterday (2 Pet. 3:8)! The high calling is nowhere in their vocabulary.

So we see that they were not able to enter, because of their unbelief (Heb. 3:19, NIV).

Second, the root word for "locust" (grasshopper) means, "to increase, multiply." This is the pupa, still in its first skin. At this juncture the insect puts forth little wings, and so is called the swarming locust.

The "grasshopper" mindset of the ten spies kept them out of the Promised Land; they were overwhelmed by this realm of "great stature" (Num. 13:25-33; Eph. 4:13). Their tasting the "firstripe grapes" (Num. 13:20) typifies the Holy Ghost Baptism, the "first-fruits" of the Spirit (Rom. 8:23), and the "earnest" of our inheritance (Eph. 1:13-14). On this Spirit-filled level we find the early traditions of the Holy Place, the Feast of Pentecost, the Charismatic realm.

The ugly tradition of staunch legalism, prevalent in classical Pentecostalism, stunts spiritual growth—a dwarf could not be a priest (Lev. 21:20). Double-minded, dualistic preaching is a horrible mixture, bouncing between law and grace, between Jesus and the devil, between the sweat of Adam (the old man, the flesh) and the savor of Christ (the new Man, the Spirit). Bogged down in the civil war of Romans chapter 7, classical Pentecostals rarely taste the glorious liberty of Romans chapter 8. But the war is over (Isa. 40:2). Jesus' death on the Cross is a finished work (John 19:30)!

Charismatic folks love to swarm from conference to conference. "Revival groupies" and blessing-seekers only want to have a "good time." Faddish and fickle, they are like the loaves and fishes crowd that followed Jesus just to see the miracles (Mark 6:52). These folks will walk away the moment they are challenged with the high calling, to eat His flesh and to drink His blood, to participate fully in the life of His flesh, His Body (John 6:35-60).

If you keep on biting and devouring each other, watch out or you will be destroyed by each other (Gal. 5:15, NIV).

Third, the "cankerworm" is the stage when the locust develops small wings that enable it to leap better, but not to fly. At the third level, this adolescent pest does a great deal of devouring and is known as the devourer or the licking locust (the lapper).

This reveals a further development of the traditions found in the second dimension. "Cankerworm" preachers move in the gifts of the Spirit, but without character and integrity. This is often seen in the hyper-faith fast lane of the "boys' club," where lapping up big contributions is expected, not just tolerated. The "love of money" (1 Tim. 6:10) and the love of titles has blinded many of these men and women to the obvious lack of real glory and anointing in their lives, their marriages, their homes, and their churches. They are too busy devouring widows' houses (Matt. 23:14), always competing with other egos as fragile as their own. They think nothing of tearing down other ministries, trying to make a small man taller by cutting a tall man's legs off. Biting and devouring others is a way of life on this level.

But these great egos only have "little wings." They scream and jump about, working the crowd for multiple offerings, but have yet to learn to mount up in real worship. Some on this level unashamedly parrot "present truth" (2 Pet. 1:12), preaching just enough of the Kingdom for their message to be palatable. They read books like this one for sermons, not for life (Matt. 4:4). These are sin-conscious, dualistic Pentecostals with a Kingdom face. They are "neo-Kingdom," trying to preach the Kingdom and move in a Third Day message with a Second Day method, practice, and application. What incredible mixture!

> *Do not let anyone who delights in false humility...disqualify you for the prize. Such a person goes into great detail about what he has seen, and his unspiritual mind puffs him up with idle notions.*
>
> *He has lost connection with the Head...* (Col. 2:18-19, NIV).

Finally, the most dangerous level is the "caterpillar," the mature locust. This final stage (reached six to seven weeks from birth) is the matured creature with its full wings. The completely mature locust is known as the consuming locust, or the finisher.

Not surprisingly, there are also traditions in the Third Dimension, the Feast of Tabernacles, the realm of Christ's finished work.[5] Far too many Kingdom preachers have been caught up in the contemporary "bishop" epidemic, wanting to be "seen of men" (Matt. 6:5; 23:5). Others only emphasize one area of truth, riding the same horse in every message. They preach reconciliation as a doctrine rather than just being a reconciler. It is true that all men have been reconciled—the provision has been made. But not all men have been automatically saved.[6] As in the Passover (Exod. 12:22), the blood must be applied! The doctrine of "inclusion," as presently taught, is dangerous.

Others preach the doctrine of sonship without having the spirit of a son. Such have professed themselves to be wise, but have become fools, exchanging the glory of the incorruptible God for an image made like to corruptible man, worshiping the creature more than the Creator (Rom. 1:21-23). Classical Pentecostals are proud of their "holiness" standards; the sonship camp arrogantly flaunts their latest "revelation." But the knowledge of a thing is not the possession of it. Committing a strange form of idolatry, these men and women worship the process of becoming like Christ, rather than bowing at the feet of the One who is changing them.

Many have made their sonship singular, not corporate, and have stopped holding Jesus as the Head. The "manifestation of the sons of God" is biblical truth (Rom. 8:14-23,29; Heb. 2:6-13). But God is not going to manifest us; He has purposed to unveil the Son, *the* Son Jesus, in and through His brethren, a *corporate* Man created in *His* image and likeness! We are partakers of the "divine nature" (2 Pet. 1:4), but we will never be partakers of Deity. Our high calling is to be *like* Him, but we will never *be* Him!

Finally, the four levels of the locust's development can also be compared with the four "horns" which "scattered" (to toss about, diffuse, winnow, fan, cast away, disperse, turn aside) Judah, Israel, and Jerusalem (Zech. 1:18-21). Moreover, it would be interesting to contrast the stages of the locust with the metamorphosis of the butterfly.[7]

Judgment of the Drunkards

The bulk of this first chapter of Joel shows the effects of Jehovah's judgment upon the land and the people. Every strata of society was impacted by this widespread desolation. National worship had waned. The economy was ruined. Their joy had withered. Three major crops had failed—the corn, the wine, and the oil.

Awake, ye drunkards, and weep; and howl, all ye drinkers of wine, because of the new wine; for it is cut off from your mouth (Joel 1:5).

We cry with Joel, "Awake, O Zion"! It's a new Day! A fresh Feast of Trumpets for the Church has begun to sound. True prophets are calling us to repent and be cleansed in the Feast Day of Atonement. It is time to afflict our souls (Lev. 16:29-31), to return to Zion, the place of the high calling.

Joel calls out first to the "drunkards," those who had abused the wine and who were usually known for their ungodly song. The "drunkards of Ephraim" (Isa. 28:1) were addressed in depth in Chapter Three. The prophet challenges these "drinkers of wine" to "weep" (moan, cry) and to "howl" (wail), along with the vinedressers and priests.[8]

There is a "time to weep" (Eccles. 3:4). The "new wine," the fresh flow of the joy and gladness of the Holy Ghost, has been "cut off" (destroyed, consumed, eliminated, removed), along with the meat (meal) and drink offerings (Joel 1:9,16).

Woe to them who are at ease (careless) in Zion (Amos 6:1). The fear of the Lord is clean (pure), but we are not clean (Ps. 19:9).[9] We have forsaken the high calling for a mess of pottage, the allurements of lesser things (Gen. 25:29-34). Sinners in Zion are startled by this sudden prophetic alarm. Fearfulness and trembling has surprised every hypocrite (Isa. 33:14). God has come to deal with the kingdoms of our hearts, with everything that we have held back from Him up till now.

Joel's indictment against the drunkards, the habitually intoxicated, is strong. We have already learned that Adam, the old nature, is asleep and drunk in the night (1 Thess. 5:3-7). We are further instructed from the lives of others in the Bible who were tipsy with wine.[10]

The "new wine" (fresh grape-juice as just trodden out; pressed-out juice) had been cut off (Compare Joel 1:10; 3:18). This is also rendered as "sweet wine" (Isa. 49:26; Amos 9:13). Its root means, "to trample, tread down; to press or crush." All this speaks of a fresh move of the Holy Ghost. Help us, oh Lord. Come slake our thirst. Show us just how dry we have become.

The Strange Nation

For a nation is come up upon My land... (Joel 1:6).

The invading locusts are called a "nation" by the prophet. Today's religious traditions have swarmed over God's "land," God's holy nation, the Church (1 Pet. 2:9). Note especially Revelation 9:1-12, the vivid description of the locust army like unto horses which comes out of the pit, and whose king is the devil. The theme of the last book of the Bible is the "revelation" or "unveiling" of Jesus Christ in and through a people, the Lamb Company. Satan, the "god of this world" (2 Cor. 4:4), is the "king" over all religion. His sole purpose is to come against the full formation of Christ in His Body (Gal. 4:19). He attacks Zion with the "imagi-nation" of false images and ideas, the mind of the flesh.

The "nation" in Joel 1:6 is a "people, nation (usually non-Hebrew); in the sense of massing, also (figuratively) a troop of animals, or a swarm of locusts." This word is elsewhere rendered in Joel as "heathen" (2:17,19; 3:11-12); "nations" (3:2); "people" (3:8); and "Gentiles" (3:9).

One of the seven angels who had the seven bowls came and said to me, "Come, I will show you the punishment of the great prostitute, who sits on many waters.

With her the kings of the earth committed adultery and the inhabitants of the earth were intoxicated with the wine of her adulteries" (Rev. 17:1-2, NIV).

Spiritual drunkards are intoxicated with the wine of the adulteries of religion. The "nation" or swarm of locusts can represent, first of all, the many "denomi-nations" and non-denominational sects that proliferate the earth today. The Bible mentions the "Mother of Harlots" with all her daughters and grand-daughters, along with all their unholy mixture of man-made traditions (Rev. 17:5).

But there are other kinds of "nations." Paul warned against the "imagi-nations," and admonished us to cast down every high thing and man-made idea that exalts itself against the knowledge of God (2 Cor. 10:3-5). Every denomi-nation is marked by its own particular package of imagi-nations! These traditional belief systems have become strange gods, idols. Denominational schools and colleges have enshrined their particular brands of falsehood.

...strong, and without number... (Joel 1:6).

The prophet further notes that this "nation" is "strong" (Compare Joel 2:2,5,11) and "without number." Man-made denominations are thus "strong in number; might, vast, numerous, countless." There are over 200 Christian denominations, not to mention all the other brands of religion in the earth.

This point is plainly illustrated in the story of two women: Peninnah and Hannah (1 Sam. 1:1-7). Peninnah has all the numbers—all the children, all the money, all the facilities. She "provokes" (troubles, vexes) "Hannah," whose name means, "grace." Peninnah still taunts today, "How many are in your church? Your network? How big is your campus? Your budget?"[11] The old order will always flaunt their numbers in our faces.

Take courage, you "sons of promise" (Gal. 4:28). As stated earlier, it does not matter how many of us there are, but rather how big a sound we are making! There *is* a high calling to Zion, and "few" there be that find the upward pathway to light and life (Matt. 7:14; 22:14).

...whose teeth are the teeth of a lion, and he hath the cheek teeth of a great lion (See Joel 1:6 and compare Rev. 9:8).

The army of invading locusts in the days of Joel had lion's "teeth"[12] that were "sharp and pointed; a cliff or sharp rock." The denominations bite and devour with jealousy and envy. Legalism, with all its rules and regulations, breeds frustration, shame, confusion, and condemnation.

But if ye bite (wound, cut, lacerate, rend with reproaches; thwart) *and devour* (eat down) *one another, take heed that ye be not consumed* (use up, spend up, destroy) *one of another* (Gal. 5:15).

The "lion" of Joel 1:6 reminds us of the devil (1 Pet. 5:8), the accuser of the brethren (Rev. 12:10), the god of this world, and the fabricator of all religion (2 Cor. 4:4). He has the "cheek teeth" (jaw teeth, fangs, incisors) of a "great lion." Interestingly, the Hebrew notes that this latter word denotes a "female lion," which is fiercer than the male. This pictures the soul, which is feminine in gender. This points back to the "strange woman" of Proverbs chapter 7, the aforementioned religious harlot of Revelation 17-18.

Kill All That Is Green

We are "trees" of righteousness, the "planting" of the Lord (Isa. 61:3). In the Bible, green is the color of resurrection life. John saw that the throne room is the green room (Rev. 4:3). The Zion Company has been called to life and immortality (see Chapter Three). In this first chapter of Joel, we see a progressive attack of these locusts upon all that is green and succulent. Trees are targeted, leaves and bark; all vegetation, young shoots, saplings and their bark; herbs and grasses; fruit, flowers; even the thatched roofs of houses!

The devil has given orders to his minions: kill everything green. Kill life. Kill the Vine. Kill the Seed. Kill Christ. Kill anything that has to do with the Holy Ghost, the Spirit of His resurrection life (Rom. 8:11).

He hath laid My vine waste, and barked My fig tree: he hath made it clean bare, and cast it away; the branches thereof are made white (Joel 1:7).

In this view, the "he" of this verse represents the corporate "man of sin" (2 Thess. 2:3-4). Note that it is "My vine" and "My fig tree" (the Lord is speaking). Religion has "laid waste" (ruined) His "vine" (also mentioned in Joel 1:22; 2:22). The "vine" is too vast a biblical subject to cover; it speaks of the life and prosperity of the Church.[13]

> *Now I beseech you, brethren, by the name of our Lord Jesus Christ, that ye all speak the same thing, and that there be no divisions*[14] *among you...* (1 Cor. 1:10).

The traditions of men have also "barked" (fragmented, splintered) His fig tree. The root word means, "to snap or crack off; to burst out in rage and anger." This keenly describes all the schisms and factions of religious Babylon (Babylon is a spirit). All of satan's ministers are men and women of war. Broken lives, broken homes and families, broken churches—broken wineskins—lay strewn upon the pathway of death (Prov. 2:18).

The "fig tree," like the "vine," is a broad subject (compare Joel 1:12; 2:22).[15] The fig was symbolic of the fruit of Israel.[16] The fig can also represent self-atonement, like the self-made coverings of Adam and Eve (Gen. 3:1-8 with Isa. 64:8). The fig tree, generally speaking, points to the fruit of the Spirit (Gal. 5:22-23), which is the nature of Jesus. Religious tradition has stripped the Church of real fruit, making it "clean bare." This word means, "to strip off, make naked in disgrace and shame." The enemy wants us to "cast" (throw) out the idea that we can be partakers of the "divine nature" (2 Pet. 1:4).

The prophet concludes verse seven by noting that the locusts had so devastated the land that the branches of the fig tree were made "white," like the leper (Num. 12:10; 2 Kings 5:27). The beauty of the House of the Lord has been replaced with the ghostly whiteness of another gospel. Jesus explained this:

> *Woe unto you, scribes and Pharisees, hypocrites! for ye are like unto whited sepulchres* (white-washed, plastered; the root means, "dust"), *which indeed appear beautiful outward, but are within* (in the heart) *full of dead men's bones, and of all uncleanness* (see Matt. 23:27 and compare Acts 23:3).

The word for "branches" means, "tendril (as entwining)." There is no channel for the life of the Vine. There is no revelation of the corporate Branch called to the top of Mount Zion, called to walk in the same sevenfold anointing as did Messiah (Isa. 11:1-2).[17]

The rest of the first chapter of Joel's prophecy shows the full effects of this judgment upon the land and the people—the full, widespread *calamity* of desolation.

ENDNOTES

1. The words "locust" or "locusts" are mentioned in Scripture a total of 28 times (see Exod. 10:1-20; Lev. 11:22; Deut. 28:38,42; 1 Kings 8:37; 2 Chron. 6:28; 7:13; Ps. 78:46; 105:34; 109:23; Prov. 30:27; Isa. 33:4; Jer. 46:23; Joel 1:4; Nah. 3:15,17; Matt. 3:4; and Mark 1:6). Note especially Revelation 9:1-12, the vivid description of the locust army like unto horses which comes out of the bottomless pit, and whose king is the devil.

2. The word "left" in Joel 1:4 suggests the "remnant" of Zion (see 2 Kings 19:30-31; 2 Chron. 30:6; Ezra 3:8; 9:8; Neh. 1:3; Isa. 1:9; 10:20-22; 11:11,16; Jer. 23:3; 31:7; Joel 2:32; Amos 5:15; Mic. 2:12; 4:7; 5:7-8; Zeph. 2:7-9; 3:13; Hag. 1:12-14; Zech. 8:6,12; Rom. 9:27; 11:5; and Rev. 12:17).

3. The word "eaten" (devoured) in Joel 1:4 is used a total of 13 times in his prophecy (see Joel 1:4 [six times]; 1:19,20; 2:3,5,25,26 [twice]). Thirteen is the biblical number denoting rebellion and anarchy.

4. *Paradosis*, the Greek word translated as "tradition" in the King James Version, is used a total of 13 times. Ten are given in a negative context (see Matt. 15:2,3,6; Mark 7:3,5,8,9,13; Gal. 1:14; Col. 2:8), and three are presented in a positive setting (1 Cor. 11:2; 2 Thess. 2:15; 3:6).

5. The prophet Ezekiel was shown the abominations of idolatry in the Outer Court, the Holy Place, and the Most Holy Place (Ezek. 8). Tradition has exchanged the glory of the incorruptible God for the glory of corruptible man in all three realms. In Rom. 1:23, the "creeping things" speak of those who crawl in the dust. The "fourfooted beasts" are quadrupeds, double-minded folks who don't know which end is up. The "birds" are dirty birds that soar in the heavenlies of the Most Holy Place, but who are unclean.

6. The apostle Paul shows this difference in Romans 5:10, KJV – "*For if, when we were enemies, we were reconciled to God by the death of His Son, much more, being reconciled, we shall be saved by His life.*" Though we have been reconciled, we must "continue in the faith" (Col. 1:21-23; compare Eph. 2:16; Heb. 2:17).

7. The Greek word *metamorphoo* means, "to change into another form, to transform." This is translated in the King James Version as "transfigured" (Matt. 17:2; Mark 9:2), "transformed" (Rom. 12:2), and "changed" (2 Cor. 3:18).

8. Joel calls for his people to "weep" (Joel 2:12,17) and to "howl" (Joel 1:11,13) elsewhere in his prophecy. As then, this is a serious day.

9. The "fear of the Lord" is the beginning of wisdom and knowledge (Ps. 11:10; Prov. 9:10; 15:33); we have exchanged that for other kinds of wisdom (James 3:15). The "fear of the Lord" is to hate evil, pride, and arrogance (Prov. 8:13); we have lost the pathway of humility. The "fear of the Lord" is strong confidence in Him (Prov. 14:26); we boast in the strength of the systems that we have built for ourselves in His name. The "fear of the Lord" is the fountain of life (Prov. 14:27); the wages of sin is death (Rom. 6:23). The "fear of the Lord" is the treasure of true riches (Isa. 33:6 with Luke 16:11); we, like the Church of Laodicea, are seemingly rich, and increased with goods, and seem to have need of nothing, not knowing that many are wretched, and miserable, and poor, and blind, and naked (Rev. 3:17).

10. Consider Eli the priest, blind and heavy of flesh (1 Sam. 1:13); Nabal the fool (1 Sam. 25:36); Elah, the irresponsible king of Israel (1 Kings 16:9); Ben-hadad, the wicked King of Syria (1 Kings 20:16); the leaders of the earth who grope in darkness (Job 12:25); the princes of Egypt (the world) (Isa. 19:14); and proud Ephraim, whose glorious beauty is fading (Isa. 28:1,3).

11. Throughout the Scripture, we see these two women. Their natures are clearly contrasted in Paul's allegory (Gal. 4:21-31), where he uses the examples of Sarah and Hagar to illustrate the "freewoman" and the "bondwoman." Other examples of these two women are Rachel and Leah, Abigail and Michal, Esther and Vashti. Note as well the "strange woman" and the "virtuous woman" of the Book of Proverbs (Prov. 7 and 31), as well as the Harlot and Bride of the Book of Revelation (Rev. 17-19). With regard to Sarah and Hagar, note the strife between Isaac and Ishmael (Gen. 21). The pattern is clear. The man of the flesh will always persecute the man of the Spirit. The nation of tradition will always come against the nation of truth.

12. This illustrates the "mystery of iniquity," the "teeth" in the mouth of the corporate "man of sin" (2 Thess. 2:1-12). Contrast the "teeth" of the Shulamite, the Church (Song 4:2; 6:6), revealing the "mystery of godliness," the Corporate Christ made flesh, Christ in all of you (Col. 1:27 with 1 Tim. 3:16)!

13. For more about the "vine," study these Scriptures (see Gen. 49:11; Ps. 80:8,14; 128:3; Song 6:11; 7:8,12; Mic. 4:4; and John 15:1-5).

14. This word for "divisions" is *schisma* and it means, "a split or gap ('schism'); a rent, cleft; metaphorically, a division, dissension" (compare Matt. 9:16; Mark 2:21; John 7:43; 9:16; 10:19; and 1 Cor. 11:28; 12:25).

15. The Hebrew word for "fig tree" means, "to stretch out" (its branches). The fig is a fruit-producing plant that could be either a tall tree or a low-spreading shrub. The size of the tree depended on its location and soil. The blooms of the fig tree always appear before the leaves in spring. When Jesus saw leaves on a fig tree, He expected the fruit (Mark 11:12-14,20-21). There were usually two crops of figs a year. Figs were eaten fresh (2 Kings 18:31), pressed

into cakes (1 Sam. 25:18), and used as a poultice (Isa. 38:21). The early ripe fig is "the hasty fruit" (Isa 28:4). Figs usually ripened in August; earlier ones in June. Figs were esteemed a delicacy (Jer. 24:2; Hos. 9:10; Mic. 7:1).

16. Study these Old Testament verses on the "fig" (see Num. 13:33; Deut. 8:8; 1 Kings 4:25; Prov. 27:18; Song 2:13; Isa. 36:6; Jer. 24:1-8; Mic. 4:4; and Hab. 3:17).

17. The Man whose name is the Branch is the many-membered Body of Christ. Jesus is the true Vine and we are the "branches" (John 15:1-5; see also Ps. 80:15; Prov. 11:28; Isa. 4:1-2; 11:1-2; Jer. 23:5-6; 33:15-16; Zech. 6:12-13; and Rev. 1:4; 3:1; 4:5; 5:6).

CHAPTER EIGHT

DESOLATION — ITS CALAMITY (JOEL 1:8-20)

Joel was God's trumpet, the mouthpiece of God to his generation. He began his prophecy with the *cry* of desolation (Joel 1:1-3). The next four verses revealed the *cause* of this devastation. The nation of locusts invading the land is a vivid picture of how religious tradition has laid waste the Christ-life throughout His Church.

The remainder of Joel 1 (verses 8-20) details the full effects of Jehovah's judgment—the *calamity* of desolation—upon the land and the people. There was no worship, no economy, and no joy. All had been stripped away, most notably the corn, the wine, and the oil!

Lament Like a Virgin

Lament like a virgin girded with sackcloth for the husband of her youth (See Joel 1:8 and compare with Amos 5:2).

Judah is compared to a virgin bewailing the death of her lover to whom she was espoused, or as a young woman lately married whose husband is suddenly taken by death. Today's Church has left the first love of her heavenly Husband (Eph. 5:22-33). She walks alone, uncovered and unprotected, content to live in a lower realm. The setting of this verse has the same flavor as the writings of the prophet Jeremiah (See Jer. 14:17; 18:13; 31:2; Lam. 2:13).

How doth the city sit solitary, that was full of people! how is she become as a widow she that was great... (Lam. 1:1).

"Virgin" means "to separate." Tradition has robbed us of the consecrated life. The Church was once pure and powerful, a "chaste virgin" with one Husband (2 Cor. 11:2). Now we are "girded"[1] with "sackcloth,"[2] clothed with mourning and humiliation.

The phrase, "the husband of her youth," points back to the time when Jehovah first brought Israel out of Egypt (Ezek. 16:1-14). It typifies the young Church in the Book of Acts that depended upon the name of her Husband Jesus (Acts 2:38; 4:18). The "youth" or "young men" pictures the Pentecostal experience, the Second Day (1 John 2:13-14).

> The meat offering and the drink offering is cut off from the house
> of the Lord... (Joel 1:9).

The meat (meal) and drink offerings (Joel 1:13; 2:24) had been "cut off" (Joel 1:5,16). These were an integral part of the nation's daily sacrifice and worship unto the Lord. People today would rather listen quietly as a professional minister does their praying for them. The family altar is a thing of the past. We haven't prayed together. Little wonder that we haven't stayed together. The divorce rate in the Church is the same as the world. The number of single-parent families continues to rise.

> For we being many are one bread, and one body: for we are all
> partakers of that one bread (See 1 Cor.10:17 and compare with
> Ruth 1:6; Matt. 6:11; 15:26; 1 Cor. 5:8).

> And wine that maketh glad the heart of man... (see Ps. 104:15
> and compare with Zech. 10:7).

> Yea, and if I be offered (as a libation of wine, a picture of
> Paul's martyrdom) upon the sacrifice and service of your faith, I
> joy, and rejoice with you all (Phil. 2:17).

In a deeper spiritual application, the "meat (meal) offering," like the Table of Shewbread in the Tabernacle of Moses, is the revelation of the Body of Christ. Its accompanying "drink offering" speaks of the joy of the Lord, as well as the poured-out life, the sacrificial life.

The prophet addresses the responsibility of this calamity first to the leaders, calling upon the "priests"[3] and the "ministers."[4] We can liken them in today's Church to the elders and the deacons.

> ...The priests, the Lord's ministers, mourn (Joel 1:9).

Calamity has struck the nation. It is time for every God-ordained leader to "mourn," to "bewail, lament" along with the land (see Joel 1:10 and compare with Gen. 37:34; Lam. 2:8). The priority of prayer and intercession must be pressed upon the people as never before.

Drought and Famine Have Destroyed the Harvest

The plague of locusts had been horrific. This national catastrophe was made worse by the distress of drought and famine. The prophet begins to intercede for the corn, the wine, and the oil. He is broken-hearted because the harvest is wasted.

The field is wasted, the land mourneth; for the corn is wasted... (Joel 1:10).

The "field" (also mentioned in Joel 1:11,12,19,20; 2:22) is "wasted," ravaged, devastated, and spoiled. The "field" is the world (Matt. 13:38). The harvest in our day is ruined because the "corn" of God's Word, the "wine" of the Lord's joy, and the "oil" of His Spirit have been cut off! These blessings have been replaced respectively by man-made teachings; by deathly quiet church services; and by humanistic, psychological cleverness.

Little wonder that the whole "land" mourns. This word in the tenth verse is different from that used in Joel 1:2,6,14. Appearing but once more in Joel 2:21, this word is tied to the Hebrew word for "Adam." The Lord's inheritance, the "land" in which He invests Himself, is humankind! God plants His nature, the Seed of His engrafted Word (James 1:21), within a people. We are the "earth" into which His Kingdom comes (Matt. 6:10). The "land" mourns. All of Adam's family is crying out for the corn, the wine, and the oil.

And the sound of a millstone (grinder) *shall be heard no more at all in thee* (Babylon) (Rev.18:22).

The "corn" (wheat, cereal, grain), also mentioned in Joel 1:17; 2:19, represents the Word of God.[5] There is no fresh "corn" in Babylon. It has been "wasted" (ravaged, ruined) in her Bible schools and seminaries (Mark 7:13) by higher criticism and liberal theology. Instead of grinding out the Word in the quietness of their study, her ministers prefer the social drinking at the local country club.

...The new wine is dried up, the oil languisheth (Joel 1:10).

We noted earlier that the "new wine" (Joel 1:5; 3:18), the fresh flow of the joy and gladness of the Holy Ghost, had been "cut off" (destroyed, consumed, eliminated, removed). The joy of the Lord is our strength (Neh. 8:10). Sadly, it has "dried up," having been replaced with the sad, mournful, ancient language of lifeless liturgy. This word means, "to be ashamed, confused or disappointed; also (as failing) to dry up as water, or to wither as herbage" (Joel 1:12,17,20).

The corn of the Word and the joy of the Lord have been wasted by religious tradition. Moreover, the "oil" of the Spirit has been decimated by the evil teaching of cessationism. Intellectual "might" and "power" has replaced the ways and means of the Holy Spirit (Zech. 4:6). The word "languisheth" means, "to be sick, weak, feeble; droop, exhausted; to fail," and clearly describes those lives, homes, and churches that continue to ignore the power of His Spirit.

Throughout the Bible, "oil" is a symbol for the anointing of the Holy Spirit. Joel mentions the "oil" later in his prophecy (Joel 2:19,24). Many key verses in the Word help us understand the importance of the "oil."[6] Oil was used for lamps, medicine, hygiene, food, in some of the offerings, and for the anointing oil.

Be ye ashamed, O ye husbandmen; howl, O ye vinedressers... (Joel 1:11).

It was He who gave some to be apostles, some to be prophets, some to be evangelists, and some to be pastors and teachers (Eph. 4:11, NIV).

The prophet next turns his attention to the "husbandmen" and the "vinedressers." Both are pictures of the five ascension-gift ministries that Jesus sent to equip and empower the Church. Still, hard-core evangelicals stubbornly refuse to recognize and acknowledge the contemporary ministries of apostles and prophets.

God's true ministers are "ashamed" (to pale, disappointed, be put to shame, confounded; see Joel 2:26-27) of watered-down Christianity. Confusion reigns throughout the old order (1 Cor. 14:33).

The word for "husbandmen"[7] means, "to dig, work the land; farmer, plowman." The "husbandmen" are seed-carriers who plant the words of life in the people of God.

The national calamity had caused the "vinedressers" (those who tend or dress vines, vineyards, or gardens)[8] to howl and weep (Joel 1:5,13). Notice in Genesis 2:15 Adam was to "dress" the Garden.

...For the wheat and for the barley; because the harvest of the field is perished (Joel 1:11).

The "wheat" or corn (Joel 2:24) is the most important cereal grass mentioned in the Bible. It was usually broadcast and then either plowed or trodden into the soil by oxen or other animals (Isa. 32:20). This grain was used for bread (Exod. 29:32), and was also eaten parched (Lev. 23:14; Ruth 2:14). Wheat was used in ceremonial offerings (Lev. 2:1; 24:5-7) and as an article of commerce (Ezek. 27:17; Acts 27:38). Jesus compared His death to a grain of wheat that must die to produce fruit (John 12:24).

Wheat is a symbol for the staff (bread) of life, of Christ, and of His righteous saints. The Feast of Weeks, another name for the Feast of Pentecost, was also called "the firstfruits of wheat harvest" (Exod. 34:22; Rom. 8:23).[9]

The Hebrew word for "barley" means, "roughness; barley (as villous or hairy)." Barley was a grain known since early times, well adapted to varied climates, ripening quickly and resistant to heat. It usually was harvested before wheat. Barley was considered a food for slaves and the very poor, held in low esteem as an inferior grain. In the Bible, barley was first associated with Egypt (Exod. 9:31). It was used as an offering of jealousy (Num. 5:15), for fodder (1 Kings 4:28), and for food (Judg. 7:13; John 6:5,13).

A measure of wheat is equivalent to three of barley (Rev. 6:6). Thus "barley" came to symbolize poverty, lowliness, and low reputation. Barley was the Passover harvest.[10]

All three Feasts—Passover, Pentecost, and Tabernacles (Deut. 16:16)—are harvest feasts. Religious tradition has cut a swathe through the barely harvest of souls in Passover, and the wheat harvest of the fruit and gifts of the Spirit in Pentecost. How tragic! Though the harvest is "ripe" and "plenteous" (Joel 3:13; Matt. 9:37-38), it has "perished." This word means, "to wander away, go astray, vanish; be lost." Zion must awake! Too many lives, homes, and churches have already been lost (John 3:16; 2 Pet. 3:9).

*The vine is dried up, and the fig tree languisheth; the pomegranate
tree, the palm tree also, and the apple tree...* (Joel 1:12).

The "pomegranate" (Deut. 8:7-9) means, "the tree (from its
upright growth) or the fruit (also an artificial ornament)." Its root
means, "to rise; be exalted or lifted up." The "pomegranate" represents
the "fruit" of the Spirit (Gal. 5:22-24).

This fruit (red when ripe) contained numerous edible seeds
(1 Pet. 1:23). The hem of Aaron's priestly blue robe was woven with
blue, purple, and red pomegranates (Exod. 28:33-34). Solomon deco-
rated the two great pillars in his Temple with the likeness of the pomegranate (1 Kings 7:18,20,42). The pomegranate is mentioned
throughout the Song of Solomon to describe the Shulamite's temples
(4:3; 6:7), the orchard (4:13; 6:11; 7:12), and the spiced wine (8:2).

The righteous shall flourish like the palm tree... (Ps. 92:12).

(The people) *took branches of palm trees, and went forth to
meet him, and cried, Hosanna: Blessed is the King of Israel that
cometh in the name of the Lord* (See John 12:13 and compare
with Rev. 7:9).

The "palm" tree was "erect; a (date) palm tree." The "palm" symbolizes victory, uprightness, strength, and that which is regal or noble.
It can also denote praise (the uplifted palms of our hands).

"Elim" (which means, "palms") was a place of refreshing (Exod.
15:27; Num. 33:9). Palms were part of the Feast of Tabernacles (Lev.
23:40; Neh. 8:15). Jericho was "the city of palm trees" (Deut. 34:3;
Judg. 1:16). The stature of the Shulamite was likened to the palm tree
(Song 7:7-8).

*Who is this that cometh up from the wilderness, leaning upon her
beloved? I raised thee up under the apple tree...* (See Song 8:5
and compare with Song 2:3,5; 7:8).

The word for "apple" tree means, "an apple (from its fragrance)."
The apple symbolizes the Word of God (John 1:1). The apple tree pictures Jesus, our beloved Bridegroom-lover.

The apple was sweet and fragrant, and was used to describe the
nose (discernment) of the Shulamite (Song 7:8). There are golden
apples (Prov. 25:11) that are suitable for shade (Song 2:3).

...Even all the trees of the field, are withered: because joy is withered away from the sons of men (Joel 1:12).

All the trees of the field are "withered" (dried up). There is no moisture, no living water for the sons of "men" (Adam). Tradition has brought a severe drought for the Word and Spirit of God. The joy and strength of the Lord has waned (Neh. 8:10). All those who "hate Zion" have withered away (Ps. 129:5-6).

As noted in verse ten, this word for "dried up" or "withered (away)" means, "ashamed, confused, or disappointed." This is what happens to the people of God when we allow our own ideas to replace the "joy" of the Christ-life. This word means, "cheerfulness; gladness, joy, exultation, rejoicing; exultation." It is taken from a root, which means, "to be bright, cheerful; to display joy," and is translated as, "gladness, joy, mirth, rejoicing."[11]

Sanctify the Leaders

In the next two verses (Joel 1:13-14), the prophet calls for the leaders (the elders and deacons) to humble themselves, to take the initiative, and to lead by example (1 Pet. 5:1-5).

Gird yourselves, and lament, ye priests: howl, ye ministers of the altar: come, lie all night in sackcloth, ye ministers of my God: for the meat offering and the drink offering is withholden from the house of your God (Joel 1:13).

God's spokesman implores the "priests," the Lord's "ministers," to pray (Joel 1:9). In the same spirit, leaders today must forsake ungodly traditions and "gird" themselves once again with truth (Eph. 6:14). The moment is serious; Joel commanded them to "lament." This is a different word from the one used in Joel 1:8 (to wail). This word means, "to tear the hair and beat the breasts (as Orientals do in grief); to wail, mourn."[12]

Like Ruth at the threshing floor, let us "lie all night" before His presence. Let us exchange our robes of bright linen for "sackcloth" (Joel 1:8). Sackcloth was worn in mourning or humiliation.

But as for me...my clothing was sackcloth: I humbled my soul with fasting... (Ps. 35:13).

It's time for every leader to repent. Why? Because the "meat (meal) offering" with its accompanying "drink offering" (as in Joel

1:8) are "withholden" (to hold back, keep back, deny, restrain, hinder) from the House of God, the Body of Christ (1 Tim. 3:15; Heb. 3:6; 1 Pet. 2:5).

Sanctify ye a fast, call a solemn assembly... (Joel 1:14).

This key verse underscores God's remedy for this national calamity. The seventh month of Israel's sacred calendar parallels the Book of Joel. The first day of the seventh month was the Feast of Trumpets; the tenth day was the Day of Atonement; and the fifteenth day was the Feast of Tabernacles. The "fast" (to cover the mouth) and the "solemn assembly" (a sacred of festive meeting) mentioned in Joel 1:14 point directly to the Feast Day of Atonement (Lev. 16), which is called "the fast" in Acts 27:9. Examples of such fasting are seen throughout the Scriptures.[13]

Interestingly, as with all truth, fasting is in three dimensions (Prov. 22:20-21). In the realm of the Outer Court (the body), we fast from natural food. In the Holy Place (the soul), we fast "mind" food (put down the newspaper and turn off the television). In the Most Holy Place (the spirit), we find that there are seasons in the lives of mature believers when we fast the feeling or sense of His manifest presence. In those times Christ must dwell in our hearts by faith (Eph. 3:16-20).

If My people, which are called by My name, shall humble themselves, and pray, and seek My face, and turn from their wicked ways; then will I hear from heaven, and will forgive their sin, and will heal their land (2 Chron. 7:14).

The prophet commands the leaders and the nation to prepare or "sanctify" this fast. Joel 2:15 repeats the admonition. This Hebrew word is *qadash* (Strong's #6942), and it means, "to be (make, pronounce or observe as) clean (ceremonially or morally); to consecrate, to sanctify, to prepare; to be hallowed, to be holy, to be separate; to be set apart, to be consecrated." It appears about 175 times in the Old Testament and is translated as "prepare" in Joel 3:9.

This accentuates the reason for blowing the trumpet and sounding the alarm. A clear word now calls us to the Day of Atonement, to be broken and contrite before the Lord. Only then can we fully return to the high calling of the Feast of Tabernacles. The people of Zion are a "sanctified" people.[14] It is time to "call" (address by name, call out to, commission, appoint) a solemn assembly (Joel 2:15,32).

As in the days of Joshua, we must set ourselves apart unto the Lord. We must posture ourselves to receive our inheritance (Josh. 3:5).

> ...gather the elders and all the inhabitants of the land into the house of the Lord your God, and cry unto the Lord (Joel 1:14).

As stated, we are in a *kairos* moment, a divinely appointed season. It is time to "gather" (in) the elders (the old or aged men) first, and then call for the rest of the congregation (Joel 2:6,16). This word means, "assemble, collect; bringing things to a common place or point." This collecting point is the "house" of "the Lord your God."[15] Leaders are being gathered by the trumpet's sounding, and it only blows once (Num. 10:4)! We must come and "cry" (cry out, call for help; to shriek from anguish or danger) unto the Lord.

The Day of the Lord

Alas for the day! for the day of the Lord is at hand... (Joel 1:15).

The "Day of the Lord" is a keynote to the Book of Joel, and is mentioned six times in his prophecy (Joel 1:15 [twice]; 2:1,11,31; 3:14). This awesome season is the Seventh Day from Adam (2 Pet. 3:8; Jude 1:14), and the Third Day from Jesus (Hos. 6:1-3; Matt. 16:21; Luke 13:32; John 2:1). Like the apostle John, may we always be "in the Spirit on the Lord's day" (Rev. 1:10).

The "Day of the Lord" is a day of reversals (Ps. 126). It is both day and night in the Earth at the same time! Joel prophesied that this season was approaching, "at hand" (near in place or time). Besides the Book of Joel, the "Day of the Lord" is mentioned another 15 times in the Old Testament.[16]

> But the day of the Lord will come as a thief in the night; in the which the heavens shall pass away with a great noise, and the elements[17] shall melt[18] with fervent heat, the earth also and the works that are therein shall be burned up...

> ...Looking for and hasting unto the coming of the day of God, wherein the heavens being on fire shall be dissolved, and the elements shall melt with fervent heat? (2 Pet. 3:10,12).

The "day of the Lord" in Peter's mind was the end of the Jewish world, the old order of his day. The Gospel of light had dawned and its "fervent heat" had set on fire the previous administration. This "fading flower" of the previous order and the "drunkards of Ephraim" (Isa. 28:1) were discussed in depth in Chapter Three.

...and as a destruction from the Almighty shall it come (Joel 1:15).

This "destruction" (violence, ravage; havoc, devastation, ruin) in the Day of the Lord is upon the old order, with all its religious lies and traditions (Isa. 13:6; Hos. 7:13). The same Flood in Noah's day that destroyed the wicked also delivered the righteous.

This righteous judgment comes from the "Almighty" or *El-shaddai*.[19] Yet in this verdict He remembers mercy. When Jesus cleansed the temple, He used a scourge of "small cords" (John 2:15).

Shad is the Hebrew word for "breast." God is neither male nor female; He is "spirit" (John 4:24). Yet both were created in His image. *El-shaddai* is the "breasted One" who manifests the mercy and compassion of God, just as a mother would love and nurse her own.

No Food, No Seed, No Joy

Is not the meat cut off before our eyes, yea, joy and gladness from the house of our God? (Joel 1:16).

The "meat," Judah's food supply had been "cut off" just like the "new wine" mentioned in Joel 1:5. Without a staple diet, there was no more "joy," no more "glee; mirth, gladness, joy, gaiety, pleasure; a glad result, a happy issue." This comes from a root meaning, "to brighten up."

"Gladness" meant "a revolution (of time); a circle; also joy." The root means, "to spin round (under the influence of any violent emotion)." That kind of excitement and exuberant praise is foreign to the traditional church. It, too, has been cut off from the Lord's House.

Then will I go unto the altar of God, unto God my exceeding joy... (see Ps. 43:4 and compare with Ps. 45:15; 65:12 and Prov. 23:24).

When there is no joy, there is no "strength." This word in Nehemiah 8:10 means, "a fortified place; figuratively, a defense; a place or means of safety, a protection, a refuge, a stronghold, a harbor."

The seed is rotten under their clods, the garners are laid desolate... (Joel 1:17).

The "seed" is the Word of God (Luke 8:11). The "seed" (kernels, grains) is "rotten" (dried up, shriveled), deceitfully veiled under the burden of "clods" of earth. Old order preachers have covered up the living Word with rotten, humanistic philosophy, the "earthy" teachings of Adam (1 Cor. 15:47-49). Chapter Three showed the professional clergy walking and talking in the sleep of death. Man-made burdens of legalism have killed the real anointing. Babylon's seed is rotten.

The "garners" are "laid desolate" (destroyed; to stun, grow numb, stupefy; be appalled). The "garner" was "a depository; storehouse; treasure-house, treasury; magazine of weapons, armory." This is a varied description and picture of the local church (Ps. 144:13; Matt. 3:12; Luke 3:17).

...the barns are broken down; for the corn is withered (Joel 1:17).

Bring ye all the tithes into the storehouse... (Mal. 3:10).

Honour the Lord with thy substance, and with the firstfruits of all thine increase:

So shall thy barns be filled with plenty, and thy presses shall burst out with new wine. (Prov. 3:9-10).

Moreover, like the walls of Jerusalem in the Book of Nehemiah, the "barns"[20] (granary, storehouse) have been "broken down." This strong word means, "to pull down or in pieces, break, destroy; to tear down, to overthrow, beat down."

If the foundations be destroyed, what can the righteous do? (Ps. 11:3).

The giving of God's tithe (the first tenth) and our offerings into the garner or the barn (the local church) is a fundamental teaching. Wicked men and woman have overthrown the foundations of the "city" (the Church, as in Matt. 5:14) by their evil teachings (Prov. 11:11). They have forsaken the Word; the "corn" is withered and dried. But a prophetic people in the spirit and power of Elijah have begun to repair the altar that has been "broken down" (1 Kings 18:30).

How Do the Beasts Groan

How do the beasts groan! the herds of cattle are perplexed, because they have no pasture... (Joel 1:18).

For we know that the whole creation groaneth and travaileth in pain together until now (Rom. 8:22).

How do the "beasts" (cattle) "groan"! How they "mourn, sigh; to groan (in pain or grief), to gasp; moan (of cattle)."

Joel's entire first chapter pulsates with the cry of *calamity*, the travail of the "whole creation." The Greek word for "groaneth" means, "to moan jointly; to experience a common calamity." It is a compound of *sun* (with or together) and *stenazo* (to be in straits, to sigh, murmur, pray inaudibly). Compare Israel's sigh and cry for deliverance from Egyptian bondage and tyranny (Exod. 2:23).

The herds of cattle are "perplexed" (entangled; confused; restless). The same word is used in the Book of Esther to describe the city when Haman's decree was published (Esther 3:15). So it is today among the nations. Turbulent masses of unregenerate humanity are like the troubled sea, when it cannot rest (Isa. 57:20).

The ways of Zion do mourn, because none come to the solemn feasts: all her gates are desolate: her priests sigh, her virgins are afflicted, and she is in bitterness (Lam. 1:4).

The locusts had devoured the land; there was no "pasture," no feeding-place (Joel 1:20; 2:22). God's people are starving for the Word of God. Few want to come to the Feast of Pentecost, let alone Tabernacles. They have no place to feed because they have walked away from the good Shepherd (John 10:1-17; Ps. 23; Ezek. 34).

...yea, the flocks of sheep are made desolate (Joel 1:18).

Because there is no spiritual food available, the people of God, the "flocks" (arrangement, muster) of sheep have become "desolate." This word means, "to perish; offend, be guilty, trespass; be punished." Traditional sin-conscious teaching and preaching has sent God's flock on a perpetual guilt trip. The curse of tradition has devoured the earth (Isa. 24:6).

O Lord, to thee will I cry: for the fire hath devoured the pastures of the wilderness, and the flame hath burned all the trees of the field (Joel 1:19).

Let us join our voices with the "cry" of the prophet. This word is translated as "call" in Joel 1:14; 2:15,32. The *calamity* is great. It is time for us all to call upon the Lord. Only He can deliver us now.

As noted, the calamity of the locusts was further aggravated and compounded. The "fire" and heat of severe drought and consequent famine "devoured" (the same word as "eaten" in Joel 1:4) the pastures of the "wilderness" (open field).

Its "flame" has burned up all the trees of the field (Joel 1:10). This word (Joel 2:3) means, "to gleam; a flash; figuratively, a sharply polished blade or point of a weapon." This same word is used to describe the tip or "head" of Goliath's (satan's) spear (1 Sam. 17:7). The devil is the "god of this world" (2 Cor. 4:4), the spirit that energizes all religious tradition.

The word for "pastures" in Joel 1:19 (Joel 1:20; 2:22) is different from that of the preceding verse. It means, "a home; an abode, an abode of shepherds, a habitation, a meadow." This is the word that David used in his famous psalm (Ps. 23:2).

The beasts of the field cry also unto thee... (Joel 1:20).

The "cry" of the creation is repeated, but here it is different. This word for "cry" means, "to long for, to pant after." It is only mentioned in one other place.

As the hart (stag or male deer) panteth after the water brooks (streams), so panteth my soul after Thee, O God (Ps. 42:1).

This is a different kind of cry for a different reason.

...for the rivers of waters are dried up, and the fire hath devoured the pastures of the wilderness (Joel 1:20).

The "rivers" of water are dried up (as in Joel 1:10,12,17). This word is *'aphiyq* (Strong's #650), and it means, "containing, a tube; also a bed or valley of a stream; also a strong thing or a hero; a ravine." Its root means, "to gather in or collect for any purpose; to receive" (Ps. 18:15; 42:1; Song 5:12; Ezek. 34:13; 36:4-6).

These "rivers of water" constitute the genuine flow of the presence of God, the pure move of His Word and Holy Spirit (Ps. 126:4). There are three of these spiritual rivers:

First, the prophetic river from the belly. The word for "flow" in John 7:38 is *rheo* (compare *rhema*, which means, "an utterance"). Second, the priestly river from the sanctuary (Ezek. 47:1-2). Third, the kingly river from the throne (Rev. 22:1-2).

And he (the godly man) *shall be like a tree planted by the rivers*[21] *of water, that bringeth forth his fruit in his season; his leaf also shall not wither; and whatsoever he doeth shall prosper* (Ps. 1:3).

The priesthood of Jesus is after the order or manner of Melshisedec (Heb. 5:1-8:6). Our Savior fills all three offices of Prophet, Priest, and King. His Church is to be conformed to His image. We are a "royal priesthood" (1 Pet. 2:9), "kings and priests" (Rev. 1:6). These rivers of truth have been obliterated by tradition. Babylon has dried up these rivers and quenched the Spirit (1 Thess. 5:19).

The prophet puts down his pen. His heart is dejected. His initial assignment was to reveal the *cry,* the *cause,* and the *calamity* of his nation's desolation. We weep with Joel as we see the spiritual barrenness in the Church today. Religious tradition has stripped away our life and strength. We hunger and thirst for the corn, the wine, and the oil.

There can be no delay. Sound the alarm! We must call a solemn assembly and sanctify a fast throughout the congregation. Trumpets must summon us all to the Feast Day of Atonement.

There is but one remedy for all this desolation—our corporate *consecration!*

ENDNOTES

1. The word "girded" used here (compare Joel 1:13) means, "to bind on" (with a belt or armor) (see Exod. 12:11; 29:9; Ps. 109:19; compare Luke 12:35; Eph. 6:14; 1 Pet. 1:13).

2. The word "sackcloth" used here (compare Joel 1:13) means, "a mesh (as allowing liquid to pass through); coarse loose cloth or sacking (sack) used in mourning or humiliation," and thus alludes directly to the Feast Day of Atonement (see Gen. 37:34; 2 Sam. 21:10; 1 Chron. 21:16; Esther 4:1-4; Job 16:15; Ps. 30:11; Isa. 22:12; 37:1-2; Jer. 4:8; 6:26; Lam. 2:10; Dan. 9:3; and John 3:5-8).

3. The word for "priests" used here (compare Joel 1:13; 2:17) is *kohen* (Strong's #3548), and it means, "officiating (at the altar in sacrificial or mediatorial duties) as a priest; to mediate in religious services (representing the people before God)." More than one-third of its over 700 references are found in the Pentateuch. Leviticus, which has about 185 references, is called the "manual of the priests" (note Isa. 61:6 with 1 Pet. 2:9; Rev. 1:6; 5:10).

4. The word for ministers" (compare Joel 1:13; 2:17) is *sharath* (Strong's #8334), and it means, "to attend as a menial or worshipper; figuratively, to contribute to; a servant or attendant." In the New Testament sense, "priests" can be

compared to elders, and "ministers" likened to deacons (see Gen. 39:4; Exod. 24:13; Josh. 1:1; 1 Kings 19:21).

5. These verses stress the importance of the "corn," the Word of God (see Zech. 9:17; Matt. 4:4; 6:10; Mark 4:28; John 12:24; and 1 Tim. 5:18).

6. There are many important verses in the Word to help us understand the importance of the "oil" (see Ps. 23:5; 89:20; 92:10; Zech. 4:11-14; Mark 6:13; Heb. 1:9; James 5:14).

7. Both the Old and New Testaments say much about the "husbandman" ministry (see Gen. 9:20; 2 Chron. 26:10; Isa. 61:5; Jer. 14:4; 31:24; 51:23; Amos 5:16; and Zech. 13:5; compare Matt. 21:33-41; John 15:1; 2 Tim. 2:6; and James 5:7).

8. This word for "vinedressers" is used elsewhere in the Old Testament (see Deut. 28:39; 2 Kings 25:12; 2 Chron. 26:10; Isa. 61:5; and Jer. 52:16).

9. Study these other verses concerning the "wheat" harvest of Pentecost (see Num. 18:12; Deut. 8:8; Ruth 2:23; 1 Chron. 21:23; Ps. 81:16; Song 7:2; Isa. 28:25; Jer. 31:12; Matt. 13:24-30; Luke 22:31; 1 Cor. 15:37; and Rev. 6:6; 18:13).

10. Study these other verses concerning the "barley" harvest of Passover (see Deut. 8:8; Judg. 7:13; Ruth 1:22; 2:17,23; 1 Kings 4:28; Isa. 28:25; Ezek. 4:12; Hos. 3:2; and John 6:9,13).

11. This word for "joy" occurs 22 times in the Old Testament (including Esther 8:16-17; Ps. 45:7; 51:8,12; 105:43; Isa. 12:3; 35:10; 51:3,11; 61:3; Jer. 15:16; 31:13; 33:9,11; and Zech. 8:19).

12. The word translated as "lament" here in Joel 1:13 is used in these cross-references (see Gen. 23:2; 50:10; Eccles. 3:4; Mic. 1:8; Zech. 12:10).

13. Note these examples of fasting in the Old Testament (see 2 Chron. 20:3; Ezra 8:21; Neh. 9:1; Esth. 4:3; 9:31; Ps. 35:13; 69:10; 109:24; Isa. 58:3-6; Jer. 36:6-9; and Zech. 8:19); and in the New Testament (Matt. 4:2; 6:16-18; 9:15; 17:21; Mark 2:20; Luke 2:37; 5:33; 18:11-12; Acts 13:3; 10:30; 14:23; 27:33; and 2 Cor. 6:5; 11:27).

14. Note these verses about His "sanctified" ones (see Gen. 2:3; Exod. 20:8; 28:3; 31:13; Lev. 25:10; 1 Sam. 16:5; 1 Kings 9:3; 1 Chron. 15:12-14; Isa. 13:3; and Jer. 1:5).

15. This phrase, "the Lord your God," is used seven times in Joel's prophecy (1:14; 2:13,14,23,26,27; 3:17).

16. The "Day of the Lord" is mentioned 21 times in the prophetic books of the Old Testament (six times in Joel; see also Isa. 2:12; 13:6,9; Ezek. 13:5; 30:3 [twice]; Amos 5:18 [twice],20; Obad. 1:15; Zeph. 1:7,14 [twice]; Zech. 14:1; and Mal. 4:5).

17. The word translated as "elements" in 2 Peter 3:10,12 is *stoicheion* (Strong's #4747), and it means, "something orderly in arrangement; a serial (basal, fundamental, initial) constituent; the elements, rudiments, primary and

fundamental principles of any art, science, or discipline." It is translated in the KJV as "elements" (Gal. 4:3,9), "rudiments" of the world (Col. 2:8,20), and the first "principles" of the Word of God (Heb. 5:12).

18. The Greek word for "melt" in 2 Peter 3:10,12 is *luo* (Strong's #3089), and it means, "to loosen; release from bonds, set free; to loosen, to undo, to dissolve anything bound, tied, or compacted together." Jesus' finished work has "broken down" the middle wall of partition (Eph. 2:14), and "destroyed" the works of the devil (1 John 3:8; compare Matt. 16:19; John. 2:19; 5:18; 11:44; Rev. 1:5; 5:2)

19. *El-shaddai* is mentioned 31 times in Job (compare Gen. 17:1; 28:3; 35:11; Exod. 6:3; Ps. 68:14; 91:1; and Ezek. 1:24; 10:5).

20. Here is every Scripture in the Bible about the "barn" (see Job 39:12; Prov. 3:10; Joel 1:17; Hag. 2:19; Matt. 6:26; 13:30; Luke 12:18,24).

21. Note these verses concerning the "rivers" (see Deut. 10:7; Prov. 5:16; 21:1; Song 5:12; Isa. 32:2; and Jer. 31:9).

THE BOOK OF JOEL

PART TWO

CONSECRATION

(JOEL 2:1-32)

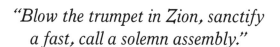

*"Blow the trumpet in Zion, sanctify
a fast, call a solemn assembly."*

CHAPTER NINE

CONSECRATION — ITS ALARM (JOEL 2:1)

The first section of Joel's prophecy to Judah and Jerusalem (Joel 1:1-20) was all about *desolation*—its cry, its cause, and its calamity.

Desolation's *cry* (Joel 1:1-3) represented the travailing groan of the "whole creation" to be delivered from bondage and futility (Rom. 8:22). Its *cause* (Joel 1:4-7) in Joel's day was a plague of locusts aggravated by severe drought and consequent famine. This pictures the plague of religious tradition that has ravaged the Church for 2,000 years. The widespread *calamity* of this desolation (Joel 1:8-20) demolished every area of life throughout Judah and Jerusalem. Man-made ideas and teachings have corrupted and contaminated biblical Christianity.

Is there a remedy? Do we have any hope for deliverance? Our only hope is for a *consecration* as widespread as the need!

Blow the Trumpet in Zion

Blow ye the trumpet in Zion... (Joel 2:1).

Cry aloud, spare not, lift up thy voice like a trumpet, and shew My people their transgression... (Isa. 58:1).

We arrive at last to the heart of our message and the title of this book. With Joel's passion, we "blow" the trumpet in Zion, and *sound the alarm* of our corporate *consecration*.

Like Isaiah, we "spare not" (hold back nothing). Once that kind of commitment is made and the Church returns to her "first love"

(Rev. 2:4), we will see the restoration of all that He has promised. The prophet repeats this opening admonition verbatim in the 15th verse of this same chapter.

This root word for "blow" means, "to blow, to clap, to strike, to sound, to thrust, to blast." It is used eight times (the number of a new beginning) in the story of the conquest of Jericho (Josh. 6:1-20).

On the morning of the third day there was thunder and lightning, with a thick cloud over the mountain, and a very loud trumpet blast. Everyone in the camp trembled (Exod. 19:16, NIV).

The word for "trumpet" in Joel 2:1 is *shophar* (Strong's #7782), and it means, "a cornet (as giving a clear sound) or curved horn; a ram's horn." It is first mentioned in Exodus 19:16, and was the Jubilee trumpet of Leviticus 25. It is noteworthy that the Jubilee trumpet was blown on the tenth day of the seventh month (in the 50th year), the same day as the Feast Day of Atonement. This will be discussed in depth in Chapter Eleven (Joel 2:12-17). The *shophar* is mentioned 14 times in Joshua 6:1-20 (the biblical number of Passover, salvation, and deliverance).

Blow the trumpet in "Zion;" this was revealed as both a *place* (the high calling) and a *people* (the corporate Overcomer) in Chapters Four and Five.

Awake, awake (open your eyes, stir up or rouse yourself); *put on thy strength, O Zion; put on thy beautiful garments, O Jerusalem, the holy city...*[1] (Isa. 52:1).

Most of the Church world, like the Shulamite (Song 5:2-7), is asleep in Adam (see Chapter Three). Both the wise virgins and the foolish virgins were sleeping (Matt. 25:1-10). Awake, O Zion, from the desolation of Chapter One! The trumpet has become an alarm. A new Day is dawning. Note this acronym; to "awake" (A-W-A-K-E) is to have:

1. Awareness of our ascension (1 Kings 5:1-4; Eph. 1:18-23).

2. Wisdom for a new order (2 Kings 3:6-12).

3. Accountability in every aspect (Matt. 13:1-23).

4. Knowledge of the Kingdom (2 Pet. 1:3-8).

5. Energy of the Spirit; or the Enterprise of the Kingdom (Acts 1:8).

Speak unto the children of Israel, saying, In the seventh month, in the first day of the month, shall ye have a sabbath, a memorial of blowing of trumpets, an holy convocation (Lev. 23:24).

And the sons of Aaron, the priests, shall blow with the trumpets... (see Num. 10:8 and compare with Num. 31:6; 1 Kings 34,39).

Sound the ram's horn at the New Moon, and when the moon is full, on the day of our Feast (Ps. 81:3, NIV).

Joel 2:1 is a key verse for the Feast of Trumpets (Num. 10:1-10; 29:1-6), which took place on the first day of the seventh month.[2]

Trumpets are calling us to the place of consecration, to return to the high calling. A clear word now summons us to the Feast Day of Atonement (the tenth day of the seventh month), to the place of *consecration*—repentance, humility, brokenness, and cleansing (Lev. 16). Only the priest could blow the trumpet. Men and women of prayer, praise, and worship are sounding this message. Like Ezekiel, who was a priest before he became a prophet, only those who can show mercy will proclaim Zion's call.

Different Words for "Trumpet"

So David and all the house of Israel brought up the ark of the Lord (to the tent in Zion) *with shouting, and with the sound of the trumpet* (see 2 Sam. 6:15 and compare with 1 Chron. 15:28).

As noted, the Hebrew word for "trumpet" in Joel 2:1 is *shophar*. Besides the reference above, it is used throughout the Old Testament in various settings.[3]

Make thee two trumpets of silver... (Num. 10:2).

And David and all Israel played before God with all their might, and with singing...and with trumpets (1 Chron. 13:8).

Another Hebrew word for "trumpet" is *chatsotserah* (Strong's #2689), and it means, "a trumpet (from its sundered or quavering note); a clarion." Its root means, "to surround with a stockade; to sound a trumpet." Besides the two references above, it also is used throughout the Old Testament.[4]

Then shalt thou cause the trumpet of the jubile to sound on the tenth day of the seventh month....

And ye shall hallow the fiftieth year, and proclaim liberty throughout all the land unto all the inhabitants thereof: it shall be a jubilee... (Lev. 25:9-10).

Compare still another Hebrew word translated 19 times in Leviticus 25, and seven times in Leviticus 27 as "Jubile." It is *yobel* (Strong's #3104), and it means, "the blast of a horn (from its continuous sound); specifically, the signal of the silver trumpets; hence, the instrument itself and the festival thus introduced (the Jubilee)." Its root means, "to flow; causatively, to bring (especially with pomp); to lead, carry, conduct, or bear along." *Yobel* is also rendered six times as "rams' horns" in Joshua chapter 6.

For if the trumpet give an uncertain sound, who shall prepare himself to the battle? (1 Cor.14:8).

I was in the Spirit on the Lord's day, and heard behind me a great voice, as of a trumpet (Rev.1:10).

The Greek word for "trumpet" is *salpinx* (Strong's #4536), and it means, "the idea of quavering or reverberation)."[5] It is taken from *salos* (a vibration; billow, wave; the tossing or swell of the sea), and is akin to *saino* (to wag [as a dog its tail fawningly]; to shake, disturb, agitate, trouble, move). Compare the primary verb *seio* (to rock or vibrate sideways or to and fro; to agitate in any direction; cause to tremble; to throw into a tremor of fear or concern; to quake for fear). The root *seio* is rendered five times as "move, quake, shake."

Again, the Feast of Trumpets was on the first day of the seventh month. They awakened the nation to prepare for the coming Day of Atonement and the harvest of the Feast of Tabernacles. So the Lord now calls His "holy nation" (1 Pet. 2:9) to return to Zion. As noted by the Hebrew words given above, there were different kinds of trumpets.

First, there was the trumpet of "rams' horns" (the *shophar*). This horn was produced from the sacrifice of the ram, an animal of substitution and consecration. Jesus was our "ram" caught in the thicket of humanity's sins (Gen. 22:13). His death produced a clear sound of resurrection. Those who are crucified with Him (Gal. 2:20) are producing the sound of His life in the earth.

Second, there were the "two trumpets of silver" (Num. 10:2). Silver is the symbol for redemption; these trumpets are blown by the redeemed and sound the message of full redemption. They were only blown by priests, a picture of the believer, especially the five fold ministries (Eph. 4:11). These trumpets were made from the silver given as atonement money (Exod. 30:11-16). Jesus' blood has a voice (Heb. 12:24).

There were two of these silver trumpets; two is the biblical number denoting witness, testimony, or covenant. This speaks of Christ in the fullness of his Body; or, the Jew and the Greek in one Body by His Cross (Eph. 1:11-16; 1 Pet. 1:14-20). There were two times that Ezekiel was told to prophesy to the dry bones (Ezek. 37:4,9)!

The trumpet symbolizes a *clear word from God* at the mouth of His God-ordained ministry—prophet and priest, male and female. This is His prophetic voice, the Word of the Lord, spoken or sung, to God's people through His servants. This is the "voice of the bridegroom" (Jer. 33:11).

Four Purposes for Blowing the Trumpet

The blowing of the trumpets is consecration's *alarm.* There is a sound that now causes Zion to awake. There were four major purposes (among nine) for blowing the trumpets (Num. 10:1-10), revealing the progressive operation of our return to Zion.

Make thee two trumpets of silver; of a whole piece shalt thou make them: that thou mayest use them for the calling of the assembly... (See Num. 10:2 and compare with Matt. 24:31).

First, the trumpets were "for the calling of the assembly." This is the purpose of gathering. We are being gathered by the voice of One in the realm of the Spirit.

...And for the journeying of the camps (See Num. 10:2 and compare with Rom. 8:14).

Second, the trumpets sounded "for the journeyings of the camps." This shows the purpose of growth. We are moving on from the adolescence and duality of the Second Day to the maturity and single-ness of the Third Day. We are growing in grace (2 Pet. 3:18). The cloud of His presence is leading the way (Num. 9:15-23).

And if ye go to war in your land against the enemy that oppres-seth you, then ye shall blow an alarm with the trumpets; and ye shall be remembered before the Lord your God, and ye shall be saved from your enemies (See Num. 10:9 and compare with 2 Cor. 10:4).

Third, the trumpets blew the alarm when it was time to "go to war." This is the principle of a great struggle. There now comes a new dimension of spiritual warfare in the heavenlies (Eph. 6:10). We are to cast down every imagination, every religious idea that exalts itself against the knowledge of God (2 Cor. 10:3-6). New levels, new devils! But we rejoice that He has already won (John 16:33).

Also at your times of rejoicing—your appointed feasts and New Moon festivals—you are to sound the trumpets... (Num. 10:10, NIV).

Fourth, the blowing of the trumpets announced the Feasts of Jehovah, especially Tabernacles, the promised assurance of a great ingathering. We are growing up from the Feast of Pentecost in the third month to the global harvest of the Feast of Tabernacles in the seventh month.

The trumpets are sounding. Zion is awakening! We have been gathered for the purpose of growth. On the other side of every great struggle, there is a great harvest!

Sound an Alarm

Blow ye the trumpet in Zion, and sound an alarm... (Joel 2:1).

Seek ye the Lord while He may be found, call ye upon him while He is near:

Let the wicked forsake his way, and the unrighteous man his thoughts: and let him return unto the Lord, and He will have mercy upon him; and to our God, for He will abundantly pardon. (Isa. 55:6-7).

Seek the Lord while He may be found. Call upon Him at the sound of His trumpet. Do it today. Hear the trumpet in these days of grace and mercy. Obey its sound before it becomes an "alarm"!

So the people shouted when the priests blew with the trumpets: and it came to pass, when the people heard the sound of the trumpet, and the people shouted with a great shout, that the wall fell down flat... (Josh. 6:20).

This key word for "sound an alarm" in Joel 2:1 is a primitive root that means, "to mar (by breaking); to split the ears (with sound), shout (for alarm or joy). This is translated seven times in the Book of Psalms as "joyful noise" (Ps. 66:1; 81:1; 95:1,2,4; 96:6; 100:1).

This same word is translated ten times as "shout" or "shouted" in Joshua chapter 6 at the fall of Jericho. Zechariah used the same word to announce the coming of Messiah the King (Zech. 9:9).

I beseech every believer, every leader, and every local church. Return to the Lord with all your heart. Every wall is about to fall. The King is coming with righteous judgment. With great zeal He will cleanse His Temple. Hear the trumpet before it becomes an alarm!

> *Blow ye the trumpet in Zion, and sound an alarm in My holy mountain: let all the inhabitants of the land tremble: for the day of the Lord cometh, for it is nigh at hand* (Joel 2:1).

> *They shall not hurt nor destroy in all My holy mountain: for the earth shall be full of the knowledge of the Lord, as the waters cover the sea* (Isa. 11:9).

His "holy mountain" (see Joel 3:17) is Zion![6]

The inhabitants of the land from every nation have begun to "tremble" at the sound of His trumpet. This word means, "to quiver (with any violent emotion, especially anger or fear); to quake, to rage, to be agitated, excited, disturbed, or perturbed" (Isa. 64:2; Jer. 33:9; 50:34; Joel 2:10; and Hab. 3:16).

> *Arise, shine; for thy light is come, and the glory of the Lord is risen upon thee.*

> *For, behold, the darkness shall cover the earth, and gross darkness the people: but the Lord shall arise upon thee, and His glory shall be seen upon thee* (Isa. 60:1-2).

> *For, behold, the day cometh, that shall burn as an oven; and all the proud, yea, and all that do wickedly, shall be stubble: and the day that cometh shall burn them up, saith the Lord of hosts, that it shall leave them neither root nor branch.*

> *But unto you that fear my name shall the Sun of righteousness arise with healing in His wings...* (Mal. 4:1-2).

The "day of the Lord" is "at hand" (near in place or time; to approach or draw near). We discussed the "Day of the Lord" in depth in the previous chapter with regard to Joel 1:15.

We noted that the "Day of the Lord" is the Seventh Day from Adam and the Third Day from Jesus. It is the Day of divine reversals. The prophets Isaiah and Malachi revealed it to be day and night, light for the righteous and darkness for the wicked, at the same time in the earth. Joel himself would see this Day as dark and gloomy, and yet as the sun rising in the dawn of a new day!

I was in the Spirit—rapt in His power—on the Lord's day, and I heard behind me a great voice like the calling of a war trumpet (Rev. 1:10, AMP).

Let us, like Joel and John, be in the Spirit on this His Day. May our ears and hearts be pierced with the sound of His trumpet, a clear word that beckons us to awake and return to the high calling in Zion.

Have you heard the trumpet, His *alarm*? Have you begun to make your consecration? If so, rejoice. You may now arise and take your rightful place in Joel's overcoming *army!*

ENDNOTES

1. These verses speak about a people who are arousing and awakening in Zion (see Deut. 32:11; Judg. 5;12; 2 Chron. 36:22; Ps. 57:8; Song 2:7; 4:16; 5:2; Isa. 50:4; 51:9,17; and Hag. 1:14).

2. Study these verses for the Feast of Trumpets (Lev. 23:23-25; Num. 10:1-10; 29:1-6; Ps. 81:3-5). Compare Lev. 25:9 (the Jubilee Trumpet); Josh. 6:4 (seven trumpets); Judg. 7:19-21 (Gideon); 2 Sam. 6:15 (the Ark); 2 Chron. 5:12-14 (the dedication of Solomon's Temple); Isa. 58:2 (the voice); Jer. 6:17 (the watchmen); 42:14 (not heard in Egypt); Joel 2:1,15 (Zion); Amos 3:6-7 (prophets); Zeph. 1:14-16 (the Day of the Lord); Zech. 9:13-14 (the sons of Zion); Matt. 24:31 (to gather his elect); 1 Cor. 14:8 (the uncertain sound); and Rev. 1:10-11 (His great voice); 4:1 (the first voice heard behind the open door or rent veil); 8:2 (the seven trumpets).

3. The Hebrew word *shophar* (trumpet) is used in these verses (see Exod. 19:16,19; 20:18; Judg. 7:16-22; 2 Sam. 6:15; Neh. 4:18,20; Ps. 47:5; 81:3; 98:6; 150:3; Isa. 58:1; Ezek. 33:3-6; Hos. 8:1; Joel 2:1,15; Amos 3:6; Zeph. 1:16; and Zech. 9:14).

4. This second word for "trumpet" is used in these verses (see 2 Kings 11:14; 1 Chron. 15:24,28; 2 Chron. 5:12-13; 13:12-14; 20:28; 29:26-28; Ezra 3:10; Neh. 12:35,41; Ps. 98:6; and Hos. 5:8).

5. The Greek word *salpinx* (trumpet) is mentioned 11 times in the New Testament (see Matt. 24:31; 1 Cor. 14:8; 15:52; 1 Thess. 4:16; Heb. 12:19; and Rev. 1:10; 4:1; 8:2,6,13; 9:14).

6. God's "holy mountain" is Zion (see Isa. 11:9; 56:7; 57:13; 65:11,25; 66:20; Ezek. 20:40; 28:14; Dan. 9:16,20; 11:45; Joel 2:1; 3:17; Obad. 1:16; Zeph. 3;11; and Zech. 8:3).

CHAPTER TEN

CONSECRATION — ITS ARMY (JOEL 2:2-11)

Chapter Two of Joel provides the answer to the nationwide dilemma of Chapter One. God's people must make a corporate *consecration!*

The previous chapter introduced consecration's *alarm.* The trumpet has blown in Zion. The Day of the Lord is at hand!

We now behold the characteristics of those who are presently repenting and making this level of commitment to the Lord, and who are returning to the high calling. Behold Zion's consecrated *army!*

The prophet uses the figure of an "army" in Joel 2:2-11 to explain the unprecedented plague of locusts Jehovah sent to judge the house of Judah. The context demands this literal application. But this detailed description of Joel's army also *prophetically* points to the corporate Overcomer, those men and women apprehended for Zion!

Day and Night at the Same Time

A day of darkness and of gloominess, a day of (thunder) *clouds and of thick darkness, as the morning spread upon the mountains...* (Joel 2:2).

The Day of the Lord is a day of "darkness" to the wicked, to those who are walking after the flesh. This word (see Joel 2:31) means, "the dark, darkness; figuratively, misery, destruction, death, ignorance, sorrow, wickedness." Its root means, "to be or become dark (as withholding light); to darken, to grow dim; to obscure, to confuse."

The Kingdom of God is a Kingdom of light, in stark contrast to the kingdom of darkness (Acts 26:18). Light represents understanding (Eph. 1:18), and darkness signifies ignorance. Remember, Adam is asleep in the darkness, but Christ is awake in the light, the morning of this new day.

To the wicked, God's day is marked by "gloominess" (duskiness, figuratively, misfortune, calamity). The root means, "to set as the sun." The Day of the Lord marks the ending of the old day, the old order. This is also a time of "thick darkness" (the gloom of a lowering sky; a heavy or dark cloud; gross darkness; to droop). In Moses' day, there was a darkness so dark that the Egyptians could feel it; but there was light at the same time among the Israelites in Goshen (Exod. 10:21-23).

Watchman, what of the night? Watchman, what of the night? The watchman said, the morning cometh, and also the night (See Isa. 21:11-12 and compare with Rom. 13:11-14; Eph. 5:14).

The "Day" of the Lord is "day" and not night! It is as the "morning" or the "dawn." Awake, O Zion! Many have asked me and other watchmen, "Are you a day preacher or a night preacher?"

My answer is, "Both. But my focus, like the watchman in Isaiah, is the morning! I preach a great big Jesus and a wee little devil, a whole lot of morning and a little bit of night (to those who need it)."

The morning of this new Day is "spread" (dispersed, broken up and spread out, stretched out) upon the "mountains" (it's still dark in the valleys). Joel's army of prayer warriors has been broken and sent throughout the nations! This also can represent the spreading of the wings of the corporate Eagle Company, or the spreading of the wings of the cherubim in the Most Holy Place.[1]

...a great people and a strong; there hath not been ever the like, neither shall be any more after it, even to the years of many generations (Joel 2:2).

Joel's overcoming army is "great"[2] and "strong" (Joel 1:6; 2:5,11). The word for "great" means, "abundant (in quantity, size, age, number, rank, quality); much, many; enough; greater than; a captain, a chief." As with David, this host of God grows in number "day by day" (1 Chron. 12:22). More and more people are hearing the sound of the trumpet, a clear word of "present truth" (2 Pet. 1:12).

First and foremost, Joel's army is a corporate entity, a "people." This word means, "a people (as a congregated unit); specifically, a tribe; hence (collectively) troops or attendants; figuratively, a flock; nation." Its root means, "to associate; overshadow (by huddling together)."

We are of the tribe of Judah, His holy flock (Ezek. 36:38). We are overshadowed by His wings in the secret place of the Most High. We are huddled together in Christ.

The Garden of Eden Before Them

A fire devoureth before them; and behind them a flame burneth: the land is as the garden of Eden before them... (Joel 2:3).

Is not My word like as a fire? (Jer. 23:29).

For our God is a consuming fire (Heb.12:29).

Jehovah's Army is heaven's "answer" for the desolation of Joel 1 because God will answer "by fire" (1 Kings 18:24)!

A fire "devoureth" (eats, feeds) before them (before their face). "Behind them" (afterward) a flame "burneth" (to lick; blaze up, scorch). Every overcomer has been in the fire. But now we are more than on fire; we are as fire, the Word made flesh, His ongoing incarnation! Our face has become one with His face (2 Cor. 3:18; James 1:18-25). The fiery passion of the Lord Himself goes before us.

Blessed are the meek: for they shall inherit the earth (Matt. 5:5).

The "land" (of promise), the earth, is before us. It belongs to the Lord (Ps. 24:1). The earth does not belong to the devil and his crowd. It rightfully belongs to Jesus Christ (Rom.8:17)! The Seed of Abraham are heirs of the "world" (Rom. 4:13; Gal. 3:16,29).

For the Lord shall comfort Zion: he will comfort all her waste places; and he will make her wilderness like Eden, and her desert like the garden of the Lord... (See Isa. 51:3 and compare with Gen. 2:8).

The land is as the (enclosed, fenced) Garden of "Eden." This word is *'Eden* (Strong's #5731), and it means, "pleasure; luxury, dainty, delight, finery." *'Eden* is used 16 times in the Old Testament.[3]

How that he was caught up into paradise, and heard unspeakable words, which it is not lawful for a man to utter (see 2 Cor. 12:4 and compare with Luke 23:43; Rev. 2:7).

"Eden," or "paradise," is also called "the third heaven" (2 Cor. 12:2). The "third heaven" is the third dimension of grace, the Most Holy Place. This highest realm is promised to "him that overcometh." The "third heaven" is Zion, the dwelling-place of God! What the apostle Paul heard there was "not lawful" (to be spoken in public). But it's lawful now!

"Paradise" is transliterated from the Greek word *paradeisos* (Strong's #3857). Of Oriental origin, it means, "a park, (specifically) an Eden." Among the Persians, an "eden" was a grand enclosure or preserve, a hunting ground, a pleasure ground or park (shady and well watered) for Persian kings and nobles.

The essential, spiritual meaning of "Eden" is clear. Eden is Paradise, the Kingdom of God on earth, the original dream and vision of the Father (Joel 2:28). Five essential principles were planted there:

First, relationship; both the man and the woman were created in His image and likeness (two were one). There was *worship.*

Second, dominion; both the man and the woman as co-regents were given authority over the earth. There was *stewardship.*

Third, productivity and creativity; both the man and the woman were called to replenish (fill, fulfill, accomplish, complete) and subdue (tread down, conquer, subjugate, bring into subjection) the earth. There was *inheritance.*

Fourth, discipline; both the man and the woman were given a choice, for there were two trees in the Garden. There was *accountability.*

Fifth, priesthood; both the man and the woman were partakers of the river in Eden, which flowed out. There was *privilege.*

And a river went out of Eden to water the garden; and from thence it was parted, and became into four heads (Gen. 2:10).

The river in Eden became "four heads." The bulk of the Book of Genesis (chapters 12-50) has to do with four men—Abraham, Isaac, Jacob (Israel), and Joseph. All were patriarchs or fathers. The "way of the tree of life" (Gen. 3:24) back into Eden "before" Joel's army will be through the fathers, the apostolic company (1 Cor. 4:15)!

...and behind them a desolate wilderness; yea, and nothing shall escape them (Joel 2:3).

Behind Joel's army is a "desolate" (devastated, astonished) wilderness (Joel 1:19-20). All who have been in the path of these chosen ones will be "astonished" at their doctrine and works (Matt. 7:28; 13:54). These overcomers have been called to lay waste to every man-made idea and teaching. Religious tradition is rooted out and pulled down (Jer. 1:10) wherever their voice is heard. Nothing shall "escape" Zion's influence (Joel 2:32). Even futurism's or dispensationalism's "escape" mentality, the any-minute pre-tribulation rapture theory, will be been burned with fire. "Whosoever" shall call upon the Lord shall be delivered (Joel 2:32).

The Appearance of Horses

The appearance of them is as the appearance of horses... (Joel 2:4).

In that day shall there be upon the bells of the horses, HOLINESS UNTO THE LORD... (see Zech. 14:20 and compare with Jer. 4:13).

The "appearance" (sight, vision, phenomenon, spectacle) of Joel's consecrated army shall be as "horses." This is the Hebrew word *cuwc* (Strong's #5483), and it means, "to skip (properly, for joy); a horse (as leaping); also a swallow (from its rapid flight); a warhorse or chariot horse."

Behold, we put bits in the horses' mouths, that they may obey us; and we turn about their whole body (James 3:3).

Throughout the Bible, the "horse" (warhorse or chariot horse) is a picture of the overcomer. The only ones who are able to deal with the desolation of Joel 1 are those who have been harnessed by the Lord, whose mouths have been bridled by His righteousness (Ps. 32:9).[4] The oldest book in the Bible has much to say about the horse. Above all, the war horse is fearless in the face of the enemy!

"Do you give the horse his strength or clothe his neck with a flowing mane?

Do you make him leap like a locust, striking terror with his proud snorting?

He paws fiercely, rejoicing in his strength, and charges into the fray.

He laughs at fear, afraid of nothing; he does not shy away from the sword.

The quiver rattles against his side, along with the flashing spear and lance.

In frenzied excitement he eats up the ground; he cannot stand still when the trumpet sounds.

At the blast of the trumpet he snorts, 'Aha!' He catches the scent of battle from afar, the shout of commanders and the battle cry (Job 39:19-25, NIV).

The Lord Jesus Christ, the Head of the Church, is Heaven's fearless Warhorse. He is the beloved Son (Matt. 3:17), the Firstborn among many brethren (Rom. 8:29), the consummate Overcomer (Rev. 3:21).

Jesus' armies are clothed with His righteousness (Rev. 19:8,14). We have heard the trumpet-blast and have caught the scent of battle. We have obeyed the shout of our Captain (Heb. 2:10). We have heard His battle cry!

If thou hast run with the footmen, and they have wearied thee, then how canst thou contend with horses? and if in the land of peace, wherein thou trustedst, they wearied thee, then how wilt thou do in the swelling of Jordan? (Jer. 12:5).

The Kingdom of God is not for half-hearted people. It is time to run with the horses, for the Jordan is swelled and overflowing in the day of harvest (Josh. 3:15). It is time to cross over.

The "horse" is a rich and vast subject of study; the characteristics of this animal are given throughout the Scriptures.[5]

...and as horsemen, so shall they run (Joel 2:4).

And the shapes of the locusts were like unto horses prepared unto battle... (Rev. 9:7).

A plague of locusts had devastated the land in Joel's day. The prophet uses the description of that invading army to illustrate the Host of the Lord. Notice the head of a locust is like that of a horse.

Joel now mentions the "horsemen." One is tempted to ask, "Where does the horse stop and the man begin?" We are One with Him (1 Cor. 6:17)! "Horsemen" means, "a steed, warhorse (as stretched out to a vehicle, not single nor for mounting; also (by implication) a driver (in a chariot); (collectively) cavalry."

It is noteworthy that "horsemen" are mentioned in connection with Elijah's translation (2 Kings 2:12). This remarkable prophet did not experience physical death (see Chapter Three).

Like the "horse," the "horsemen" are mentioned throughout the Old Testament.[6] So shall they "run" (swiftly; dart, rush), as in Joel 2:7,9.

A Strong People Set in Battle Array

Like the noise of chariots on the tops of mountains shall they leap... (Joel 2:5).

This Army comes with the "noise" (sound, voice, as in Joel 2:11; 3:16) of "chariots." The patriarch Joseph rode in the "second chariot" because Pharaoh was king of Egypt (Gen. 41:42-43). The corporate Overcomer is second only to Jesus, for our King will always have the preeminence (Col. 1:18). We wear the ring of His authority, and are clothed in the fine linen of His righteousness. Those called to Zion even wear His gold, partaking of His "divine nature" (2 Pet. 1:4).

These chariots are moving on the "tops" or "heads" of the mountains. We are moving about on the heads of kingdoms, and will bring the Word of the Lord to heads of state.

Joel's army of consecrated ones is sent forth to minister His "anger" and "rebuke" upon the "refuge of lies" (Isa. 28:14-18; 66:15). We are horses that "leap," that stamp, spring about (wildly or for joy)." This is also rendered as, "dance, jump, skip." This same word is used to describe David's "dancing" when the Ark was brought to Zion (1 Chron. 15:29; 2 Sam. 6:14-16), and by the prophet Nahum who mentioned prancing horses and "jumping" chariots (Nah. 3:2).

> *...like the noise of a flame of fire that devoureth the stubble, as a strong people set in battle array* (Joel 2:5).

> *And the house of Jacob shall be a fire, and the house of Joseph a flame, and the house of Esau for stubble, and they shall kindle in them, and devour them; and there shall not be any remaining of the house of Esau...* (see Obad. 1:18 and compare with Nah. 1:10; Mal. 4:1).

This Host moves with a "noise" (voice, sound) of a "flame of fire" (Joel 2:3) that devours the "stubble" (dry straw, chaff). The traditions of men are as stubble. Babylon's preaching is very dry.

Joel's army is a "strong" people (Joel 1:6; 2:2). They are "set (in battle) array" (set in a row; arranged, put in order; prepared, furnished). This is an ordered and disciplined people ready for the "battle" (war; the engagement).

Before their face the people shall be much pained: all faces shall gather blackness (Joel 2:6).

She (Nineveh) is *pillaged, plundered, stripped! Hearts melt, knees give way, bodies tremble, every face grows pale* (Nah. 2:10, NIV).

Before their "face" (presence) the "people" (plural; the nations) shall be much "pained" (tortured, distressed). All faces shall gather "blackness" (glow, heat; the flush of anxiety). Joel's army shall restore the fear of the Lord to the Church.

They shall run like mighty men... (Joel 2:7).

This great Host of dedicated warriors shall "run" (Joel 2:4,9) like "mighty men" (Joel 3:9-11). This is the word *gibbowr* (Strong's #1368), and it means, "powerful; by implication, warrior, tyrant; a strong man, brace man." This is also rendered as "champion, chief, valiant man." This was "a warrior (emphasizing strength or ability to fight); one who prevails."

The *gibbowr* is a proven warrior, a hero; the elite military corps. These were "mighty men of valour" (Josh. 10:7; 1 Chron. 5:24; 12:20-23; 1 Sam. 16:18; 2 Sam. 23:8-23). The "mighty men" who suffered with the renegade David in the caves later reigned with King David in the palaces of Zion (Rom. 8:17-18).

They Shall Climb Every Wall

...they shall climb the wall like men of war... (Joel 2:7).

These overcomers are Special Forces. These "men" (notable men of high degree) of war are expert climbers, able to scale any obstacle. To "climb" is "to ascend, go up; be high; mount; grow up or go over; to excel, to be superior to; to be exalted." It aptly applies to those apprehended for the "high (upward) calling." This word *alah'* is akin to *'olah* (the burnt offering), and to *El-elyon*, the "Most High God" of the Most Holy Place. Melchizedek, the forerunner of the king-priest ministry, was "the priest of the Most High God" (Gen. 14:18-20).

Joel's army are climbers by virtue of their inward nature. There are creeping vines and there are climbing vines. Like Joseph (Gen. 49:22), we innately reach for the highest realm by virtue of Him who lives within. No box can contain us. No wall can withstand us.

> *And Saul cast the javelin; for he said, I will smite David even to the wall with it...* (1 Sam. 18:11; 19:9-10; 20:25,33).

The "wall" (to join; a wall of protection) of Joel 2:7 represents religious systems and paradigms. On a more practical note, these walls can speak of unholy alliances, confederacies and conspiracies. Angry leaders vexed with demons are always trying to pin godly men to their systems. By Oriental custom, when Saul threw the javelin at David, he released the lad from his jurisdiction. Later, he even hurled the spear at his son Jonathan. Thus, when David left the old order, he was not in rebellion. But when Jonathan stayed at the house and table of his father, he was!

> *...these cities were fenced with high walls, gates, and bars...* (see Deut. 3:5 and compare with Prov. 18:11; Matt. 23:27; Acts 23:3; 2 Cor. 10:3-6).

Every denomination is a walled city. Most are prisons of legalism that have captured our youth by the very size of their institutions. Sadly, years may pass before one is aware that he or she has been trapped by the old order.

God is at war with every man-made wall. Jesus rent the veil and destroyed the "middle wall of partition" at the Cross (Matt. 27:51; Eph. 2:14). He now sends His prophets to progressively "mop up" the operation. Prophet Ezekiel dug through the wall (Ezek. 8:7-9). Prophet Daniel wrote words of judgment on the wall (Dan. 5:5). Joel's prophetic army climbed all over the wall (Joel 2:7). Prophet David leaped over the wall (2 Sam. 22:30). Finally, prophet Joshua shouted and the wall fell (Josh. 6:5). Every religious wall is coming down in Jesus' name!

> *...and they shall march every one on his ways, and they shall not break their ranks* (Joel 2:7).

The Army of God is disciplined, well-trained, and devoted to one another. They each "march" (walk) "on his ways." This word means, "road; manner, habit, way; course of life; mode of action." Compare the Greek word *hodos*, translated as "way" in John 14:6 and Acts 19:9; 22:4. Each of us is to walk on "His" way!

When thou dost lend thy brother any thing, thou shalt not go into his house to fetch his pledge (Deut. 24:10 and compare with Deut. 15:6-8).

When we follow His footsteps (1 Pet. 2:21; 2 Cor. 12:18), we will not "break" our ranks. This word means, "to pawn; causatively, to lend (on security); figuratively, to entangle; to interchange." We refuse to use or abuse one another, especially in the area of finances. Joel's army is made of honest folks, men and women of great integrity and reliability.

The word for "ranks" here in Joel 2:7 means, "a well-trodden road; also a caravan; to journey, to go, to keep company with; way, path, course, conduct, manner (recurring life event)." This is also rendered "race, rank, traveler, troop."

The name of "Gad" means, "a troop cometh." There is a company of men and women sprinkled throughout the nations who are all walking the same upward "path" to Zion! We are following the Lamb into the Holy of Holies (Rev. 14:4; Heb. 6:19-20). Jesus is the "strong man" and we are running His "race" (Ps. 19:5).

This well-worn path, laid out by Abraham and Paul and others, is the ascended life. This way of life is above to the wise; we have departed from the religious hell beneath (Prov. 15:24). We are now coming forth, every man in his own order (rank or assignment; class; the arrangement of a troop) (1 Cor. 15:23).

Neither shall one thrust another; they shall walk every one in his path... (Joel 2:8).

They do not jostle each other; each marches straight ahead... (Joel 2:8, NIV).

Do nothing out of selfish ambition or vain conceit, but in humility consider others better than yourselves.

Each of you should look not only to your own interests, but also to the interests of others. (Phil. 2:3-4, NIV).

Mature believers do not "thrust" (press, crowd, entangle, or oppress) one another. By love we prefer and serve each other (Gal. 5:13). In the previous verse, we walk in "His" ways. Here we walk (go) in "His" path. This "path" is a "thoroughfare, turnpike; viaduct, staircase; raised way, a public road," and is translated 20 times as "highway" or "highways" (Prov. 16:17; Isa. 11:16; 35:8; 62:10). Joel's army is also the Firstfruits Company (Rev. 14:1-5) that goes before the people of God to prepare the highway, much as John heralded the coming of Jesus (Isa. 40:3).

> *...and when they fall upon the sword, they shall not be wounded* (Joel 2:8).

Nothing can stop or hinder this army. They are never offended by the "sword"[7] (Joel 2:10) of His Word (Eph. 6:17; Heb. 4:12). They are not easily offended or "wounded" (to break off, plunder; to finish, or stop; to cut off, to sever; to violently make gain of).

We walk in a spiritual immunity, having been given "power" (authority) over all the "power" (ability) of the enemy (Luke 10:19). We have nothing to fear. The enemy is afraid of us (Josh. 2:9-11).

> *They shall run to and fro in the city; they shall run upon the wall, they shall climb up upon the houses; they shall enter in at the windows like a thief* (Joel 2:9).

Note the progressive motion of Joel's host: they march upon the city, then scale the wall, then climb upon the houses, and then enter the windows! God is relentless in His righteous judgments.[8]

Heaven's hordes run to and fro, greedily coursing like a beast of prey. They are coming to the "city," the Church (Matt. 5:14), and are about to run upon every man-made wall and to climb up (Joel 2:7) upon (into) every denominational house! The words of this prophetic army are going to enter the "windows," the hearts and ears, of every tribe and people. This word means, "perforated; a piercing of the wall." All this will be done like a thief, with the element of surprise. "Sudden destruction" is about to hit the harlot church, and, in spite of their cherished eschatology, "they shall not escape" (1 Thess. 5:3-4).

Lights Out for the Old Order

> *The earth shall quake before them; the heavens shall tremble...* (Joel 2:10).

> *Whose voice then shook the earth: but now he hath promised, saying, Yet once more I shake not the earth only, but also heaven.*

> *And this word, Yet once more, signifieth the removing of those things that are shaken, as of things that are made, that those things which cannot be shaken may remain* (See Heb. 12:26-27 and compare with Hag. 2:6-7).

Every purpose of the Lord shall be performed against Babylon (Isa. 51:29). The "earth," the natural realm, shall "quake" before this Host. This is the same word translated as "tremble" in Joel 2:1. Apostles have been known to cause earthquakes (Acts 16:25-26).[9]

For we wrestle not against flesh and blood, but against principalities, against powers, against the rulers of the darkness of this world, against spiritual wickedness in high places (Eph. 6:12).

The "heavens," the spiritual realm, as well shall "tremble." This is a different word that means, "to undulate (as the earth, the sky, or a field of grain) through fear; to quake or shake; to cause to leap or spring as a horse or locust."[10]

...the sun and the moon shall be dark, and the stars shall withdraw their shining: (Joel 2:10).

This verse shows that the raising up of Joel's army means "lights out" for the old order (Micah 3:6)!

The sun and the moon shall be "dark" (Joel 3:15) or "ashy, dark-colored; by implication, to mourn (in sackcloth or sordid garments)." Here is described the death of the previous order. The stars shall "withdraw" (take away or remove) their "shining" (brilliancy, brightness; to glitter; to illuminate).

But unto you that fear my name shall the sun of righteousness arise with healing in his wings... (Mal. 4:2).

The righteous shine as the "sun," for the Son is the "sun" (Joel 3:15). This word is *shemesh* (Strong's #8121), and it means, "to be brilliant; the sun; by implication, the east; figuratively, a ray, (archaic) a notched battlement; sunrise, sun-rising, east; pinnacles, battlements, shields (as glittering or shining)."[11]

And God made two great lights; the greater light (the sun) *to rule the day, and the lesser light* (the moon) *to rule the night: he made the stars also* (Gen. 1:16).

The word for "moon" (Joel 2:31; 3:15) means, "a month (lunar cycle), the moon; a calendar month." The moon is but a reflection of the sun. The sun can also be likened to grace, and the moon to the law. The moon can also symbolize powers of darkness (Eph. 6:12). A "lunatic" literally means one who is under the moon's influence. Babylon's doctrines are crazy, as are some who teach them.[12]

And they that be wise shall shine as the brightness of the firmament; and they that turn many to righteousness as the stars for ever and ever (see Dan. 12:3 and compare with Job 38:7).

The word for "stars" (Joel 3:15) is *kowkab* (Strong's #3556), and it means, "(in the sense of blazing); a star (as round or as shining); figuratively, a prince." The characteristics of the "stars" are revealed throughout the Old Testament.[13]

Again, Joel 2:10 is prophetic imagery that declares "lights out" for the old order, with all its religious tradition!

Immediately after the tribulation of those days shall the sun be darkened, and the moon shall not give her light, and the stars shall fall from heaven, and the powers of the heavens shall be shaken (Matt. 24:29).

Matthew 24:21-24,29 describes God's people enduring a time of tribulation and pressure. The "tribulation" prophesied by Jesus in Matthew 24:29 marked the end of Judaism (A.D. 67-70). The 12 tribes of natural Israel are described as the "sun" and the "moon" (Gen. 37:9-10). The cosmic imagery describing the judgment and vindication of God meant "lights out" for the old order (Matt. 21:42-43; 1 Pet. 2:9-10). There is no revelation or understanding of the things of the Spirit in the old order (1 Cor. 2:9-16; Eph. 1:18).

Note the similar parallel language (imagery) of the Old Testament describing the end of Babylon (Isa. 13:9-10); the end of Edom (Isa. 34:4-5); and the end of Israel (Amos 5:18-22; 8:9).

Who Can Abide the Day of the Lord?

And the Lord shall utter His voice before His army: for His camp is very great... (Joel 2:11).

What will ye see in the Shulamite? As it were the company of two armies (Mahanaim, or two "dancing" armies – one here and one there!). (See Song 6:13 and compare with Song 6:4,10; Ezek. 1:24; Rev. 19:19).

This classic passage (Joel 2:2-11) has vividly described Joel's army, the corporate Overcomer destined for Zion. This new creation Man is totally devoted to the Lord. We are "His" army, "His" camp. We only have ears for "His" voice (Josh. 24:24; John 10:3-4; Heb. 4:7).

The Lord shall "utter" (give) His "voice" ("noise" in Joel 2:5) "before" (in the face of) His army. The New International Version says that the Lord "thunders at the head of His army."

The word for "army" in Joel 2:11 (Joel 2:20,25) is *cheyl* (Strong's #2426), and it means, "an army or host; also an entrenchment; a rampart, a fortress, a wall; a force, whether of men, means or other resources; wealth, virtue, valor, strength; might, ability, efficiency." This word is translated as "strength" in Joel 2:22.

Jehovah's "camp" (of an armed host) is very great (Joel 2:2,13; 3:13). Joel's army is the "camp of the saints" (Rev. 20:9).

> *...for He is strong that executeth his word: for the day of the Lord is great and very terrible; and who can abide it?* (Joel 2:11).

> *But the people that do know their God shall be strong, and do exploits* (see Dan. 11:32 and compare with Exod. 12:12; Ps. 149:7-9; Jer. 23:5).

He is "strong" (Joel 2:2,5) that "executeth" (does) His Word. The Kingdom of God is a kingdom of words. Joel's host is a prophetic army. The creative Word of the Lord is in our hearts and mouths to adjudicate the purposes of God. We declare and decree the Word of the Lord (Job 22:28 and 1 Sam. 3:19).

> *He is thy praise, and He is thy God, that hath done for thee these great and terrible things...* (see Deut. 10:21 and compare with Ps. 47:2; 66:3).

The "Day of the Lord" (Joel 1:15; 2:1, 31; 3:14) is "great" (large in magnitude and extent) and very "terrible." This word (Joel 2:31) means, "to fear; morally, to revere; stand in awe of; causatively, to astonish, terrify, frighten." This Day is "great" for the righteous, but "terrible" for the wicked!

> *...behold, heaven and the heaven of heavens cannot contain Thee; how much less this house which I* (King Solomon) *have built!* (see 2 Chron. 6:18 and compare with Isa. 40:12).

Who can "abide" the Day of the Lord? Only He can! Only the corporate Overcomer, as we allow God to be big in us, as His anointing is "without measure" (John 3:34). Who shall stand when He appears (Nah. 1:6; Mal. 3:2)? He will! And the only reason that we are still standing is that He is standing in us.

The word for "abide" in Joel 2:11 means, "to keep in, contain, hold in, restrain; hence, to measure, calculate; figuratively, to maintain, sustain, support, endure." This is also rendered as "comprehend."

Zion, the high calling, is above and beyond the grasp and comprehension of mere men. Those who make up Joel's great army will do so by His inward empowerment and His anointing (Zech. 4:6). God is bigger than anything that man can imagine (Eph. 3:20). He has broken out of every man-made theological and eschatological box (old paradigms). Again, who will abide the Day of the Lord? He will—in His people!

Lord, who shall abide in thy tabernacle? who shall dwell in thy holy hill (of Zion)? (Ps. 15:1).

The only answer to the national chaos and desolation of Judah is for the people to make a fresh *consecration* to the Lord. The only hope for creation is the Lord through His glorious Church, and the only cure for the sins of the Church is for all of us to fall at His feet!

Now that we have Joel's army for a model and pattern of such radical discipleship and complete surrender, it is time to call the people to prayer—Zion's *appeal*. Once God has restored the Tabernacle of David, a people for His Name, he can then go after the residue of men, the remnant of Edom (Amos 9:11-12; Acts 15:13-17).

ENDNOTES

1. Concerning the Cherubim, study these verses (see Exod. 25:20; 37:9; Deut. 32:11; 1 Kings 6:27; 2 Chron. 3:13; Isa. 40:31; and Ezek. 1:6-11).

2. Joel's army is "great" (see Joel 2:11,13; 3:13; compare 2 Tim. 2:20; Titus 2:13; Heb. 4:14; 7:4; 12:1; 13:20).

3. This Hebrew word for "Eden" is mentioned 16 times in the Old Testament (Gen. 2:8,10,15; 3:23-24; 4:16; 2 Chron. 29:12; 31:15; Isa. 51:3; Ezek. 28:13; 31:9,16,18 [twice]; 36:5; Joel 2:3; compare 2 Kings 19:12; Isa. 37:12; Ezek. 27:23; and Amos 1:5).

4. The late Bill Britton wrote a classic tract, *The Harness of the Lord*. It is available by writing to his daughter Becky Volz at P.O. Box 707, Springfield, MO 65801; Email: harness707@aol.com

5. The "horse" is mentioned throughout the Scriptures (see Deut. 17:15-16; 1 Kings 4:26; 2 Kings 2:11; Esther 6:8-11; Ps. 20:7; 32:9; 33:17; 147:10;

Prov. 21:31; 26:3; Jer. 4:13; 5:8; 8:6,16; 12:5; 46:4; Nah. 3:2; Hab. 1:6; Zech. 1:8-11; 6:1-8; 10:3; 14:20; James 3:3; and Rev. 6:1-8; 9:7; 19:11-21).

6. The "horsemen" are mentioned throughout the Old Testament (as in Gen. 50:9; Exod. 14:26-28; 1 Sam. 8:11; 1 Kings 4:26; 10:26; 2 Kings 2:12; 2 Chron. 8:9; Ezra 8:22; Neh. 2:9; Isa. 28:28; Jer. 46:4; Ezek. 23:6; Hos. 1:7; Joel 2:4; Hab. 1:8; compare Acts 23:23,32; Rev. 9:16).

7. These verses reveal the "sword" of His Word (Gen. 3:24; Rev. 1:16; 2:12,16; 19:15,21.

8. The Lord is the Plowman who has put His hand to us, and will not look back (Luke 9:62 with Ps. 138:8; Jer. 29:11; Zech. 4:9; Phil. 1:6)!

9. For more about "earthquakes," note these verses (see 1 Kings 19:11-12; Isa. 29:6; Amos 1:1; Zech. 14:5; Matt. 24:7; 27:54; 28:2; Mark 13:8; Luke 21:11; and Rev. 6:12; 8:5; 11:13,19; 16:18).

10. Compare Joel 3:16, where this word is translated as "shake" (see also Judg. 5:4; Ps. 68:8; 77:18; Jer. 8:16; 10:10; 50:46).

11. Note these verses about the "sun" (see Ps. 19:4; 74:16; 84:11; 136:8; Song 6:10; Matt. 13:43; 24:29; Mark 13:24; Acts 2:20; 27:20; 1 Cor. 15:41; James 1:11; and Rev. 1:16; Rev. 6:12; 8:12; 10:1).

12. Note these Scriptures about the "moon' (see Gen. 37:9; Deut. 33:14; Josh. 10:12-13; Job 25:5; Ps. 8:3; 81:3; 104:19; 136:9; Song 6:10; Isa. 24:23; 60:19-20; Jer. 31:35; and Rev. 21:1; 21:23).

13. Note these characteristics of the "stars." They were made by the Creator God (Gen. 1:16), and chosen to be the Seed of Abraham (Gen. 15:5; 22:17; 26:4). Messiah is the Star out of Jacob (Num. 24:17). The stars fight against the enemies of the Lord (Judg. 5:20); appear and go forth to their places (Neh. 4:21); are sealed by the Lord (Job 9:7); are high and exalted (Job 22:12; Obad. 1:4); are a picture of the sons of God (Job 38:7); have been ordained by the Lord (Ps. 8:3); rule in the night seasons (Ps. 136:9; Jer. 31:35); are called by name (Ps. 147:4); praise the Lord (Ps. 148:3); and are a picture of those who are wise (Dan. 12:3).

CHAPTER ELEVEN

CONSECRATION — ITS APPEAL (JOEL 2:12-17)

We have heard the *alarm,* and beheld His *army,* His firstfruits to return to Zion. They will lead the way for the rest of the people.

Now this section (Joel 2:12-17) is the most pivotal and critical of Joel's entire prophecy. It is Jehovah's *appeal* through the prophet for the people of Zion to return to His paths.

After having shown to Jerusalem and Judah the desolation of their entire society, the Lord now strongly urges His people to rend their hearts and not their garments, to "turn" (return) to Him with all their being! A merciful and gracious God stands ready to forgive.

The courageous trumpeter tearfully pleads for a fresh *consecration* before the Lord. He calls his people to a time of national mourning and repentance, to the Day of Atonement. The young virgin is to mourn, for she has no husband. The husbandmen are to mourn, for they have no harvest, no firstfruits. The priests are to mourn, for they have nothing to offer in sacrifice.

The devastating plague of locusts that ravaged Judah has been likened to the hellish plague of religious tradition that has wasted the Church and the high calling to Zion. Now we must fall on the Stone and be broken (Matt. 21:44). We must afflict our souls. We must come to the Feast, and not empty-handed (Deut. 16:16).

The Feast Day of Atonement

Joel's trumpet woke us up. The gospel of the Kingdom has been contaminated, doctrinally (duality and mixture) and politically (the "bishop" epidemic). The Church must be cleansed and restored. We have come to the tenth day of the seventh month. The primary scriptures that explain the Feast Day of Atonement are Leviticus 16:1-34; 23:27-32; Numbers 29:7-11; and Hebrews 9:1-10:39.

> *Also on the tenth day of this seventh month there shall be a day of atonement: it shall be an holy convocation unto you; and ye shall afflict your souls, and offer an offering made by fire unto the Lord* (Lev. 23:27).

We are to "afflict" (humble, bow down) our "souls" (intellect, emotions, and will). This baptism of "fire" is to purify the Body of Christ.

> *When the Lord shall have washed away the filth of the daughters of Zion, and shall have purged the blood of Jerusalem from the midst thereof by the spirit of judgment, and by the spirit of burning* (Isa. 4:4).

This "filth" (excrement, dirt, and pollution) is the "dung" of Philippians 3:8. That Greek word means, "what is thrown to dogs; refuse, rubbish, garbage, dregs; worthless and detestable." We must be "purged" (rinsed) afresh by His blood (see Prov. 30:12; Isa. 28:8).

The Scriptures present the principle of the *Day of Atonement* in a number of ways. Many other Bible pictures parallel this paradigm:

1. The Baptism of Fire (Matt. 3:7-12; 1 Cor. 3:1-15).
2. The Spirit of Judgment and Burning (Isa. 4:1-6).
3. The Day of the Lord (Joel 2:1-2; Mal. 4; 2 Pet. 3:10-12).
4. The Whole Burnt Offering (Lev. 1; Ps. 51:19).
5. The Threshingfloor (Ruth 3; 1 Chron. 13;15;21).
6. The Circumcision of the Heart (Deut. 30:6; Rom. 2:28-29).
7. The North Wind (Song 4:12; John 16:8-11).
8. The Time of Jacob's Trouble (Gen. 32:24-32; Jer. 30:7-8).
9. The Cleansing of the Temple (John 2; Matt. 21).
10. The Mount of Transfiguration (Matt. 17).
11. The Garden of Gethsemane (Luke 22:40-48).

12. The Transformation of the Soul (1 Pet. 1:9).

13. The Renewing of the Mind (Rom. 12:1-2).

In this purging, the fire consumes everything except the Seed, the Christ (1 Cor. 3:13; Gal. 3:16). Those who comprise the Hundredfold Company (Matt. 13:23) are reduced to "nought"—this is the "are not" Company (1 Cor. 1:18-31). *He* is all that is left! In this Day of Atonement, God's fire cooks all the "crud" (everything we've not let Him deal with) to the top, lifting the lid off everything (1 Cor. 3:13-15). The kingdoms of the heart are exposed and dealt with.

His purpose is to remove these idols from our lives, to forgive them, to remit them. The Greek word for "forgiveness" means, "to release up, out, and away from the prison"! Those with a sin-conscious mindset may be overwhelmed by this experience ("What's wrong with me?"). But when a new plant breaks through the earth, the "dirt" flies!

The Hebrew word for "atonement" is *kippur* (Strong's #3725), and it means, "expiation (only in plural)." This is the Day of Propitiation or Expiations. Its root is *kaphar*, and it means, "to cover (specifically with bitumen or pitch); figuratively, to expiate or condone, to placate or cancel; to purge, to make reconciliation; to pacify, to propitiate." The latter is rendered in the King James Version as "appease, make an atonement, cleanse, disannul, forgive, be merciful, pacify, pardon, purge (away), put off, (make) reconcile (-liation)."

This "holy convocation" (Lev. 23:27) was most solemn; it was the Day of national and sanctuary cleansing. This Feast was fulfilled historically in Jesus' finished work at the Cross, and will be fulfilled experientially in His Body, the Church (1 John 4:17). Jesus made a complete, once-for-all atonement, but we have yet to fully appropriate and receive all that His Atonement has provided.

Now when much time was spent, and when sailing was now dangerous, because the fast (Day of Atonement) *was now already past, Paul admonished them...* (Acts 27:9).

This holy day was marked by fasting, which is the afflicting of the flesh and the subjugation of bodily appetites (see Joel 1:14). This was a Day for the afflicting of the "soul" (*nephesh* in Hebrew and *psuche* in Greek). Our intellect, emotions, and will comprise what we think, our opinions; what we feel, our feelings; and what we want, our desires. All these things must be brought and laid at the foot of His Cross.

And when He had made a scourge of small cords, He drove them all out of the temple, and the sheep, and the oxen; and poured out the changers' money, and overthrew the tables;

And said unto them that sold doves, Take these things hence; make not My Father's house an house of merchandise (John 2:15-16 and Matt. 21:12-13).

Jesus cleansed the Temple not once, but twice, at the beginning and at the end of His public ministry. In the scheme of the Feasts, there is a double cleansing. In the First Day, in Passover, there is an outward washing with blood and water; in the Third Day, in Tabernacles, there is an inward purging with fire. God cleansed His Temple, the Church, at the very beginning of this age (the ministry of Jesus), and will again purify His people at the end of this age (through His sons, Joel's army).

Then shalt thou cause the trumpet of the Jubile to sound on the tenth day of the seventh month, in the day of atonement shall ye make the trumpet sound throughout all your land (Lev. 25:9).

Finally, the Year of Jubilee, the year of Liberty (Ezek. 46:17), the Year of Release (Deut. 15:9; 31:10), also took place on the tenth day of the seventh month, the *same day* that the High Priest went beyond the veil on the Day of Atonement. The "glorious liberty" of the sons of God will be a reality (Rom. 8:21).

Turn With All Your Heart

Therefore also now, saith the Lord, turn ye even to me with all your heart... (see Joel 2:12 and compare with Hos. 6:1-2).

Jesus said unto him, Thou shalt love the Lord thy God with all thy heart, and with all thy soul, and with all thy mind. This is the first (foremost) and great commandment (see Matt. 22:37-38 and compare with Mk. 12:30).

The first word of Joel 1:12 is "therefore." Thus Joel 2:12-17 is based upon Joel 1:1-2:11. These six verses illustrate real prayer and intercession, upon which everything now pivots.

Judah is commanded to "turn" (Joel 2:13; 3:1,4,7) to her God with all her heart. This word is *shuwb* (Strong's #7725), and it means, "to turn back; adverbial, again; return, come back; to restore, to refresh, to repair (figurative); to bring back, to make requital, to pay (recompense); to reverse, to revoke." The basic meaning of the verb is movement back to the point of departure (unless there is evidence to the contrary). This is the Hebrew word for "restore."

Restore unto me the joy of Thy salvation...(see Ps. 51:12 and compare with Isa. 1:26; 42:22).

Then and now, God's people are to turn to Him with "all" (whole, totally, everything) their heart (inner man). This phrase "all your heart" or "all thine (thy) heart" is found nine times in the Book of Deuteronomy.[1] Nine is the biblical number of finality and centers in the finished work of His Cross (Luke 23:44-46; John 19:30). To love, serve, and obey on this level is only possible through the crucified life (Gal. 2:20), by His inward empowering and enabling.

...and with fasting, and with weeping, and with mourning: (Joel 2:12).

This kind of prayer is accompanied by "fasting" (Joel 1:14; 2:15). Fasting is intensified prayer.

...His anger endureth but a moment; in His favour is life: weeping may endure for a night, but joy cometh in the morning (Ps. 30:5).

We are to humbly come with "weeping" (Joel 1:5; 2:17), and "moan; to bewail, to cry, to shed tears; lament (in grief or humiliation)."[2] This is the "time to weep" (Eccles. 3:4).

O daughter of my people, gird thee with sackcloth, and wallow thyself in ashes (roll in the dust): *make thee mourning* (for the dead), *as for an only son, most bitter lamentation...* (Jer. 6:26).

The Day of Atonement is further marked by "mourning" (Joel 1:9), by "lamentation and wailing." The root means, "to tear the hair and beat the breasts (as Orientals do in grief)."[3]

And rend your heart, and not your garments, and turn unto the Lord your God... (Joel 2:13).

Because thine heart (King Josiah) *was tender, and thou didst humble thyself before God... and didst rend thy clothes, and weep before me; I have even heard thee...* (2 Chron. 34:27).

As with King Josiah, we are to "rend" (tear or split in pieces) our hearts, not just our garments (a sign of great grief and mourning), as we "turn" (Joel 2:12) to the Lord. Compare these other examples of such contrition: Joshua and Caleb (Num. 14:6); King

Hezekiah (2 Kings 19:1); Mordecai (Esther 4:1); and Barnabas and Paul (Acts 14:14).

> *...for He is gracious and merciful, slow to anger, and of great kindness, and repenteth him of the evil* (Joel 2:13).

> *And the Lord passed by before him* (Moses), *and proclaimed, The Lord, The Lord God, merciful and gracious,* [4] *longsuffering, and abundant in goodness and truth* (Exod. 34:6).

Return to the Lord with confidence, for he is "gracious;" He will "bend or stoop in kindness to an inferior; pity; to favor, bestow; causatively, to implore (move to favor by petition)." Make your petitions known unto Him (1 John 5:15). He is "merciful" (compassionate), "slow" (long) to "anger." This latter word means, "the nose, nostril; to breathe hard; be enraged, displeased; wrath."

> *In a little wrath I hid My face from thee for a moment; but with everlasting kindness will I have mercy on thee, saith the Lord thy Redeemer* (See Isa. 54:8 and compare with Ruth 2:20).

Moreover, our God is of "great" (abundant) "kindness." He will "bow the neck in courtesy to an equal; steadfast love; grace; mercy." This word is frequent in the Psalms (over 130 times, 26 times alone in Psalm 136, where it is translated as "mercy." *The Septuagint* nearly always renders this Hebrew word with *eleos* (mercy). Three basic meanings of the word always interact: "strength," "steadfastness," and "love."

> *If so be they will hearken, and turn every man from his evil way, that I may repent Me of the evil, which I purpose to do unto them because of the evil of their doings* (Jer. 26:3).

If we turn to God, He will "repent" Himself of this "evil" (moral evil, harm, calamity). This latter word is translated as "wickedness" in Joel 3:13. The word "repenteth" (Joel 2:14) means, "to repent, comfort; to sigh, breathe strongly; by implication, to be sorry, (in a favorable sense) to pity, console, to be sorry, to be moved to pity, to have compassion." It indicates a change of heart or disposition, a change of mind, a change of purpose, or (emphatically) the change of one's conduct. [5]

> *Who knoweth if He will return and repent, and leave a blessing behind him; even a meat offering and a drink offering unto the Lord your God?* (Joel 2:14).

If we will return to Him, He will "return" (Joel 2:12) to us, and "repent" (Joel 2:13). Beyond this, as with Ruth (Ruth 2:16), God will "leave" (as a gift from the surplus) a "blessing" (benediction, prosperity) behind Him, even a meat (meal) offering and a drink offering (Joel 1:9,13). This would signify that our priestly fellowship around His Table of Shewbread is to be restored. This also pictures the bread and the wine of the New Testament Eucharist, the Lord's Supper (1 Cor. 11:23-30)!

Sanctify a Fast, Call a Solemn Assembly

Blow the trumpet in Zion, sanctify a fast, call a solemn assembly (Joel 2:15).

The prophet repeats Joel 1:14 and 2:1, bringing a threefold witness of the solution to his nation's desolation. God's three greatest spokesmen—Moses, Paul, and Jesus—all declared that by the mouth of two or three witnesses would everything be established (Deut. 19:15; Matt. 18:16; 2 Cor. 13:1).

Blow the trumpet in Zion (Joel 2:1)! "Sanctify a fast, call a solemn assembly" (Joel 1:14). Again, this references the Feast Day of Atonement. There are to be no exceptions, for the prophet begins to call *everyone* to the Feast.

Gather the people, sanctify the congregation, assemble the elders... (Joel 2:16).

Joel begins his plea. He is anointed to "gather" (Joel 1:14) the "people" (Joel 2:2,5,6). God always wants to gather His own (Matt. 23:37). Then he commands to "sanctify" (Joel 1:14; 3:9) the "congregation" (assembly, company, multitude, convocation). Joel's first task is to "assemble" (Joel 2:6; 3:2,11) the leaders, the "elders" (Joel 1:14). The "elders" are to lead the prayer meeting!

...gather the children, and those that suck the breasts: let the bridegroom go forth of his chamber, and the bride out of her closet (Joel 2:16).

Once the leaders (fathers) are in place, the Lord calls for the sons, the (young) "children." Those who "suck" (suckle, nurse) the "breasts" have undeveloped faith and love (1 Thess. 5:8), immature righteousness and judgment (Exod. 28:15; Eph. 6:14). Even these babies who demand a certain bottle (pacifier) are called.

Joel then calls for the "bridegroom"[6] to come out of his "chamber" (Ps. 19:5). This was "an apartment; a room, a parlor, an innermost (or inward) part, within." The verb means, "to enclose (as a private room)." The noun is also translated as, "bedchamber, inner chamber."[7] No level of human intimacy can compare with communion with God in the "secret place" (Ps. 18:11; 81:7; 91:1).

Likewise, the "bride"[8] is to come forth from her "closet." This was "a canopy: a chamber, a room; a divine protection (figurative). Its root means, "to cover; by implication, to veil, encase, protect; to overlay, wainscoted, covered with boards or paneling."

Though ye (Israel, Jehovah's Bride) *have lien among the pots* (of Egypt), *yet shall ye be as the wings of a dove covered with silver, and her feathers with yellow gold* (Ps. 68:13).

Again, we are closest to God in the private place of prayer.

Let the priests, the ministers of the Lord, weep between the porch and the altar, and let them say, Spare thy people, O Lord, and give not thine heritage to reproach, that the heathen should rule over them: wherefore should they say among the people, Where is their God? (Joel 2:17).

The "priests" (Joel 1:9,13) and the "ministers," the elders and the deacons, are to lead by example. They are admonished to "weep" (Joel 1:5; 2:12) between the "porch" (the vestibule of the Temple) and the (brazen) "altar" (of sacrifice). This was the location of the Brazen Laver in the Mosaic Tabernacle and the Molten Sea in Solomon's Temple. This was the place of sanctification, washing, and cleansing. The priests are urged to re-fill the empty Laver with their tears, and then bathe in it!

And I commanded the Levites that they should cleanse themselves, and that they should come and keep the gates, to sanctify the sabbath day. Remember me, O my God, concerning this also, and spare me according to the greatness of Thy mercy (see Neh.13: 22 and compare with Ps. 72:13; Jonah 4:10-11).

The prayer is to a simple one: "Spare" us, O God! This word means, "to cover, to compassionate; pity, regard." God's "heritage" (Joel 3:2; Ps. 16:6; 1 Pet. 5:3) is His people, His possession, His "inheritance; something inherited; an heirloom; an estate, patrimony or portion; a possession or property."

But Judah had known nothing but desolation and "reproach" (Joel 2:19), only "disgrace, scorn, and shame." The root means, "to pull off, to expose (by stripping); figuratively, to carp at, defame; to taunt, to blaspheme, to defy, to jeopardize, to rail, to upbraid."[9]

Because of this pitiful condition, then and now, the "heathen" (Joel 1:6) are mocking the people of God. But they are not to "rule" (to exercise dominion) over us, or be able to taunt us with their words, "Where is their God?"[10]

Again, Joel 2:12-17 is a most essential passage, a *rhema* word to our generation. The only answer to the desolation of Chapter One of his prophecy is real prayer from the heart!

If My people, who belong to Me, humble themselves and pray and seek My presence, turning from their evil ways, I will listen up in heaven and forgive their sins and heal My land (2 Chron. 7:14, Moffatt).

Consecration's *appeal* turns the whole situation from trouble to triumph! This *affects* everyone and everything!

ENDNOTES

1. To love God with "all" our heart is found nine times in the Book of Deuteronomy (see Deut. 4:29; 6:5; 10:12; 11:13; 13:3; 26:16; 30:2,6,10).

2. These Scriptures deal with our "weeping" (see Gen. 45:2; Ezra 3:13; Esther 4:3; Ps. 102:9; Isa. 22:4,12; Jer. 3:21; 9:10; 31:9,15,16; compare Matt. 26:75; Luke 7:38; 19:41; 22:62; John 11:35; 1 Cor. 7:30; Phil. 3:18; and Rev. 5:4).

3. Compare these verses for "mourning" (see Esther 4:3; Isa. 22:12; Amos 5:16-17; Mic. 1:8; and Zech. 12:11).

4. Note these cross-references that tell about our "gracious" God (see 2 Chron. 30:9; Neh. 9:17,31; Ps. 86:15; 103:8; 111:4; 112:4; 116:5; 145:8; and Jon. 4:2).

5. Consider these other verses that deal with His repentance (see Exod. 32:12-14; Deut. 32:36; 2 Sam. 24:16; 1 Chron. 21:15; Jer. 18:8; 26:3; and Jon. 3:9-10; 4:2).

6. Note these Scriptures about the "bridegroom" (see Isa. 61:10; 62:5; Jer. 33:11; Matt. 9:15; 25:1-10; John 2:9; 3:29; and Rev. 18:23).

7. Note these verses about the "chamber" (see Gen. 43:30; 1 Kings 1:15; 1 Chron. 28:11; Prov. 24:4; Song 1:4; 3:4; and Isa. 26:20).

8. Note the verses for the "bridegroom" and add these for the "bride" (see Gen. 49:18; Jer. 2:32; 7:34; 16:9; 25:10; and Rev. 21:2.9.17).

9. Note these verses where "reproach" is mentioned (see Gen. 30:23; Neh. 2:17; Ps. 69:19-20; Isa. 54:4; and Ezek. 36:30).

10. "Where is their God?" (compare 2 Kings 2:14; Job 35:10; Ps. 42:3,10; 79:10; 115:2; Mic. 7:10; and Mal. 2:17).

CHAPTER TWELVE

CONSECRATION — ITS AFTEREFFECT (JOEL 2:18-27)

The previous chapter revealed the essential necessity of prayer and intercession in the Day of Atonement, the *appeal* of our consecration. The verses now set before us show how this now *affects* everyone and everything.

When the Lord turned again the captivity of Zion, we were like them that dream.

Then was our mouth filled with laughter, and our tongue with singing: then said they among the heathen, The Lord hath done great things for them (Ps. 126:1-2).

Everything now turns. After the real prayer of Joel 2:12-17, there is deliverance and blessing for the land (Joel 2:19-20); for the beasts (Joel 2:22); for the children of Zion (Joel 2:23); for the harvest supply of wheat, wine, and oil (Joel 2:24-26); and, most importantly, for worship (Joel 2:27)!

The Land is Blessed Again

Then will the Lord be jealous for His land, and pity His people (Joel 2:18).

What a huge word—*"then"!*

"Then..." When? After the repentance and cleansing of the Day of Atonement, after the time of fasting and prayer, we receive the unlimited blessing of the Feast of Tabernacles! God spares His sons, His "jewels" (Mal. 3:17).

Once more the Lord is "jealous" for His "land." As noted, the "land" is mentioned 12 times throughout the prophecy (Joel 1:2,6,14; 2:1,3,10,18,20,30; 3:2,16,19). This is God's number for divine order and government. Up till now, everything has been out of order (the number 11).

God is "jealous" for His land, the earth. He is "zealous; jealous or envious; provoked or excited to jealous anger" (Ezek. 39:25; Zech. 1:14; 8:2).

It is of the Lord's mercies that we are not consumed, because his compassions fail not.

They are new every morning: great is thy faithfulness (Lam. 3:22-23).

His mercies are new every morning. Our Father will ever "pity" or "have compassion on, or spare" His family for the sake of His great Name (Ezek. 36:21). It's all about Him, not about us.

Yea, the Lord will answer and say unto his people, Behold, I will send you corn, and wine, and oil, and ye shall be satisfied therewith: and I will no more make you a reproach among the heathen: (Joel 2:19).

For the people shall dwell in Zion at Jerusalem: thou shalt weep no more: He will be very gracious unto thee at the voice of thy cry; when He shall hear it, He will answer thee (see Isa. 30:19 and compare with Jer. 33:3).

When we call upon the Lord, He will "answer" us. This word means, "to eye or to heed, pay attention; by implication, to respond; by extension, to begin to speak; specifically to sing, shout, testify, announce; respond, reply."[1] Indeed, His eye is on the "sparrows" (little birds); how much more His chosen (Matt. 10:29-31).

Whenever His people repent and commit themselves afresh to His service, God sends plenty of the "corn" of his Word, the "wine" of His joy, and the "oil" of His Spirit" (Joel 1:10). We are "satisfied" (filled, fulfilled) with His goodness. Nothing in this world can compare with the things of God. Natural blessings will never slake our thirst or fulfill the cry of our hungry hearts (Matt. 5:6).

And the Lord said unto Joshua, This day (because of their covenantal obedience of circumcision) *have I rolled away the reproach of Egypt from off you...* (Josh. 5:9).

Once we have received these blessings of His Word and Spirit, the "reproach" (Joel 2:17) of the "heathen" (Joel 1:6) is removed. The world will no longer mock the children of God.

But I will remove far off from you the northern army... (Joel 2:20).

As far as the east is from the west, so far hath He removed our transgressions (of following after tradition) *from us* (see Ps. 103:12 and compare with Jer. 50:20).[2]

Thanks be to God! He will "remove far off" (put far away; see Joel 3:6) from us the reproach of all these religious traditions that have, like the horde of locusts, stripped and devoured the land. Every hindrance to the high calling will be removed! The prophet Nahum declared that the rising of the sun (Mal. 4:2) in this new Day will cause the locusts to "flee away" (Nah. 3:17).

This "northern army" of locusts had been brought in on the wings of the north wind, which was cold, barren, and biting (Job 37:9). Religious tradition leaves the human heart cold and hard.

On a positive note, the north wind reveals the operation of the Holy Spirit in the conviction of sin (Song 4:16; John 16:8-11). The north wind kills everything except the evergreens, everything except Christ, who is our life. As noted in Joel 2:2-12, this army of locusts pictures the prophetic army of God, who come out of the north, out of Zion (Ps. 48:1-2; 75:6-7; Isa. 14:13; 41:25).

...and will drive him into a land barren and desolate, with his face toward the east sea, and his hinder part toward the utmost sea, and his stink shall come up, and his ill savour shall come up, because he hath done great things (Joel 2:20).

God is about to "drive" (push off, thrust, banish) these locusts of man's tradition into a land that is "barren" (parched, dry, solitary) and "desolate" (Joel 2:3). How fitting! This wilderness has its "face toward the east sea" (the Dead Sea), and its "hinder part toward the utmost (western) sea" (the Mediterranean Sea). These traditions face the place of death and stagnation. Similarly, this is the same direction to which Adam was driven out of the Garden after the Fall (Gen. 3:24).

Religion has turned its back on the Most Holy Place and the resurrection life of God. Like Orpah (whose name means, "turning the back"), many have refused to leave the land of Moab, the place where they do not have to change (Jer. 48:11-12).

Religion, like dead locusts, causes a bad "stink" (stench, foul odor). This word (Isa. 34:3; Amos 4:10) is derived from the word for "cistern" (pit). Traditions are "broken cisterns" that can hold no water of His Word (Jer. 2:13).

In Chapter Three of this writing, we learned that Adam is asleep in the night, walking and talking in his sleep! Adam is dead, and, like Lazarus, was dead for four days. This represents 4,000 years, from Adam till Christ (Gen. 2:21; John 11:39; 2 Pet. 3:8). These man-made traditions, these dead locusts, stink!

This "ill savour" (to putrefy, decompose, rot), like the smell of dead flesh (Gen. 7:21-23) shall come up (ascend), because "he" (the corporate man of sin) hath done "great" (proud) things. The New King James says, "monstrous things." The New English Bible adds, "proud deeds." This is the lot of all those who arrogantly oppose God and do harm to His people.

Fear not, O land; be glad and rejoice: for the Lord will do great things (Joel 2:21).

We need not "fear" or dread (Isa. 43:1; 2 Tim. 1:7). When these traditions (the locusts) have been removed, the land (earth) will be "glad" and "rejoice" (brighten up, to make gleesome). The word for "glad" (Joel 2:23) means, "to spin round (under the influence of any violent emotion); rejoice, exult."[3]

Tabernacles is a feast of great joy, gladness, and rejoicing. The Lord has done "great things for us" (Ps. 126:1-3)[4] (in contrast to the work of the enemy mentioned in the previous verse).

Be not afraid, ye beasts of the field: for the pastures of the wilderness do spring, for the tree beareth her fruit, the fig tree and the vine do yield their strength (Joel 2:22).

God blesses the "beasts" (Joel 1:18,20) of the "field" (Joel 1:10), the cattle and livestock. Our prayer has turned His blessings. There is new life everywhere. The "pastures of the wilderness" (Joel 1:19-20) "spring" (sprout, shoot, grow green). Every tree bears "fruit," the "fruit" of the Spirit (Gal. 5:22-24). The "fig tree and the vine" (Joel 1:7,12) yield (give) their "strength." This word is translated as "army" in Joel 2:11,25. Everything is green again, full of His life.

The Former Rain and the Latter Rain

All these blessings happened in Joel's day because the seasonal rains returned. Rain upon us, O God! The promise declared in this next verse is only made to a covenantal, governmental people—"the children (sons) of Zion."

> *Be glad then, ye children of Zion, and rejoice in the Lord your God: for he hath given you the former rain moderately...* (Joel 2:23).

We are to be "glad" and "rejoice" (Joel 2:21). He has "given" (bestowed, granted by His grace) the "former rain." This word is *mowreh* (Strong's #4175), and it means, "an archer; also teacher or teaching." This is the early rain or the "first rain" (Deut. 11:14). Its root *yarah* (Strong's #3384) means, "to flow as water (to rain); transitively, to lay or throw (especially an arrow, to shoot); figuratively, to point out (as if by aiming or directing the finger), to teach."

Compare the active participle *yowreh* (Strong's #3138), which means, "sprinkling; hence, a sprinkling (or autumnal showers); the early rain, the autumn shower." Note these key verses that mention the "former rain."

> *Then shall we know, if we follow on to know the Lord: His going forth is prepared as the morning; and He shall come unto us as the rain, as the latter and the former rain unto the earth* (see Hos. 6:3 and compare with Ps. 84:7; Rom. 1:17; 2 Cor. 3:18; Jer. 5:24).

> *Be patient therefore, brethren, unto the coming of the Lord. Behold, the husbandman waiteth for the precious fruit of the earth, and hath long patience for it, until He receive the early and the latter rain* (James 5:7).

This "former rain," the early rain of autumn, is the rain that prepares the arid soil for the seed. It begins gradually in late October until early December, and comes generally from the west or southwest (Luke 12:54). At no period in the winter, from the end of October to the end of March, does rain entirely cease.

The former autumn rain comes "moderately." This word is *tsedaqah* (Strong's #6666), and it means, "rightness, righteousness, rectitude, justice, virtue, prosperity." Thus, the "former rain moderately"

(Joel 2:23) literally means, "the teacher of righteousness" (preparing the soil of our heart to walk all the way to Zion)!

The "former rain" corresponds to the "firstfruits" (Rom. 8:23) and the "earnest" (Eph. 1:13-14) of the fullness of the "latter rain" (see below). This "teacher of righteousness" points ahead to two major Third Day truths.

The righteous shall flourish as a branch (Prov. 11:28).

First, the righteous (Corporate) Man whose name is the Branch (Isa. 11:1-2; Jer. 23:5-6; 33:15-16; Zech. 6:12-13; John 15:1-4).

To whom (Melchisedec) *also Abraham gave a tenth part of all; first being by interpretation King of righteousness, and after that also King of Salem, which is, King of peace;* (Heb. 7:2).

Second, the righteous king-priest ministry after the order (manner, similitude) of Melchisedec (Gen. 14:18-20; Ps. 110:4; Heb. 5:1-8:6; 1 Pet. 2:9).

...and he will cause to come down for you the rain, the former rain, and the latter rain in the first month (Joel 2:23).

God will cause to "come down" (bring down, send down) the former rain, and the "latter rain." This word is *malqowsh* (Strong's #4456), and it means, "the spring rain; figuratively, eloquence; the March and April rains which mature the crops of Palestine." Its root *laqash* (Strong's #3953) means, "to gather the after crop or latter growth; to glean, to take the aftermath, to take everything; to despoil, to gather everything from, to strip."

This "latter rain," the later spring showers, especially in March, matures the crop for the harvest. Compare the verses given above on the "former rain," and then note these additional key verses that mention the "latter rain."

That I will give you the rain of your land in his due season, the first rain and the latter rain, that thou mayest gather in thy corn, and thy wine, and thine oil (Deut. 11:14).

In the light of the king's countenance is life; and his favour is as a cloud of the latter rain (see Prov. 16:15 and compare with Job 29:23; Jer. 3:3).

Ask ye of the Lord rain in the time of the latter rain; so the Lord shall make bright clouds, and give them showers of rain, to every one grass in the field (Zech. 10:1).

To summarize, the consecrated prayer of Joel 2 was the answer to the desolation of Joel 1. The blowing of the trumpets brought us to the Day of Atonement. Our full surrender to the Lord in that day brings the blessings of the Feast of Tabernacles and the global outpouring of the early and the latter rains.

The glory of this latter house shall be greater than of the former, saith the Lord of hosts... (Hag. 2:9).

The "former rain" was the planting rain, and was historically poured out in the Book of Acts (2:1-4) during the "former," or early part of this age. This represents the "former" Feasts of Passover and Pentecost.

The "latter rain" was the harvest rain, and is presently being poured out (Eph. 4:11-13) during the "latter" part of this age. This represents the "latter" Feast of Tabernacles.

Moreover, the Lord promised to pour out *both* the former rain and the latter rain in the "first" (*month* is in italics; it is not in the original text). This word means, "first in place, time, or rank; primary, foremost." Both rains will be sent down into and then flow out from the "first." This alludes to the people of the high calling, for this is the "Firstfruits Company" that John saw standing with the Lamb on Mount Zion (Rev. 14:1-5).

The Jewish Civil Year began in the end of the religious calendar. The end of one thing is the beginning of another. Jesus is our Head, the First of the "first." He is the "beginning of the creation of God" (Rev. 3:14). His "brethren," His Body (Rom. 8:29; Heb. 2:6-13) are the rest of the "first."

And the floors shall be full of wheat... (Joel 2:24).

This verse describes the abundant harvest that comes from this global outpouring. The wheat of His Word shall fill the "floors," the threshingfloor; any open area; barn floor, grain floor" (Deut. 15:14). At the threshingfloor, Ruth received the full measure of her inheritance (Ruth 3:2). At the threshingfloor, King David paid the "full price" by doing everything God's way (2 Sam. 24:24 and 1 Chron. 21:24 with 2 Sam. 6:1-8).

Till we all come in the unity of the faith, and of the knowledge of the Son of God, unto a perfect man, unto the measure of the stature of the fulness of Christ (Eph. 4:13).

The *aftereffect* of our return to the Lord will be floors "full" of wheat. This word means, "to fill, to be full; a fullness, an abundance; accomplished, ended; to consecrate, to fill the hand; to be armed, to be satisfied." The latter rain brings in the fullness of the harvest.[5] The anointing that rests upon Messiah and the Man whose name is the Branch is "without measure" (John 3:34), the sevenfold fullness of the Spirit (Isa. 11:1-2; Rev. 1:4; 3:1; 4:5; 5:6).

There shall be an handful of (such) *corn in the earth upon the top* (head) *of the mountains* (kingdoms)... (Ps. 72:16).

The word for "wheat" in Joel 2:24 is a different word from that used in Joel 1:11. It means, "in the sense of winnowing, grain of any kind (even while standing in the field); by extension, the open country." This word is also rendered as "corn" (Gen. 41:49; Ps. 65:13; Prov. 11:26). Its root means, "to clarify (brighten), examine, select; to purify, select, polish, choose, purge, cleanse, or test (prove)." Thus it reveals the purity of the mature harvest.

Joel 2:24, KJV ...*and the fats shall overflow with wine and oil.*

Thou shalt furnish (supply) *him* (your brother) *liberally...out of thy winepress: of that wherewith the Lord thy God hath blessed thee thou shalt give...* (Deut. 15:14).

The "fats" shall overflow abundantly with excess. These were "excavated troughs (dug out); specifically, a wine-vat (whether the lower one, into which the juice drains; or the upper, in which the grapes are crushed); a wine-press." The "winepress" is a biblical picture of overflowing, abundant joy![6]

...*I* (Jesus) *am come that they might have life, and that they might have it more abundantly* (John 10:10).

The wine vats shall "overflow" (Joel 3:13) and "run over; to water; to be abundant." This is the realm of "more than enough."[7] God's mercy and grace are abundant (2 Cor. 4:15; 1 Pet. 1:3). There will be "plenty" of corn, wine, and oil in the Feast of Tabernacles (Joel 2:26).

Consecration *affects* everything in our lives. Besides the abundance of corn, the vats overflow with the "wine" of His joy and the "oil" of His Spirit (Joel 1:10; 2:19).

> *And I will restore to you the years...* (Joel 2:25).

> *Whom shall he teach knowledge? and whom shall he make to understand doctrine? them that are weaned from the milk, and drawn from the breasts* (Isa. 28:9-10).

> *For precept must be upon precept, precept upon precept* (ordinance, commandment), *line upon line* (the cord for measuring the boundaries of the inheritance), *line upon line; here a little, and there a little* (Matt. 4:4; 2 Pet. 1:12).

God through His prophet now promises to "restore" the years! This verb is *shalam* (Strong's #7999), and is akin to the noun *shalom*, the Hebrew word for "peace" (compare with the Greek word for "salvation," which is *soteria*). *Shalom* means, "to be safe and sound (in mind, body or estate); figuratively, to be completed or finished; by implication, to be friendly; to be in a covenant of peace, to be at peace; to make whole or good, to restore, to make compensation." This word is used 18 times in Exodus 22:1-15.[8]

In spite of the traditions of men, God has already begun to restore the "years," beginning with Martin Luther to the present. God has been speaking "precept upon precept" and moving forward "line upon line" since the 16th century (Isa. 28:9-10). At any given time in the earth, there is a proceeding Word of "present truth" (Matt. 4:4; 2 Pet. 1:12). Note this historical overview of restored biblical truth:

1. Martin Luther (1517) – justification by faith.
2. The Anabaptists (1524) – water baptism by immersion.
3. John Wesley (1738) – sanctification.
4. A. B. Simpson (1875) – divine healing.
5. Charles Parham, William Seymour (1906) – Holy Ghost baptism.
6. George Hawtin (1948) – the laying on of hands and Eph. 4:11.
7. David Schoch (1950s) – the Tabernacle of David.
8. Bill Britton, G. C. McCurry (1960s) – biblical Sonship.

9. This author, many others (1970s to the present) – the present
   reality of the truths of the Most Holy Place, the Third Day.

*Therefore leaving the principles of the doctrine of Christ, let us go
on unto perfection; not laying again the foundation of repentance
from dead works, and of faith toward God,*

*Of the doctrine of baptisms, and of laying on of hands, and of res-
urrection of the dead, and of eternal judgment* (Heb. 6:1-2).

This familiar passage also shows this restoration of the years, out-
lining the same period of Church history. Repentance and faith are the
two elements of conversion (Martin Luther). Faith toward (upon) God
also embraces the Anabaptists and Wesley. The doctrine of baptisms
includes the Anabaptists and the Pentecostals at Azusa Street (1906).
The laying on of hands marked the Latter Rain Revival of 1948-56,
and the restoration of the fivefold ministries.

This continued during the 1950s (the evangelists), the 1960s
and 1970s (the pastors and the teachers), the 1980s (the prophets),
and the 1990s (the apostles). The era known as the resurrection of
the dead began in 1990. The season of eternal judgment in the earth
is yet to come.

*...that the locust hath eaten, the cankerworm, and the cater-
piller, and the palmerworm, my great army which I sent among
you* (Joel 2:25).

*For the earth shall be filled with the knowledge of the glory of the
Lord, as the waters cover the sea* (see Hab. 2:14 and compare
with Isa. 6:3).

Centuries of devastating tradition, pictured by the four devel-
oping stages of the locust (Joel 1:4), the "great army" (Joel 2:11)
which was "sent" (to let go) among us, will give way to the glory of
God filling and permeating the nations!

*And ye shall eat in plenty, and be satisfied, and praise the name of
the Lord your God, that hath dealt wondrously with you: and my
people shall never be ashamed* (Joel 2:26).

*Thou preparest a table before me in the presence of mine enemies:
thou anointest my head with oil; my cup runneth over* (see Ps.
23:5 and compare with Ps. 78:19; Prov. 3:10; Luke 15:17).

God's table is full! In the Feast of Tabernacles, we shall "eat (feed) in plenty,"[9] as did the four lepers of Samaria mentioned in Chapter Two of this writing (2 Kings 6:25; 7:1).

This is in direct contrast to the previous famine (Joel 1:4,19,20). Folks who follow after tradition are starved to death for real spiritual food. But we shall be "satisfied" (Joel 2:19), and "praise" the name of the Lord. This word is *halal* (Strong's #1984) and is the source of "Hallelujah." It means, "to be clear (of sound, but usually of color); to shine, to flash forth light; hence, to make a show, to boast, to glory, to sing (praise); and thus to be (clamorously) foolish, to make into a fool, to act like a madman; to rave; causatively, to celebrate" (Ps. 148:1-7,13-14; 150:1-6).

Now that we have turned back to God and His ways, He has "dealt" (done) "wondrously" with us. This word means, "to distinguish; by implication, to be (causatively, make) great, difficult, wonderful; to be marvellous, to be wonderful, to be surpassing, to be extraordinary, to separate by distinguishing action; to show oneself wonderful or marvelous." It is translated as "too hard" in Genesis 18:14.[10]

The hand of the Lord has moved again for us. We shall never again be "ashamed" (Joel 1:11; 2:27). God has brought an end to our confusion and reproach.

> *And ye shall know that I am in the midst of Israel, and that I am the Lord your God, and none else: and My people shall never be ashamed* (Joel 2:27).

> *Cry out and shout, thou inhabitant of Zion: for great is the Holy One of Israel in the midst of thee* (Isa. 12:6).

God is in the "midst"[11] (the center, among) His people "Israel," His company of prevailing princes (Joel 3:2,16). This name means, "he will rule as God; God prevails; contending or striving for God; dominion or rulership with God; prevailing prince." The name "Hebrew" (from Eber, as in Gen. 10:21), and "Jew" (from Judah, as in Gen. 29:35) are man-given; "Israel" is God-given (Gen. 32:24-32). There is no one beside the Lord!

> *I am the Lord, and there is none else, there is no God beside Me: I girded thee, though thou hast not known me:*

That they may know from the rising of the sun, and from the west, that there is none beside me. I am the Lord, and there is none else (Isa. 45:5-6).

The prophet repeats, "My people shall never be ashamed" (Joel 1:11; 2:26). "Emmanuel" (God with us) is among us (Isa. 7:14; Matt. 1:23)!

Thus concludes the section showing how Judah's consecration *affected* every area of their national life and brought the restoration of the years.

The closing verses of this chapter, Joel 2:28-32, are the key verses to his entire prophecy. We cannot turn from our desolation and make a fresh commitment to the Lord in our own strength. We must be empowered and enabled by the *anointing* of His Spirit!

Endnotes

1. Note these verses where God brings an "answer" to His people (see Gen. 41:16; Ps. 27:7; 86:7; 91:15; 102:2; 108:6; 143:1; and Isa. 65:24).

2. God will pardon and remove our iniquity (compare Isa. 43:25; Jer. 31:34, Mic. 7:18; 1 John 1:7).

3. These are some key verses where this word for "glad" is used (Ps. 48:11; 149:2; Song 1:4; Isa. 35:1-2; 61:10; 65:19; Zeph. 3:17; and Zech. 9:9).

4. The Lord has done "great things" (see 1 Sam. 12:24; 2 Sam. 7:23; 1 Chron. 17:19; Job 5:9; 9:10; 37:5; Ps. 71:19; Mark 3:8; 5:19-20; and Luke 1:49).

5. The latter rain brings in the "fullness" of the harvest (see Ps. 16:11; 24:1; John 1:16; Eph. 1:10,23; 3:19; 4:13; and Col. 1:19; 2:9).

6. Note these Scriptures that mention the "vats" or the "winepress" (see Num. 18:27,30; 2 Kings 6:27; Prov. 3:9-10; Isa. 5:2; 16:10; Jer. 48:33; and Zech. 14:10).

7. God's blessings "overflow" abundantly (see Ps. 36:6; 132:15; Isa. 35:2; 55:7; Rom. 5:20; 2 Cor. 8:7; 9:8; Eph. 3:20; 1 Thess. 3:12; 4:1; Titus 3:6; and 2 Pet. 1:8,11).

8. This word for "restore" is used elsewhere (see Lev. 5:16; 6:5; 24:18,21; Ruth 2:12; 1 Kings 9:25; 2 Kings 4:7; Neh. 6:15; Ps. 62;12; Prov. 6:31; 11:31).

9. There is "plenty" in the Feast of Tabernacles (see Gen. 27:28; 41:29-31; 1 Kings 10:11; 2 Chron. 31:10; Job 22:25; 37:23; Prov. 3:10; 29:19; and Jer. 44:17).

10. The word "wondrously" is used in these other verses (see Exod. 3:20; 34:10; Josh. 3:5; 1 Chron. 16:9,12,24; Ps. 40:5; 107:8; 118:23; Prov. 30:18; Isa. 28:29; Mic. 7:15).

11. Our God is "in the midst" (see Matt. 18:20; Luke 2:46; 24:36; John 19:18; 20:19,26; Acts 2:22; Heb. 2:12; and Rev. 1:13; 2:1; 5:6 with Ezek. 3:15; Hos. 11:9; Zeph. 3:15,17; Zech. 2:10-11; John 1:14).

CHAPTER THIRTEEN

CONSECRATION — ITS ANOINTING (JOEL 2:28-32)

We come now to the key passage of the Book of Joel. These five verses (Joel 2:28-32) constitute the singular prophetic passage that is directly fulfilled in the New Testament (Acts 2:14-21). Joel is the Prophet (Trumpet) of Pentecost! Blow the trumpet in Zion! Sound the alarm!

Zion will awake as we have a fresh experience with the Holy Ghost, the Spirit of resurrection life and power. Only the Holy Spirit can reveal and expose the *desolation* and true condition of the Church (Joel 1), empower us to *consecration* and a full commitment in the Feast Day of Atonement (Joel 2), and facilitate the *restoration* of all that God has promised in the Feast of Tabernacles (Joel 3).

And it shall come to pass afterward, that I will pour out My Spirit upon all flesh... (Joel 2:28).

And it shall come to pass in the last days, saith God, I will pour out of My Spirit upon all flesh... (Acts 2:17).

The Pentecostal outpouring of Acts 2 is but the "firstfruits" (Rom. 8:23) and the "earnest" (Eph. 1:13-14) of His fullness. What Peter described that historical day was *"out of"* all that Joel envisioned!

The addition of the preposition "of" is the difference. This primary preposition *apo* means, "away from, denoting origin; used of the place whence anything is, comes, befalls, or is taken; also used of the origin of a cause." This "cause" is for the Holy Ghost to awaken Zion (Joel 1), to cleanse Zion (Joel 2), and to restore Zion (Joel 3).

Thayer's Greek Lexicon adds that *apo* is used of separation of a part from the whole, where of a whole some *part* is taken. That which fell upon the men and women in the Upper Room was but a part of all that Joel saw and declared. Pentecost is in part.

Peter preached Pentecost. That firstfruits anointing was bestowed "out of" all that Joel declared—the outpouring of the Spirit "upon all flesh"! Joel proclaimed a third Feast, of which Pentecost is but a taste! That fullness of outpouring for the whole earth remains to be seen and experienced in the global harvest of the Feast of Tabernacles, and is the Spirit "without measure" (John 3:34). This was the anointing that rested upon Jesus. It will be poured out upon Zion's overcoming company, empowering them to move into the high calling!

All With One Accord

And when the day of Pentecost was fully come, they were all with one accord in one place

And suddenly there came a sound from heaven as of a rushing mighty wind, and it filled all the house where they were sitting (Acts 2:1-2).

God's Spirit moves in seasons and cycles. Pentecost lays the foundation for the present-day Feast of Tabernacles, and sets forth the fundamental ingredients of this third move of God.

In the Upper Room at Jerusalem, the 120 who tarried were all with "one accord." This is the Greek word *homothumadon*. It is a compound of *homou* (the same) and *thumos* (passion). Those early saints were together, waiting for the promise with the "same passion"! "Suddenly" (unawares, unexpectedly), right out of Heaven, there came a "sound" or noise like the roar of the sea waves. This rushing wind was borne along with great might and force.

This "sound" changed everything, and brought a new covenant with a new administration (2 Cor. 3-4). This "rushing mighty wind" was the very Breath of God, the passionate "blast" of His nostrils (Exod. 15:8; Job 4:9; Ps. 18:15). Centuries before, God breathed His name "Jah" (the "H" sound) into "Abram" (high or exalted father) and into "Sarai" (dominative, contentious, quarrelsome), empowering them to become "Abra-H-am" (father of a multitude) and "Sara-H" (noble-woman, princess, lady queen) (Gen. 17:5,15)!

But ye shall receive power (dunamis), *after that the Holy Ghost is come upon you: and ye shall be witnesses unto Me...* (Acts 1:8).

That I may know Him, and the power (dunamis) *of His resurrection...* (See Phil. 3:10 and compare with Rom. 8:11).

The primary Greek word describing the "power" of the Holy Spirit is *dunamis* (Strong's #1411), and it means, "force; specially, miraculous power; strength, inherent power residing in a thing by virtue of its nature; ability." Its root *dunamai* means, "to be able or possible: to be capable, strong, and powerful." *Dunamis* is used 120 times in the New Testament, the exact number of men and women in the Upper Room (Acts 1:15)! It is translated as, "ability, abundance, might, (worker of) miracles, power, strength, violence, mighty (wonderful) work." The "power" of the Holy Ghost is God's "ability."

It Shall Come to Pass Afterward

And it shall come to pass afterward... (Joel 2:28).

And it shall come to pass in the last days... (Acts 2:17).

Joel prophesied that this outpouring would "come to pass." This word means, "to exist, to become, to happen, take place, be brought about." This is akin to another word meaning, "to breathe or to be." Again, the wind of God's Spirit is His breath. We could translate this as, "God will breathe...!"

Joel said that this outpouring would take place "afterward." This is a compound of two Hebrew words:

1. The word *'achar* (Strong's #310), which means, "the hind part; after, after that."

2. The word *ken* (Strong's #3651), which means, "set upright; just, right, honest, true, veritable; rightly or so, thus or there fore; certain, fixed, stable" (2 Cor. 1:20). Its root means, "to be erect (stand perpendicular); hence to set up, whether literal (to establish, fix, prepare, apply), or figurative (appoint, render sure, proper or prosperous)." David "prepared"[1] a place in Zion for the Ark of the Covenant (2 Chron. 1:4).

This outpouring of the Spirit takes place "afterward," *after* the time of *righteous preparation* (the right thing to do); *after* the time of corporate fasting and prayer in the Feast Day of Atonement

(Joel 1:14; 2:15); and *after* the corporate *"amen"* and agreement of the people of God.

Peter in Acts 2:17 referred to this same season as "the last days." The Greek word for "last" is *eschatos*, and it means, "last, final, farthest, uttermost, or extreme."

> *Hath in these last days spoken unto us by His Son, whom He hath appointed heir of all things, by whom also He made the worlds* (Heb.1:2).

Contrary to popular dispensational views of eschatology, "the last days" mentioned by Peter referred to "the last days" of the Old Covenant, "the last days" of Levitical Judaism. This application is consistent with every other Old Testament (Gen. 49:1; Isa. 2:2; Mic. 4:1) and New Testament usage (2 Tim. 3:1; James 5:3; 2 Pet. 3:3). Compare the phrase, "latter days."[2]

> *...that I will pour out My Spirit upon all flesh...* (Joel 2:28).

> *For I will pour water upon him that is thirsty, and floods upon the dry ground: I will pour My Spirit upon thy seed...* (see Isa. 44:3 and compare with Prov. 1:23; Ezek. 39:29; Zech. 12:10).

God promises here to "pour out" His Spirit (down) upon "all flesh" (humankind). This word for "pour out" (Joel 2:29; 3:19) means, "to spill forth, shed, gush out (a libation or liquid metal); intensively, to sprawl out" (Ezek. 39:29).

God will do this pouring out through His mature Church, Zion! We are His "windows (floodgates) of heaven" (Mal. 3:10). Just as the prophet Elijah stretched himself and "sprawled out" upon the widow's son (1 Kings 17:21), so this ministry will empower the next generation and the generations to come!

> *And the earth was without form, and void; and darkness was upon the face of the deep. And the Spirit of God moved upon the face of the waters* (See Gen. 1:2 and compare with Job 27:3; 33:4).

"My spirit" is *ruwach* (Strong's #7307), and it means, "wind; by resemblance breath, (or violent) exhalation; the Shekinah; to smell, scent, perceive odor, thus to accept (discern); used of a horse or delight (metaphor)."

This awesome outpouring of His Spirit is to be upon "all" (the whole; any, each, every, anything; totality, everything) "flesh," upon every nation, tongue, and tribe.[3] The glory of the Lord shall be revealed, and all flesh shall see it together (Isa. 40:5)!

> *...and your sons and your daughters shall prophesy, your old men shall dream dreams, your young men shall see visions:* (Joel 2:28).

> *And the Spirit of the Lord will come upon thee* (Saul), *and thou shalt prophesy with them, and shalt be turned* (turn about or over; changed, transformed) *into another man* (1 Sam. 10:6).

Historically, in Acts 2 and at Azusa Street, we now understand that there is no gender prejudice in a genuine Pentecostal outpouring. The "sons" (*ben*) and the "daughters" (the feminine form of *ben*) shall "prophesy." This is the word *naba'* (Strong's #5012), and it means, "to prophesy, speak (or sing) by inspiration (in prediction or simple discourse); under the influence of the divine Spirit." First mentioned in 1 Samuel 10:6, *naba'* is found in the Hebrew text about 115 times.

> *As for these four* (Hebrew) *children, God gave them knowledge and skill in all learning and wisdom: and Daniel had understanding in all visions and dreams* (see Daniel 1:17 and compare with Dan. 5:12,16).

The "old men" (Joel 1:2) are to dream "dreams" (with prophetic meaning) so that the young men can see visions. The noun appears about 65 times and in all periods of biblical Hebrew.[4]

> *Then shall the virgin rejoice in the dance, both young men and old together: for I will turn their mourning into joy, and will comfort them, and make them rejoice...* (see Jer. 31:13 and compare with Prov. 20:29; Zech. 9:17).

The "(selected) young men" are to have visions. The root means, "to try, examine (by implication) select, elect, prefer, choose out, decide for." The 44 occurrences of this word signify the fully developed, vigorous, unmarried man. The period during which a "young man" is in his prime could possibly be the period during which he is eligible for the draft—age 20 to 50.[5]

> *According to all these words, and according to all this vision, so did Nathan speak unto David* (2 Sam. 7:17).

"Visions" is the Hebrew word *chizzayown* (Strong's #2384), and it means, "revelation, expectation by dream; a vision (in the ecstatic state); an oracle, a prophecy (in divine communication)." Its root means, "to see as a seer; to gaze at; to look, behold; mentally, to per-ceive, contemplate (with pleasure); specifically, to have a vision of." This noun, which occurs ten times, refers to a prophetic "vision" and divine communication.[6]

And also upon the servants and upon the handmaids in those days will I pour out My spirit (Joel 2:29).

Again, there is no gender prejudice in this outpouring. It comes upon the "servants" (bondservant, slave) and upon the "handmaids" (bondwomen, female slave). The Greek counterparts are *doulos* and *doule*. "Those days" are the "last days" (Joel 2:28; Acts 2:17).

As noted above, Peter in Acts 2:17 declared that He would pour out "of" His Spirit, out "of" all that Joel prophesied in Joel 2:28. When comparing Acts 2:18 with Joel 2:29, this truth is repeated. Peter also adds these words, "and they shall prophesy."

But he that prophesieth speaketh unto men to edification, and exhortation, and comfort.

He that speaketh in an unknown tongue edifieth himself; but he that prophesieth edifieth the church (1 Cor. 14:3-4).

All of God's people are to prophesy by the Spirit (Num. 11:29). The Greek word *propheteuo* (Strong's #4395) means, "to foretell events, divine, speak forth by divine inspiration, exercise the prophetic office; to predict; to utter forth, to declare, a thing which can only be known by divine revelation; to break forth under sudden impulse in lofty discourse or praise of the divine counsels." This is taken from *pro* (fore, in front of, prior) and *phemi* (make known one's thoughts, speak or say).[7]

And I will shew wonders in the heavens and in the earth... (Joel 2:30).

And the Lord brought us forth out of Egypt with a mighty hand, and with an outstretched arm, and with great terribleness, and with signs, and with wonders (Deut. 26:8).

God wants to "shew" (give) wonders. "Wonders" in the "heav-ens" (the realm of Spirit) and in the "earth" (Joel 2:10; 3:16) accom-pany a genuine outpouring of the Holy Spirit. These "wonders" are the signs of the Holy Ghost in the Feast of Pentecost. The Hebrew word for "wonders" means, "conspicuousness; a miracle; a token or omen; a portent." Its root means, "bright, beautiful." This word signifies a special display of divine power.[8]

God also bearing them (that heard Him) *witness, both with signs and wonders, and with divers miracles, and gifts of the Holy Ghost, according to His own will* (Heb. 2:4).

The Greek word for "wonders" is *teras* (Strong's #5059), and it means, "a prodigy or omen; a portent; a miracle performed by anyone; something strange, causing the beholder to marvel, is always used in the plural, is always rendered "wonders," and generally follows signs. A sign is intended to appeal to the understanding, a "wonder" appeals to the imagination, for its power indicates its source as supernatural.[9]

And these signs shall follow them that believe... (Mark 16:17).

This beginning of miracles (semeion) *did Jesus in Cana of Galilee, and manifested forth His glory; and His disciples believed...* (John 2:11).

Peter adds in Acts 2:19 that God will show "signs" in the earth beneath. The Greek word *semeion* (Strong's #4592) means, "an indication; a sign, a mark, a token, a miracle; an unusual occurrence, transcending the common course of nature (by which God authenticates the men and women sent by Him).[10]

...blood, and fire, and pillars of smoke (Joel 2:30).

...He (Jesus) *that cometh after me...shall baptize you with the Holy Ghost, and with fire* (Matt. 3:11).

And there appeared unto them cloven tongues like as of fire, and it sat upon each of them (Acts 2:3).

"Blood" and "fire" are essential ingredients of a genuine Pentecostal experience. The "blood" is the basis of the "fire" (a symbol for the Holy Spirit). Calvary predicated Pentecost. "Blood" and "fire" are also the two cleansing agents in the Feast of Passover and the Feast Day of Atonement.

And the Lord went before them by day in a pillar of a cloud, to lead them the way; and by night in a pillar of fire, to give them light; to go by day and night (see Exod. 13:21 and compare with John 16:13; Rom. 8:14).

Who is this (the Shulamite) *that cometh out of the wilderness like pillars of smoke, perfumed with myrrh* (death) *and frankincense* (resurrection), *with all powders of the merchant?* (Song 3:6).

The "pillars" of smoke are a direct allusion to the pillar of cloud by day and the pillar of fire by night that led Moses' "church" through the wilderness (Acts 7:38)! The word for "pillars" means, "a pillar, a column; a palm-like spreading at the top."

And the Lord will create upon every dwelling place of mount Zion, and upon her assemblies, a (pillar of) *cloud and smoke by day, and the shining of a flaming fire by night: for upon all the glory shall be a defence* (Isa. 4:5).

"Smoke" in the Bible has two basic meanings:

First, it is a symbol for God's glory and presence (2 Sam. 22:9; Job 41:20; Isa. 6:4). God Himself is a smoking furnace (Gen. 15:17).

Second, it is a symbol for the victory of a finished work, the acceptance of the burnt sacrifice, and the end of the old order.[11]

The sun shall be turned into darkness, and the moon into blood, before the great and the terrible day of the Lord come (Joel 2:31).

Peter in Acts 2:20 calls this season the "notable" (conspicuous, manifest, illustrious) Day of the Lord.

The "sun" and the "moon" were discussed in Joel 2:10. The outpouring of the Holy Ghost on the Day of Pentecost meant "lights out" for the Levitical system!

But they (Israel) *rebelled, and vexed His Holy Spirit: therefore He was turned to be their enemy, and He fought against them* (see Isa. 63:10 and compare with Lam. 5:15; Gal. 5:17).

The sun shall be "turned" into "darkness" (Joel 2:2). This word means, "to turn about or over; by implication, to change, overturn, return, pervert; to overthrow, to overturn; to change, to transform; turning from side to the other." This is exactly what happens when God turns on the old order. Jesus overthrew the tables of the money-changers, and God is about to turn the tables on Babylon. The dance and the party are almost over for Belshazzar and his palace crowd! The prophetic fingers of a Man's "hand" are writing His Word; wicked knees are knocking together (Dan. 5:5-6; Eph. 4:11).

Again, this verse (Joel 2:31), like Joel 2:10, has several applications:

Dispensationally, the gospel of the Kingdom meant "lights out" for the previous administration of Old Testament Judaism. Malachi 4:5 declares that Elijah would also come "before" that Day. John the Baptist was the forerunner who began to spell out the demise of the old order (Matt. 3:1-12; 17:13).

> *Immediately after the tribulation of those days shall the sun be darkened, and the moon shall not give her light, and the stars shall fall from heaven, and the powers of the heavens shall be shaken* (Matt. 24:29).

Moreover, Matthew 24:21-24,29 describes God's people enduring a time of "tribulation" (pressure; metaphorically, oppression, affliction, or distress). The "tribulation" prophesied by Jesus in Matthew 24:29 marked the end of Judaism (A.D. 67-70). The 12 tribes of natural Israel are described as the "sun" and the "moon" (Gen. 37:9-10).

Again, this cosmic imagery describing the judgment and vindication of God meant "lights out" for the old order (Matt. 21:42-43; 1 Pet. 2:9-10). Note the similar parallel language of the Old Testament describing the end of Babylon (Isa. 13:9-10); the end of Edom (Isa. 34:4-5); and the end of Israel (Amos 5:18-22; 8:9).

> *And the God of peace shall bruise* (tread down, trample, crush completely, shatter, break in pieces, conquer) *satan under your feet shortly...* (Rom. 16:20).

Historically, the light of the apostolic Church of the Book of Acts went out. The Roman Church evolved, and continued throughout the Dark Ages until Martin Luther and the Protestant Reformation (1517).

Ecclesiastically, the "moon" (the power of darkness) was "turned" (over) to "blood" (the Hebrew word is *dam*). In 1969, man literally walked on the moon. Jesus completely walked all over the kingdom of darkness. Now, through Christ's finished work, "Adam" (humankind) will put the devil underfoot! The Sun-Clothed Woman (the Church) has the "moon" under her feet (Rev. 12:1-5).

> *...before the great and the terrible day of the Lord come* (Joel 2:31).

The "Day of the Lord" (Joel 1:15; 2:1,11; 3:14) is both "great" (Joel 2:11,25) and "terrible" (Joel 2:11). As noted, it is both Day ("great" for the people of God), and night ("terrible" for the children of darkness) at the *same time*. The same Flood that destroyed the wicked, elevated Noah and his family to inherit the earth.

And it shall come to pass, that whosoever shall call on the name of the Lord shall be delivered: for in mount Zion and in Jerusalem shall be deliverance, as the Lord hath said, and in the remnant whom the Lord shall call (Joel 2:32).

And whosoever liveth and believeth in Me shall never die. Believest thou this? (John 11:26).

God's promise is sure. All this will "come to pass" (Joel 2:28). God is no respecter of persons or faces (Acts 10:34; 1 Pet. 1:17), for "whosoever" shall "call on" (cry out to) the Name of the Lord shall be "delivered." This word means, "to be smooth, to escape or slip away (as if by slipperiness) from any kind of danger; to release or rescue; to bring forth young, give birth."[12] It describes the righteous remnant.

And the remnant that is escaped of the house of Judah shall again take root downward, and bear fruit upward:

For out of Jerusalem shall go forth a remnant, and they that escape out of mount Zion... (see Isa. 37:31-32 and compare with Ezra 9:8).

In "Mount Zion" and in "Jerusalem" (Joel 3:1,6,16,17,20) shall be deliverance. "Jerusalem" is the "habitation of peace," and is the Church (Heb. 12:22). The word "deliverance" in this verse means, "an escaped portion, remnant."[13] This same word is translated in Joel 2:3 as "escaped."

Except the Lord of hosts had left unto us a very small remnant, we should have been as Sodom, and we should have been like unto Gomorrah (Isa. 1:9).

There shall be deliverance in the "remnant" whom the Lord shall "call" (Joel 1:14; 2:15) with the high calling! Only those who have repented and experienced the Day of Atonement will partake of Tabernacles. Only a free man can set a man free!

For this we say unto you by the word of the Lord, that we which are alive and remain (left over, survive) unto the coming of the Lord shall not prevent them which are asleep (1 Thess. 4:15).

And this word, Yet once more, signifieth the removing of those things that are shaken, as of things that are made, that those things which cannot be shaken may remain (Heb. 12:27).

The word for "remnant" is *sariyd* (Strong's #8300), and it means, "a survivor; what is left." Its root means, "to puncture (and slip out); to escape or survive; remain."[14] Contrary to popular fiction, it is the righteous that remain, and are "left behind." According to Jesus, the wicked are taken in judgment and the righteous are left (Matt. 24:37-41)! Whose report will you believe (Isa. 53:1)?

The trumpet has sounded. We have heard the alarm. *Desolation* has been swallowed up by *consecration*. The Day of Atonement now leads us to the full and complete *restoration* of the Feast of Tabernacles.

...Shall not the Judge of all the earth do right? (Gen. 18:25).

Whatever one's view of Heaven or hell is, rest assured in this: no one is going to get away with anything! Throughout the earth and among all men, there will be divine *vindication...*

ENDNOTES

1. This word is translated as "prepared" in these verses (see 1 Kings 5:18; 6:19; 1 Chron. 9:32; 15:1-2,12; 22:5; 29:2-3; and Ps. 9:7; 74:16; 103:19; 147:8).

2. Compare the phrase, "latter days" (see Num. 24:14; Deut. 4:30; 31:29; Jer. 23:20; 30:24; 48:47; 49:39; Ezek. 38:16; Dan. 2:28; 10:14; and Hos. 3:5).

3. This outpouring is upon "all flesh" (see Ps. 65:2; 136:25; 145:21; Isa. 49:26; 66:16,23-24; Jer. 25:31; 32:27; Zech. 2:13; and Luke 3:6; John 17:2; and Acts 2:17).

4. Note these Scriptures that deal with "dreams" (Gen. 37:8,19; 41:12,15; Num. 12:6; Deut. 13:1-5; 1 Sam. 28:6; 1 Kings 3:5; Jer. 23:28; compare Matt. 1:20; 2:12,13,19,22; and Acts 2:17). A dream is a "night vision" (Gen. 46:2; Dan. 2:19; 7:27,13; Acts 16:9; 18:9).

5. These verses mention the "young men" (see Exod. 30:14; Num. 1:3; 4:3,23,35,39,43,47; compare Ruth 3:10; 1 Sam. 8:16; 9:2; 24:2; 26:2; 1 Kings 12:21; Ps. 89:19; Isa. 23:4; 62:5; and Amos 2:11).

6. Note these Scriptures that deal with "visions" (see Gen. 15:1; Job 4:13; 7:14; 20:8; 33:15; Ps. 89:19; Prov. 29:18; Isa. 22:1,5; Ezek. 1:1; Dan. 7:1; 10:1; Obad. 1:1; and Zech. 13:4; compare Luke 1:22; Acts 2:17; 9:10-12; 10:3; 16:9-10; 18:9; 26:19; 2 Cor. 12:1; and Rev. 9:17).

7. God wants His people to "prophesy" (see Acts 19:6; 21:9; 1 Cor. 11:4-5; 13:9; 14:1-5,24,31,39; 1 Pet. 1:10; Jude 1:14; and Rev. 10:11;11:3).

8. Note the "wonders" of the Old Testament (see Exod. 4:21; 7:3; Deut. 4:34; 26:8; 1 Chron. 16:12; Neh. 9:10; Ps. 78:43; 105:5,27; Isa. 8:18; Jer. 32:21; Ezek. 24:24; and Zech. 3:8).

9. Note the "wonders" of the New Testament (see Acts 2:19,22,43; 4:30; 5:12; 6:8; 7:36; 14:3; 15:12; Rom. 15:19; and Rev. 12:1-3).

10. The New testament says much about "signs" (see Matt. 12:38-39; 24:24; Mark 16:17-20; Luke 2:12,34; John 3:2; 11:47; Acts 2:19,22,43; 4:30; 5:12; 6:8; and Rom. 15:19).

11. "Smoke" is a symbol for the victory of a finished work, the acceptance of the burnt sacrifice, and the end of the old order (see Josh. 8:20-21; Judg. 20:38,40; Ps. 37:20; 68:2; 102:3; Isa. 9:18; 34:10; 51:6; Hos. 13:3 and Nah. 2:13).

12. Whosoever shall call upon the name of the Lord shall be "delivered" (see Ps. 22:5; 33:17; 41:1; 89:48; 107:20; 116:4; 124:7; Isa. 66:7; Dan. 12:1; and Zech. 2:7).

13. This word for "deliverance" is used in these verses (see Gen. 45:7; 2 Chron. 12:7; Neh. 1:2; Isa. 4:2; 10:20; 37:31-32; Ezek. 14:22; and Obad. 1:17).

14. Note these verses on the "remnant" (see Judg. 5:13; Isa. 1:9; Jer. 31:2; compare Amos 5:15; Mic. 2:12; 4:7; 5:3-8; Hag. 1:12-14; Zech. 8:6,12; and Rom. 9:27; 11:5).

THE BOOK OF JOEL

PART THREE

RESTORATION

(JOEL 3:1-21)

———✦———

"...for the Lord dwelleth in Zion."

CHAPTER FOURTEEN

RESTORATION — ITS VINDICATION (JOEL 3:1-8)

Joel's prophecy now comes full circle. The complete *desolation* of Judah and Zion (the high calling) in Joel 1:1-20 brought forth the sound of the trumpet, calling us to the much-needed *consecration* of Joel 2:1-32. After this Day of Atonement comes the Feast of Tabernacles (Lev. 23:27,39), the global *restoration* that is described in Joel 3:1-21. This third and final section (Joel 3:1-8) begins with the Lord's *vindication*. He judges every strange "nation" that has dared to raise its voice against Zion.

Captivity is Turned

For, behold, in those days, and in that time, when I shall bring again the captivity of Judah and Jerusalem (Joel 3:1).

When the Lord brought back the captives to Zion, we were like men who dreamed (Ps. 126:1, NIV).

"Behold"—this announcement is a revelation. Zion's restoration will take place "when" (not if) "in those (New Testament) days" (Joel 2:29; 3:14,18), and "in that (appointed) time" (Ps. 102:13), that *kairos* moment of His visitation. We have now come to the season for a Third Reformation.

The Lord will "bring again" the captivity of "Judah" (the First-fruits Company) and "Jerusalem" (the Church, as in Joel 3:6,20). This again is the Hebrew word which means, "to restore or bring back." It is also translated in the Book of Joel as "turn" (Joel 2:12-13) and "return" (Joel 2:14; 3:4,7).

That then the Lord thy God will turn thy captivity, and have com-
passion upon thee, and will return and gather thee from all the
nations... (see Deut. 30:3 and compare with Eph. 4:8).

The "captivity" refers to the "exile; concretely, prisoners, captives;
figuratively, a former state of prosperity." The root word means, "to
transport into captivity; take captive; carry or lead away."[1]

Among whom also we all had our conversation in times past in the
lusts of our flesh, fulfilling the desires of the flesh and of the mind;
and were by nature the children of wrath... (Eph. 2:3).

In Joel's day, the people of Judah and Jerusalem would eventually
be carried captive to Babylon and be scattered among the nations.

Our "captivity" (enslavement to the god of this world) was turned
primarily in the finished work of Jesus Christ. Then consider the
Babylonian captivity of the Church during the religious confusion of
the Dark or Middle Ages. From the days of Martin Luther (1517) to
the present, God has progressively restored the "years" (Joel 2:25), and
gathered us from among strange "nations."

Gather Every Nation

I will also gather all nations... (Joel 3:2).

Turn you at My reproof (correction): *behold, I will pour out*
My Spirit unto you, I will make known My words unto you
(Prov. 1:23).

No one will be exempt in the Day of the Lord. God has determined to "gather" (Joel 2:6,16; 3:11) and judge "all nations," all flesh
(Joel 2:28). The "nations" are mentioned throughout the prophecy
(Joel 1:6; 2:17,19; 3:8-12). As God continues to pour out His Spirit, the
pure Word of the Kingdom will increasingly vindicate His righteous
name and bring cleansing to every "nation." As with all other biblical
truths, there is a threefold paradigm concerning the "nations." As
revealed to the prophet in Ezekial 8, there are "abominations" (idols) in
all three dimensions.

But the natural man receiveth not the things of the Spirit of
God: for they are foolishness (silliness, absurdity) *unto him:*
neither can he know (perceive) *them, because they are spiritu-*
ally discerned (scrutinized, investigated, examined, judged)
(1 Cor. 2:14).

First, the Outer Court, the evangelical realm, is crowded with many *denomi-nations*. This dimension deals with the body (the natural realm). Here we see the divided Church. The religious doctrine and methodology of all these groups is "strange" to the Lord.

> *Casting down imaginations, and every high thing that exalteth itself against the knowledge of God, and bringing into captivity every thought to the obedience of Christ;* (2 Cor. 10:5).

Second, the Holy Place, the Pentecostal realm, is overrun with many *imagi-nations*. This is the dimension of the soul. Here we see divided minds. These imaginations and human reasonings are "estranged" from His thoughts, His mind. The stinking thinking of the Adamic mindset alienates itself from the mind of Chirst.

> *The prophets prophesy lies in my name: I sent them not, neither have I commanded them, neither spake unto them: they prophesy unto you a false vision and divination* (to determine by magic; oracle, including its fee), *and a thing of nought, and the deceit of their heart* (see Jer.14:14 and compare with Rom. 1:21-23, NIV).

Third, the Most Holy Place, the Kingdom realm, has been contaminated by unholy *divi-nations*. This is the dimension of the spirit. Here we see divided hearts. These men and women were originally apprehended for the high calling, to partake of His "divine nature" (2 Pet. 1:4) in Zion. But they have corrupted themselves, and become a "strange god" in and of themselves.

> *Who changed* (exchanged) *the truth of God into* [the] *lie, and worshipped and served the creature* (Adam) *more than the Creator* (Christ)... (Rom. 1:25).

Every "denomi-nation" has its own flavor, marked by its own "imagi-nation" (doctrine). This ultimately leads to its own "divi-nation," its own idea of who God is. Men and women have conformed God to their own image, so that their perception of God can corroborate and substantiate their teachings and ways of living. Thus we have an evangelical Jesus, a Pentecostal Jesus, and even a Kingdom Jesus. All of that has sinned and come short of His glorious Person and power (Rom. 3:23)!

> *...and will bring them down into the valley of Jehoshaphat...* (Joel 3:2).

The Lord will certainly bring every strange nation "down" (Joel 2:23; 3:11) and deal with them in the "valley" of Jehoshaphat. The awakening of Zion and our return to the high calling will bring about His dealings with every spirit of antichrist, every covenant-breaker.

Awake, awake; put on thy strength (force, security, majesty, praise), *O Zion; put on* (Christ) *thy beautiful* (priestly) *garments* (Exod. 28), *O Jerusalem, the holy city: for henceforth there shall no more come into thee the uncircumcised* (exposed, projecting loose, uncurtailed), *and the unclean* (foul, impure, defiled) (Isa. 52:1).

The "valley" in verse two was "a vale (broad depression); lowland, an open country." The root word means, "to be deep, make profound." This "valley" is between our ears! As He pled with Gomer the prostitute (Hos. 2:1-15), God will arbitrate with every "nation."

The name "Jehoshaphat" is rendered, "the Lord is Judge; Jehovah has judged; the government of Jehovah; whom Jah sets right; rectitude of Jehovah." This is the name of one of Judah's kings (1 Kings 15:24; 2 Chron. 17-20), and a valley near Jerusalem that is the symbolical place of ultimate judgment.

According to Jewish tradition, the Valley of Jehoshaphat was that deep ravine of the Kidron Valley between Jerusalem's Temple and the Mount of Olives through which the Kidron Creek flowed. There are differing ideas as to the full significance of this Valley (See Joel 3:14 and compare Zechariah 14:1-4 with Revelation 19:11-21).

...and will plead with them there for My people and for My heritage Israel... (Joel 3:2).

For by fire (the Holy Ghost) *and by His sword* (the Word) *will the Lord plead with all flesh...* (Isa. 66:16).

God will "plead" with every nation there for His "people" (Joel 2:16-17) and for His "heritage" (Joel 2:17) Israel. This word for "plead" in Joel 3:2 is *shaphat* (Strong's #8199), and it means, "to judge, pronounce sentence (for or against); by implication, to vindicate or punish; by extension, to govern; passively, to litigate; to act as law-giver or judge or governor; to decide controversy; to execute judgment."

Shaphat refers to the activity of a third party who sits over two parties at odds with one another. This third party hears their cases against one another and decides where the right is and what to do about it (he functions as both judge and jury). In some cases this "judging" really means delivering from injustice or oppression. *Shaphat* is also used of a process whereby order and law are maintained within a group.[2] Our God is the Judge of all the earth (Gen. 18:25; Acts 10:42; Heb. 12:23).

All this is done for His heritage "Israel" (Joel 2:27; 3:16). This name means, "he will rule as God; God prevails; contending or striving for God; dominion or rulership with God; prevailing prince" (Gen. 32:24-32; Gal. 6:16). Every overcomer is an "Israelite indeed" (John 1:47).

> ...*whom they have scattered among the nations, and parted My land* (Joel 3:2).

Religious traditions, like the horde of locusts, have "scattered" (dispersed) the people of God among the denominations, imaginations, and divinations. They have "parted" His land, His inheritance, His Church. This word means, "smooth (figuratively); by implication (as smooth stones were used for lots) to apportion or separate; to divide, share, or plunder; to allot, apportion, assign, divide up, or distribute; to be smooth, slippery, or deceitful; to flatter." Truth has been plundered.

> *They part my* (Messiah's) *garments among them, and cast lots upon my vesture* (Ps. 22:18).

Jesus' seamless robe, like Aaron's "blue robe" (Exod. 28:4,31-35), covered His body, and pictures the unity of the Body of Christ. Those who "part" and "divide" His garments crucify to themselves the Son of God afresh, and put Him to an open shame (Heb. 6:6).

Jesus adds and multiplies. The devil subtracts and divides; he is the "god" of all the world's religions with their traditions (2 Cor. 4:4). He is the king of hell from whence these locusts came (Rev. 9:1-11). Religious confusion has devastated and "divided"[3] the Church.

We Have Sold Out the Children

> *And they have cast lots for My people, and have given a boy for an harlot...* (Joel 3:3).

Religion is driven by the "love of money" (1 Tim. 6:10). The strange "nations" have "cast" (handled, thrown) "lots" for the "people" (Joel 2:2; 3:2). As noted, its preachers love to play the numbers game of "nickels, noses, and names." This word for "lots" means, "to be rough (as a stone); a pebble, a lot (small stones being used for that purpose); figuratively, a portion, destiny or thing assigned (as if determined by lot); pebbles used for making decisions, for discovering the will of God." Exactly what casting the "lot" involved is not known.[4]

...and traded boys for prostitutes... (Joel 3:3, NIV).

The New King James Version adds that they "have given a boy as payment for a harlot." Religious systems traffic in the young. The things that literally go on behind cloistered walls are scandalous. Children have been used and abused. The "boy" was "a lad or offspring; a child, a son, a boy, a youth."[5] It differs from *ben* (son), which specifies the parental relationship. These children were vulnerable, "boys" without a father.

God loves the young. Jesus ministered often to "little children" (Matt. 19:13-14). He sternly warned not to "offend" them (Matt. 18:6). This Greek word is *skandalizo* (reference the English, "scandal"). In recent years, many of these ungodly practices have been publicly exposed and dealt with.

Yea, they sacrificed their sons and their daughters unto devils,

And shed innocent blood, even the blood of their sons and of their daughters, whom they sacrificed unto the idols of Canaan: and the land was polluted with blood (see Ps. 106:37-38 and compare with Exod. 34:14-15).

The "harlot" in Joel 3:3 was "highly-fed and therefore wanton; those who commit adultery (usually of the female); figuratively, spiritual prostitution, to commit idolatry, serve other gods; to commit fornication, to be a harlot, to play the harlot."[6] This is the common term for spiritual backsliding. The Book of Hosea and the story of Gomer's unfaithfulness exemplify this. Israel was married to Jehovah in the Old Testament (Jer. 3:14). From the beginning and throughout her long history, she constantly played the harlot, and went after other gods.

...and sold a girl for wine, that they might drink (Joel 3:3).

...they sold the righteous for silver, and the poor for a pair of shoes (see Amos 2:6 and compare with Zech. 11:12-13).

The harlot church knows no shame. She has also "sold" out (Joel 3:6-8) the daughters to her whorish systems. This word means, "to sell, literally (as merchandise, a daughter in marriage, into slavery), or figuratively (to surrender); to be given over to death."[7] This word expresses the act of betrayal, as Judas in the Gospels (Matt. 26:46-48).

The "girl" was a "lass, damsel; a marriageable girl." The strange "nations" sold the "sons" and the "daughters" who were meant to receive the outpouring of Joel 2:28-32! God is jealous for the children. God's Word assures us that the streets of Zion are destined to be full of boys and girls (Zech. 8:5).

And they lay themselves down upon clothes laid to pledge by every altar, and they drink the wine of the condemned in the house of their god (Amos 2:8).

They sold the girls "for wine" (Joel 1:5) that they might "drink" (imbibe, get drunk, intoxicated).[8] These are like the "drunkards of Ephraim" (Isa. 28:1) described in Chapter Three. Babylon's priests, intoxicated with power and authority, have mocked the Eucharist, getting drunk at the table of the Lord. The harlot systems merchandise the "souls of men" (Rev. 18:10-13). Then and now, the House of the Lord is defiled with those who sell doves (Matt. 21:2; Mark 11:11,15; John 2:16).

Leaders in America and the Church today have sold out the children and youth to their secular and religious whore houses and schools, their worldly trappings (distractions) and entertainment. The word "muse" means "to think." Babylon has fed the children a steady diet of "amusement"—they don't have to think. Consider all the video and computer games of gratuitous violence. To those of you who are hooked on that stuff, I ask, "Would you do in the real world what you do in your virtual world?"

Joel 3:3 is a most vivid picture. These spiritual child slavery rings are big business, and have polluted the minds and hearts of our children. God is angry, ever jealous for the new generation. He is about to roar out of Zion to *vindicate* His own.

We Don't Need the World's Help

Yea, and what have ye to do with me, O Tyre, and Zidon... (Joel 3:4).

The prophet now turns his attention to Tyre and Zidon. Joel boldly asks for the Lord, "Now what have you against Me?"

So Hiram (king of Tyre) gave Solomon cedar trees and fir trees according to all his desire.

And the Lord gave Solomon wisdom, as he promised him: and there was peace between Hiram and Solomon; and they two made a league (covenant, alliance, pledge) together (1 Kings 5:10,12).

And Tyrus did build herself a strong hold, and heaped up silver as the dust, and fine gold as the mire of the streets (Zech. 9:3).

"Tyre" (rock) was the Phoenician seaport city on the Mediterranean coast.[9] "Zidon" (to hunt or catch fish) was an ancient Phoenician city on the Mediterranean coast north of Tyre.[10]

Tyre and Zidon represent the help of the world, especially with regard to money. These are business people with no real heart for Zion. Their entrepreneurship is for selfish agendas, not the purpose of God. The moneychangers are still selling doves. The Christian music industry, in spite of widespread corruption and shady competition, looms large in the eyes of starry-eyed youth.

And his (Samuel's) sons walked not in his ways, but turned aside after lucre (plunder, unjust gain; profit acquired by violence), and took bribes (donations, gifts, rewards), and perverted (bent, turned away) judgment (1 Sam. 8:3).

...not greedy of filthy lucre (sordid, eager for base or shameful gain) (1 Tim. 3:3,8; Titus 1:7; 1 Pet. 5:2).

The prophet fearlessly thunders out to anyone who wants to buy their way into the Kingdom, "To hell with your useless money, your filthy lucre. Character cannot be bought through the laying on of hands, and your hands are not clean!"

...and all the coasts of Palestine? will ye render Me a recompence? and if ye recompence me, swiftly and speedily will I return your recompence upon your own head; (Joel 3:4).

Joel now prophesies to the coasts (circuit, region, borders) of "Palestine," which means, "rolling, migratory; the land of sojourners." The root is rendered, "to roll in ashes or dust (as an act of mourning)." This word is translated as, "Palestina, Palestine, Philistia, Philistines."[11] This was the general territory on the west coast of Canaan or the entire country of Palestine. The older name for "Palestine" was "Canaan."

Adam is a man of dust (1 Cor. 15:44-49). To wallow in the "dust" is to wallow in self. Moreover, the Philistines were perpetual enemies of Judah, and typify demons (Eph. 6:12). Goliath, their champion (1 Sam. 17), is a picture of satan.

The Lord asks of these worldly forces, "Will you render Me a recompense (repayment, retaliate; ill treatment)?" He tells them that if they dare turn on His might and power, He will "swiftly" (lightly, rapidly) and "speedily" (hurriedly, promptly, hastily) return their arrogance upon their own head!

> *Because ye have taken My silver and my gold, and have carried into your temples My goodly pleasant things:* (Joel 3:5).

> *The silver is Mine, and the gold is Mine, saith the Lord of hosts* (Hag. 2:8).

The prophet addresses the Philistines, the enemies of Judah. They had pilfered the silver and the gold (for their idols, as in Ps. 115:4; Isa. 2:7; Hab. 2:19). They had "carried" into their "temples" (palaces; large public buildings) His "goodly" (finest, prized) "pleasant" (delightful, desirable) things. For example, the Ark of the Covenant was carried into the temple of Dagon, their fish-god (1 Sam. 5).

> *The children also of Judah and the children of Jerusalem have ye sold unto the Grecians, that ye might remove them far from their border* (Joel 3:6).

The sons of "Judah" (praise) and "Jerusalem" (Joel 3:1,20) have also been sold out. Again, the secular and religious worlds delight in the love of money. The music business and the mega-churches have lured away and hired the biggest, best and most talented folks for themselves, spoiling the Body of Christ.

> *He brought me up also out of an horrible pit, out of the miry clay...* (see Ps. 40:2 and compare with Ps. 69:2).

> *And I will set a sign among them, and I will send those that escape of them unto the nations, to... Javan, to the isles afar off, that have not heard my fame, neither have seen my glory; and they shall declare my glory among the Gentiles* (Isa. 66:19).

Our seed has been "sold" (Joel 3:3) to the "Grecians." These were "Javanites, or descendants of Javan," which is derived from a word meaning, "dregs, mud, mire" (Gen. 10:4; 1 Chron. 1:5-7; Ezek. 27:13,19).

These "mud and mire" people are "heathen" and mock spiritual things (John 12:20; 1 Cor. 1:22-24). Our youth, the sons of Zion, are bogged down in the lower realms. We will never change filthy minds and habits with worldly methods of "evangelism." If we entertain the heathen to entice them to the altar, we will have to keep them entertained.

The results of this kind of compromise are evident. Our young people have been removed "far" (Joel 2:20) from the "border" (region, territory) of Zion's high calling. Their lives are void of the Word of God and the ways of the Spirit.

> Behold, I will raise them out of the place whither ye have sold them, and will return your recompence upon your own head: (Joel 3:7).

But rejoice! God will turn the captivity of our youth and *vindicate* His purposes for their lives! As He did with Joseph (Gen. 37:20-29), the Lord will "raise" them out of the pits into which they have been "sold" (Joel 3:3,6), and return the "recompence" of every enemy back on their own heads (Joel 3:4).

> Awake, awake; put on thy strength, O (sons and daughters of) Zion... (Isa. 52:1).

The word for "raise" (Joel 3:9,12) in Joel 3:7 means, "to open the eyes; to wake (literally or figuratively); to rouse or stir oneself, to incite."[12] This word occurs about 80 times in the Old Testament. Just as the prophet Elijah raised the widow's son, so the Lord is awakening our sons and daughters, our boys and girls (1 Kings 17:21)! Our God is going to reach into every strange, alien, and worldly place to bring a new generation back to Zion!

> And I will sell your sons and your daughters into the hand of the children of Judah, and they shall sell them to the Sabeans, to a people far off: for the Lord hath spoken it (Joel 3:8).

Our young people are our most prized possession. This verse reveals God's ultimate *vindication!* He is going to "sell" (Joel 3;3,6,7) the sons and daughters of every strange "nation" (Joel 3:2) into the hands of "Judah" (praise). They will become the property of the "Sabeans," who were Shebaites, descendant of "Sheba," which means, "seven, oath." This is the revelation of *covenant!* This idea is "far off" from the world. Sheba was a nation in southern Arabia, now known as Yemen (Job 1:15; Isa. 45:14; Ezek. 23:42).

And the nations of them which are saved shall walk in the light of it (the City): *and the kings of the earth do bring their glory and honour into it* (Rev. 21:24).

The Day of the Lord is a day of reversals (Ps. 126). The children and youth of the world are going to be re-captured in the name of the Lord. They will be turned over to a life of "praise" and become benefactors of the New Covenant. In this mega-harvest of the Feast of Tabernacles, God will deal with every antichrist spirit that the worldly Church has created, and spoil the fruit of all their labors.

The nations of the earth are going to bring their glory and "honour" (money, valuables) into the City of God. The most valuable commodity they have is their children! The kids are coming to Zion!

God's day is the time of His *vindication,* the epoch in which He brings everyone and everything into the *valley* of decision to be judged.

ENDNOTES

1. The Lord will turn back the "captivity" of His people (see Job 42:10; Ps. 14:7; 85:1; 126:4; Jer. 29:14; 33:7,11; Hos. 8:11; Amos 9:14; and Zeph. 3:20).

2. Consider these usages of *shaphat* (see Isa. 43:26; Jer. 2:35; 25:31; 51:36; Ezek. 20:35-36; 38:22).

3. Note these references for this word for "parted" or "divided" (see 1 Kings 16:21; Ps. 5:9; 55:21; Prov. 2:16; 7:5; 29:5; Dan. 11:39; and Hos. 10:2).

4. These verses deal with the casting of "lots" (see Lev. 16:8; Num. 33:54; Josh. 18:10; Ps. 16:5;125:3; Prov. 16:33; 18:18; Dan. 12:13; Obad. 1:11; and Nah. 3:10).

5. These Scriptures mention the "boys," the children (see Gen. 21:8; 25:27; Exod. 1:17; 2:1-9; Ruth 4:16; 2 Sam. 12:18; and Isa. 9:6).

6. Both Testaments mention the "harlot" (see Deut. 23:18; Judg. 2:17; Prov. 6:26; 7:10; Prov. 23:27 [with Matt. 15:14]; 29:3; Isa. 1:21; Jer. 2:20; 3:1-8; Ezek. 16:15-22; and Rev. 17-18).

7. Babylon "sells" souls (Nah. 3:4; compare Gen. 37:27-28; Exod. 21:7-8; Judg. 2:14; 1 Kings 21:20,25; 2 Kings 17:17; Esther 7:4; Isa. 52:3; Ezek. 48:9-14; and Amos 2:6).

8. Babylon's crowd loves to get drunk (see Gen. 9:1; Lev. 10:8-9; Prov 4:17; 23:20,29-31; Isa. 5:11; 28:1,7; and Hos. 9:4).

9. Note these Scriptures that mention "Tyre" (see Josh. 19:29; 2 Sam. 5:11; 1 Kings 5:1-18; 7:13; 9:11-12; Isa. 23:1; Jer. 47:4; Ezek. 26:1-7; 27:1-8; Amos 1:9-10; and Zech. 9:2-3).

10. Note these verses that mention "Zidon" (see Gen. 10:19; Isa. 23:2,4,12; Jer. 47:4; Ezek. 27:8; 28:21-22; and Zech. 9:2).

11. Note these verses on "Palestine" (see Exod. 15:14; 2 Chron. 21:16-17; Ps. 60:8; 83:7; 87:4; 108:9)

12. Consider these verses where this word for "raise" is used (see Judg. 5:12; 2 Chron. 36:22; Ps. 35:23; 57:8; Song 4:16; 5:2; Isa. 42:13; 51:9; 52:1; Hag. 1:4; and Zech. 2:13; 9:13).

CHAPTER FIFTEEN

RESTORATION — ITS VALLEY (JOEL 3:9-15)

Out of widespread desolation, God separated His righteous remnant, the Army of the Lord (Joel 2:2-11). Once His sons judge themselves righteously in the Feast Day of Atonement, they will be qualified to rule and reign with Him. They form the divine instrument that Jehovah will use in the Day of the Lord to mete out His righteous judgments. The previous chapter began to set forth His *vindication* against all those who have come against Zion. Now He commands His servants to assemble the multitudes into the *valley* of decision.

Because He hath appointed (set, fixed) *a day, in the which He will judge the world in righteousness* (with justice) *by that man whom He hath ordained* (marked out, appointed, specified)... (Acts 17:31).

Enoch, the seventh from Adam, prophesied about these men: "See, the Lord is coming with thousands upon thousands of His holy ones

to judge everyone, and to convict all the ungodly of all the ungodly acts they have done in the ungodly way, and of all the harsh words ungodly sinners have spoken against Him" (Jude 1:14-15, NIV).

To him who overcomes and does My will to the end, I will give authority over the nations—

He will rule them with an iron scepter... (Rev. 2:26-27, NIV).

The "Man" who judges the earth is both Head and Body, Jesus and His brethren, "His holy ones." His "saints" have the honor to execute the "judgment written" (Ps. 149:9). The apostle Paul clearly announced that the saints would even "judge angels" (1 Cor. 6:3).

> *But the Lord shall endure for ever: He hath prepared His throne for judgment.*

> *And He shall judge the world in righteousness, He shall minister judgment to the people in uprightness* (Ps. 9:7-8).

The Bible has much to say about this "eternal (perpetual) judgment" (Heb. 6:1-2).[1] The patriarch Noah brought God's judgments to his generation (Heb. 11:7; 2 Pet. 2:5). The prophet Ezekiel told of the Man with the writer's inkhorn and his six friends, who purged the land of everyone except those intercessors marked by the Lord (Ezek. 9). The corporate Manchild Company (Rev. 12:1-5), discussed in depth in Chapter Five, shares the authority of Jesus' throne to judge and rule (shepherd) the nations.

Prepare War

Proclaim ye this among the Gentiles; Prepare war... (Joel 3:9).

The alarm has sounded. Zion's sons have been called to the battle (Num. 10:9). Joel 3:9-15 tells of a "holy" war, a "sanctified" war.[2] The Seventh Day from Adam is the Third Day from Jesus. God has determined to keep His own commandment, to remember the "Sabbath day," and to keep it "holy" (Exod. 20:8). He sets apart this holy war to the finish, not relenting until all have come through the *valley* of decision.

The trumpet is to "proclaim" this sound among the Gentiles. This word was translated as "call" in Joel 1:14; 2:15,32. The "gentiles" of Joel 3:9 are the "nation(s)" of Joel 1:6; 3:2; the "heathen" of Joel 2:17; 3:11-12; and the "people" of Joel 3:8. They include the "nations" discussed in Joel 3:2—the denominations, the imaginations, and the divinations. All these are summoned to the *valley!*

It is time to "prepare" for war (Joel 2:5,7). This word was translated as "sanctify" in Joel 1:14; 2:15-16. We have come out of Egypt and through the wilderness. Now is the time to inherit the land, to cross over, to "prepare" or "sanctify" ourselves to receive His promise (Josh. 3:5). His holy army has been prepared to execute His vengeance.

> *...wake up the mighty men, let all the men of war draw near; let them come up:* (Joel 3:9).

"Wake up" the mighty men. This word is used again in Joel 3:12, and was translated as "raise" in Joel 3:7. This trumpet-blast is a double wake-up call.

I have commanded My sanctified ones, I have also called My mighty ones for Mine anger... (Isa. 13:3).

First, the "mighty men" of Joel 3:9 are the "mighty men" of Joel 2:7, God's Army of mature sons. They are the "strong" ones of Joel 3:10, and the "mighty ones" of Joel 3:11 who will stretch the bow. These warriors of Heaven are coming down to the *valley* to judge the nations!

Second, the "mighty men" can point to the proud, arrogant heroes from every arena of the earth. When God changed the order in Noah's day, He dealt with the "giants" (Gen. 6:4). These were the Nephilim, the fallen ones, bullies and tyrants. These proud warriors of earth are coming down to the *valley* to be judged!

The "men" of war are to "draw near" (approach, present themselves). This different word for "men" is *enosh,* and it means, "mortal, ordinary." This is in direct contrast to *ish* (a notable man of high degree). The Army of Zion is made up of "ordinary men." Yet corporately they are His "mighty and strong one, which [is] as a tempest of hail and a destroying storm...a flood of mighty waters...the overflowing scourge" (Isa. 28:2,15). We described this instrument of judgment in Chapter Three, "One Among a Thousand." God calls for His Host to "come up" (Joel 2:7,9; 3:12).

Beat your plowshares into swords... (Joel 3:10).

The Lord is determined to deal with every denomination, imagination, and divination (Joel 3:2)! Once His holy war is accomplished— the full, complete appropriation of His finished work—the Lord will rule in Zion. This eventual reversal of the order of things (swords back into plowshares, and pruning hooks back into spears) is described by both Isaiah and Micah.

And it shall come to pass in the last days, that the mountain of the Lord's house shall be established in the top of the mountains, and shall be exalted above the hills; and all nations shall flow unto it.

And many people shall go and say, Come ye, and let us go up to the mountain of the Lord, to the house of the God of Jacob; and He will teach us of His ways, and we will walk in His paths: for out of Zion shall go forth the law, and the word of the Lord from Jerusalem.

And He shall judge among the nations, and shall rebuke many people: and they shall beat their swords into plowshares, and their spears into pruninghooks: nation shall not lift up sword against nation, neither shall they learn war any more (see Isa. 2:2-4 and compare with Mic. 4:1-3).

Plowshares beaten into swords, and pruning hooks beaten into spears, are symbols of *war*. The opposite description by Isaiah and Micah describe the time of *peace* in the Feast of Tabernacles.

"Beat" (strike, smite, hammer) every plowshare into a sword. This word is rendered as "beat (down, to pieces), break in pieces, crushed, destroy, discomfit, smite, stamp." It was used to describe the destruction of the golden calf (Deut. 9:21) and the brazen serpent (2 Kings 18:4). God will deal with every idol in the *valley!* There He will "beat down" every foe from before His face (Ps. 89:23).

When I have bent Judah for me, filled the bow with Ephraim, and raised up thy sons, O Zion, against thy sons, O Greece, and made thee as the sword of a mighty man (Zech. 9:13).

The "plowshare" was "a hoe or other digging implement" (the "coulter" of 1 Sam. 13:20-21). The plowshares are to be beaten into "swords." This word (see Joel 2:8) means, "drought; also a cutting instrument (from its destructive effect), as a flint knife, dagger, sword, chisel, or other sharp implement." It is rendered in the King James Version as, "axe, dagger, knife, mattock, sword, tool."[3]

...and your pruninghooks into spears: let the weak say, I am strong (Joel 3:10).

"Pruning hooks" were small knives with curved blades used for pruning grapevines (Isa. 18:5). In this time of war in the *valley*, they are to beaten into "spears" (lances, as thrown; javelins, bucklers).[4]

But He said to me (Paul), "My grace is sufficient for you, for my power is made perfect in weakness." Therefore I will boast all the more gladly about my weaknesses, so that Christ's power may rest on me.

That is why, for Christ's sake, I delight in weaknesses, in insults, in hardships, in persecutions, in difficulties. For when I am weak, then I am strong (2 Cor. 12:9-10, NIV).

Don't be afraid, Zion. God has made you ready for this Day. You were "weak" (frail) in Adam. The root of this Greek word means, "prostrate, disabled; by implication, to overthrow, decay." But now you are "strong" in Christ. Joel's "strong" ones are the same as the "mighty men" (Joel 2:7; 3:9), His "mighty ones" (Joel 3:11). God will empower the weak, like Hannah (1 Sam. 1), who have had no children, to birth a prophetic Manchild Company who will bring the nation back to God (see Isa. 54:1-11).

Assemble yourselves, and come, all ye heathen, and gather yourselves together round about: thither cause thy mighty ones to come down, O Lord (Joel 3:11).

The Lord is going to deal with every worldly hero from every arena of society, the "heavy hitters," the movers and shakers. The season of judgment is accelerating. He continues to invite them all down to the *valley.*

Through His prophet, Jehovah commands them to "assemble" (hasten). All the "heathen," the "nations" of Joel 3:2, are to "come" (Joel 1:13). They are to "gather" (Joel 2:6,16; 3:2) themselves "round about" (in a circuit; from every side) to be judged (Joel 3:12).

Why are all the "nations"—the denominations, imaginations, and the divinations—to be gathered "thither" (there)? Because there in the valley, the Lord's "mighty ones" (Joel 2:7; 3:9-10) are to "come down"! This word means, "to sink, descend; to press or lead down; penetrate; to stretch a bow" (Ps. 18:34; Jer. 21:13). The bow is a symbol for covenant.

He trains my hands for battle; my arms can bend a bow of bronze (Ps. 18:34, NIV).

Behold, I am against thee, O inhabitant of the valley...saith the Lord; which say, Who shall come down against us? or who shall enter into our habitations? (Jer. 21:13).

Joel's army, the corporate Overcomer, the Manchild Company, is like David. They can handle the bronze bow—brass is a symbol for judgment. The "nations" are haughty, as were the "drunkards of Ephraim" (Isa. 28:1). Babylon sits as a defiant "queen" (Jer. 44:15-27;

Rev. 18:7). But the sons of Zion, the "arrows" of the Lord, will bring her down (Ps. 77:17; Jer. 50:14; 51:11; Zech. 9:13-14).

The Valley of Jehoshaphat

Let the heathen be wakened, and come up to the valley of Jehoshaphat: for there will I sit to judge all the heathen round about (Joel 3:12).

These "heathen" are the "nations" of Joel 3:2 and the "gentiles" of Joel 3:9. They are to be "wakened" (Joel 3:7,9) by Zion's alarm. All the great men and women who have walked after the lust of the flesh, the lust of the eyes, and the pride of life (1 John 2:15-17), are now ordered to "come up" or ascend (Joel 3:9) because their stink has "come up" to God's nostrils (Joel 2:20)! All are to come to the *"valley"!*

The "valley of Jehoshaphat" (Joel 3:2) has several applications. The five choices that are made in this "valley of decision" are given below in the exegesis of Joel 3:14.

It is in this valley that the Lord will "sit" (down as judge). This word is translated as "inhabitants" in Joel 1:2,14; 2:1. There He, along with His brethren, will "plead" with all the "heathen," all the "nations" (Joel 3:2) "round about " (Joel 3:11).

Put ye in the sickle, for the harvest is ripe: come, get you down; for the press is full, the fats overflow; for their wickedness is great (Joel 3:13).

But when the fruit is brought forth, immediately he putteth in the sickle (gathering-hook), *because the harvest is come* (Mark 4:29).

"Put in" (send for) the "sickle" (to reap).[5] There is an apostolic sickle in the "valley of decision" (Joel 3:14). The "harvest" or crop (Joel 1:11) is "ripe" (done). There are two harvests in Revelation 14: the harvesting of the "wheat" (Rev. 14:14-16) and the harvesting of the "tares" (see Rev. 14:17-20 and compare with Matt. 13:24-30,37-44).

And the angel thrust in his sickle into the earth, and gathered the vine of the earth, and cast it into the great winepress of the wrath of God.

And the winepress was trodden without the city, and blood came out of the winepress, even unto the horse bridles, by the space of a thousand and six hundred furlongs (see Rev. 14:19-20 and compare with Rev. 19:15).

We are to "get down" (Joel 3:2), for the "press" is full (fulfilled, abundance) and "the fats overflow" (Joel 2:24). The "press" was a winepress or vat for holding and pressing out grapes.[6] The "wickedness" or "evil" (Joel 2:13) of the "nations" (Joel 3:2) is "great" (Joel 2:2,11,13). The harvest of judgment is ripe.

The Valley of Decision

Multitudes, multitudes in the valley of decision: for the day of the Lord is near in the valley of decision (Joel 3:14).

There are innumerable "multitudes" in the "valley of decision." The "Day of the Lord" (Joel 1:15; 2:1,11,31) is "near" or "at hand" (Joel 1:15; 2:1).

The "multitudes" are mentioned twice, for this is a witness or testimony against them. This word means, "a noise, tumult, crowd; also disquietude, wealth; murmur, roar, crowd, abundance, tumult, sound, rush; confusion." Its root means, "to make a loud sound; to be in great, lively commotion or tumult, to rage, war, moan, clamor; growl, to be disquieted, to be moved, to be in an uproar; to be in a stir, to be in a commotion; greatly agitated; to be boisterous, to be turbulent." This is the hum or roar of a great throng.[7]

All the "nations" (Joel 3:2) will be brought to the valley of "decision." This word is *charuwts* (Strong's #2742), and it means, "incised or (active) incisive; hence a trench (as dug), gold (as mined), a threshing-sledge (having sharp teeth); (figuratively) determination; also eager." Its root means, "to point sharply, (literally) to wound; figuratively, to be alert, to decide; to determine." Every denomination, imagination, and divination is to be brought to the threshing floor. All that Jehovah has determined is about to come to pass.

The threshing floor is the place of sifting and separation, the place of judgment. David, the man of Zion, learned to pay the "full price" of doing everything God's way at the threshing floor (2 Sam. 6:6-10; 24:24; 1 Chron. 13:9-13; 21:24)!

And if it seem evil unto you to serve the Lord, choose you this day whom ye will serve... (Josh. 24:15).

And Elijah came unto all the people, and said, How long halt ye between two opinions? if the Lord be God, follow Him: but if Baal, then follow him... (1 Kings 18:21).

There are five "decisions" that all of humankind must make in the "valley of decision." The Valley of Jehoshaphat was connected with:

1. The Mount of Olives (Gethsemane, the "olive-press"). This is the decision to surrender our will to God's will.

2. The Valley of Berachah ("blessing"), where Jehoshaphat and his people gathered to "bless" God for a battle won by praise (2 Chron. 20:20-26). This is the decision to let God fight every battle.

3. The place where the Jews historically buried worn-out rolls of Scripture. This is the decision to honor and reverence the Word of God.

4. King Melchizedeck's Dale (Gen. 14:17) or Valley of Shaveh ("plain of the double, of equalization, resemblance, of adjustment"), as identified by the Jewish historian Josephus. This is the decision to identify with the "more excellent ministry," the king-priest ministry of forgiveness and blessing (Heb. 5:1-8:6).

5. Absalom's monument (2 Sam. 18:18), which was in the same vicinity. This is the decision to honor true spiritual authority.

This "valley of decision" is present as well as future. It centers at the Cross, where Jesus was flanked between two thieves, two decisions. One chose to preserve himself; the other chose to be forgiven and restored to Paradise, the Kingdom.

A quality decision is one that is made but once. With regard to the five applications of the Valley of Jehoshaphat given above, choose you this day to:

1. Surrender your will to the will of God.

2. Praise God in every circumstance.

3. Love and study the Word of God.

4. Forgive everyone for everything.

5. Submit to the King and His Kingdom.

[God] *hath reconciled us to himself by Jesus Christ, and hath given to us the ministry of reconciliation;*

To wit, that God was in Christ, reconciling the world unto Himself, not imputing their trespasses unto them; and hath committed unto us the word of reconciliation.

Now then we are ambassadors for Christ, as though God did beseech you by us: we pray you in Christ's stead, be ye reconciled to God (2 Cor. 5:18-20).

His "royal priesthood" (1 Pet. 2:9), the king-priest ministry out of Zion, presently stands in the earth and "pleads" (Joel 3:2) with men to women to be reconciled to God!

The sun and the moon shall be darkened, and the stars shall withdraw their shining (Joel 3:15).

This present or future Kingdom operation of reconciliation in the "valley of decision" means lights out for the old order (Joel 2:10,31), the abolishing of an old administration, an old mindset, an old way of thinking and living (Luke 21:25; Rev. 8:12).

God's restoration saw its *vindication* in the *valley*. Once this is accomplished, the Lord will dwell in Zion in complete *victory!*

ENDNOTES

1. Jesus and His brethren will judge the earth in righteousness (see Ps. 50:1-6; 98:9; John 5:22-27; 16:11; Rom. 2:16; 3:6; 1 Cor. 4:5; 1 Pet. 2:23; and Rev. 22:12).

2. This is a holy, "sanctified" war (see Gen. 2:3; Exod. 20:8; 28:3; 31:13; Lev. 25:10; 1 Sam. 16:5; 1 Kings 9:3; 1 Chron. 15:12-14; Isa. 13:3; and Jer. 1:5).

3. This word for "sword" is first used in Genesis 3:24 (compare Eph. 6:17; Heb. 4:12; and Rev. 1:16; 2:12,16; 19:15,21).

4. Note these places where "spears" are mentioned (see Num. 25:7; 1 Chron. 12:8,24; 2 Chron. 11:12; 14:8; 25:5; 26:14; Neh. 4:13,16,21; and Jer. 46:4).

5. The "sickle" is mentioned 12 times in the Bible, denoting a governmental or kingdom operation (see Deut. 16:9; 23:25; Jer. 50:16; Joel 3:13; Mark 4:29; and Rev. 14:14-19).

6. Note these verses about the "press" (see Judg. 6:11; Neh. 13:15; Isa. 63:2; Lam. 1:15; compare Num. 18:27,30; Deut. 15:14; and Isa. 5:2).

7. Note these verses about the "multitudes" (see 1 Sam. 4:14,19; 2 Sam. 18:29; Ps. 65:7; Jer. 47:3; Ezek. 26:13; and Amos 5:23).

Chapter Sixteen

Restoration — Its Victory (Joel 3:16-21)

The prophet Joel began His message to Judah and Jerusalem by describing the nationwide *desolation* that had gripped the land (Joel 1:1-20). The only solution for this catastrophe was the complete *consecration* of its priests and people (Joel 2:1-32). Once this commitment to prayer, fasting, and cleansing had been made, Jehovah began His *restoration* of the years (Joel 3:1-21).

This restoration was marked by His *vindication* in the *valley* of decision. The final verses of Joel's prophecy (Joel 3:16-21) reveal the consummation of His purposes, the Lord dwelling in Zion in complete *victory!*

The Feasts of the Lord (Lev. 23; Deut. 16), especially the last three feasts in the seventh month, are outlined in the Book of Joel. Joel 2 opens with the Feast of Trumpets—sound the alarm! It continues with the "fast," the "solemn assembly" of the Feast Day of Atonement (Joel 2:12-17). The consequent Feast of Tabernacles[1] is revealed in Joel 2:18-27 and again here in Joel 3:16-21.

These last five verses of Joel's prophecy also describe the spoils of Zion's "holy war" (Joel 3:9-11). Those who have been called by the Lord's trumpet (Joel 2:1,15) have been ordained to *become* the Lord's trumpet in the earth!

The Lord Shall Roar Out of Zion

The Lord also shall roar out of Zion, and utter his voice from Jerusalem; and the heavens and the earth shall shake: but the

Lord will be the hope of his people, and the strength of the children of Israel (Joel 3:16).

The Lord shall roar from on high, and utter his voice from his holy habitation; he shall mightily roar upon (on behalf of, on account of) *His habitation; He shall give a shout, as they that tread the grapes, against all the inhabitants of the earth* (See Jer. 25:30 and compare with Hos. 1:10; Amos 1:2; 3:4-8).

The Lord shall "roar" (rumble, moan) out of Zion, the Most Holy Place, and "utter" (give) His "voice" (sound, noise) from "Jerusalem" (Joel 2:32; 3:1,6, 20). The word for "roar" is used of a lion, a conqueror, and Jehovah (Yahweh) Himself; it also denotes a cry of distress. Jesus is the Lion King of the tribe of Judah (Rev. 5:5) whose "testimony" (witness) is the "spirit of prophecy" (Rev. 19:10). The corporate Overcomer, those apprehended for the "high calling" (Phil. 3:12-14), make up the Lion Company who prophesy out of Zion!

This roar shall cause the "heavens and the earth to shake" (Joel 2:10,30). But the Lord shall be the "hope" of his "people" (Joel 3:2-3). This word means, "a refuge or a shelter (from rain or storm, from danger)." Its root means, "to flee for protection; figuratively, to confide in, to put trust in."[2]

And there shall be a tabernacle (in Zion) *for a shadow in the daytime from the heat, and for a place of refuge, and for a covert from storm and from rain* (see Isa. 4:6 and compare with Ps. 46:1; Isa. 25:4; Jer. 17:17).

The Lord shall be the "strength" of the "children" (sons) of "Israel" (Joel 2:27; 3:2; Gen. 32:24-32). His "strength" is "a fortified place; figuratively, a defence; a place or means of safety, a protection, a refuge, a stronghold; fastness, a harbor." Its root means, "to be stout; to be strong; to prevail, to make firm, to strengthen."[3] We live in an unshakeable Kingdom. The Seed is safe. The end is secure.

The Lord is good, a strong hold in the day of trouble; and He knoweth them that trust in Him (see Nah. 1:7 and compare with Ps. 48:1-2; Neh. 8:10; Col. 1:27).

The Lord himself is like the fortress (rock) of Zion. He is the hope, the glory, and the strength of His people!

God Comes To Dwell With Man

So shall ye know that I am the Lord your God dwelling in Zion,
My holy mountain... (Joel 3:17).

The simple meaning of the Feast of Tabernacles is that God tabernacles Himself in a people—His "dwelling" is in Zion! This principle of incarnation flows throughout the Bible—God comes to dwell with man! This truth has two primary dynamics:

First, God goes "from tent to tent and from one tabernacle to another," as revealed to David (1 Chron. 17:5; Ps. 84:7; Rom. 1:17; 2 Cor. 3:18). God is always on the move; the Scriptures speak of His "goings" (Ps. 68:24; Ezek. 43:11; Mic. 5:2). He moves especially as wind on water (Gen. 1:2), or as the Spirit on the Word.

Second, as God moves "from tent to tent," the glory of each proceeding House increases—"the glory of this latter House shall be greater than of the former" (Hag. 2:9). The second of these principles is revealed in the following Old Testament examples (note the historical progression):

1. God dwelled in the Garden of Eden with Adam and Eve, walking in the "cool" (*ruach* or "spirit") of the day (Gen. 3:8).

2. God walked with the patriarchs, with Noah (Gen. 6:9), Abraham (Gen. 17:1; 18:1), Isaac (Gen. 26:24), and Jacob (Gen. 35:1).

3. God dwelled in the Tabernacle of Moses (Exod. 40:33-34).

4. God dwelled in the Tabernacle of David (see 2 Sam. 6;17; 1 Chron. 16:1-4,27,39; 17:1-6; Amos 9:11-12; Acts 15:15-18).

5. God dwelled in the Temple of Solomon (1 Kings 8:10-13; 2 Chron. 5).

6. God dwelled in the post-exilic Temple of Zerubbabel (Ezra 6:15; Hag. 2:9).

7. God dwelled in Herod's Temple until Jesus (the glory of it) departed from it (Matt. 23:37-24:2 with 1 Sam. 4:15-22).

This pattern of God moving from house to house with ever-increasing glory continues in the New Testament:

1. God dwelled in Jesus Christ, who then "dwelt" or "tabernacled" among us as the Pattern Son, the "House" for the Father

(John 1:14; 14:2; 2 Cor. 5:18-19; Col. 1:19; 2:9). He is Emmanuel—"God with us" (Isa. 7:14; 8:8; Matt. 1:23), the Incarnate Word.

2. God dwells in the Church, the Body of Christ, the real Temple and eternal building or habitation of the Spirit (1 Cor. 3:9-16; 2 Cor. 6:16; Eph. 2:21). The Church is His ongoing incarnation! We are His *naos*, His "inner sanctuary."

3. God will dwell in the completed and glorified House of the Lord (Ezek. 40-48; Rev. 21-22). This finalizes the cycle, returning to Eden (Joel 2:3), to "paradise" (Luke 23:43; 2 Cor. 12:4; Rev. 2:7).

God's permanent "dwelling" is in Zion (Ps. 132:13-14; Joel 3:16-21)!

The principle is clear. Throughout the Scriptures, God comes to dwell "with" man, "among" man, and "in" man. The Bible does not emphasize the going of the Church, but the "coming" of the Lord. It does not teach about the disappearance of the Church, but the "appearing" of the Lord (see 1 Tim. 6:14; 2 Tim. 1:10; 4:1,8; Titus 2:13; 1 Pet. 1:7)!

> *Behold, the tabernacle of God is with men, and He will dwell with them, and they shall be His people, and God Himself shall be with them, and be their God* (Rev. 21:3).

The Lord Dwells in Zion

So shall ye know that I am the Lord your God dwelling in Zion, My holy mountain... (Joel 3:17).

The father has always wanted a family for Himself, a Bride for His Son, and a Temple for His Spirit.

This verse pictures the Lord permanently abiding in His people, individually and corporately. The consummate *victory* of Joel 3:16-21 is that God lives in the people whom His love has conquered! His resting place is Zion in the Feast of Tabernacles. His overcoming people will have fully entered the Sabbath rest of the Lord. At that point, there is no more mixture, for every strange "nation" (Joel 3:2) has been dealt with in the "valley of decision" (Joel 3:14).

We shall "know" (ascertain by seeing) that the Lord God has His "dwelling" in Zion, His "holy mountain" (Joel 2:1).

And let them make Me a sanctuary (Moses' Tabernacle); *that I may dwell among them* (Exod. 25:8).

For thus saith the high and lofty One that inhabiteth eternity, whose name is Holy; I dwell in the high and holy place (of Zion), *with him also that is of a contrite and humble spirit...* (Isa. 57:15).

...I am returned unto Zion, and will dwell in the midst of Jerusalem: and Jerusalem shall be called a city of truth... (Zech. 8:3).

The word for "dwelling" in Joel 3:17 is *shakan* (Strong's #7931), and it means, "lodging; to reside or permanently stay to settle down, to abide, to dwell, to tabernacle, to reside; to make settle down, to establish; to lay, to place, to set, to fix." Its root means, "to lie down (for rest, sexual connection, lodging, decease, or any other purpose)." *Shakan* is a word from nomadic life, meaning "to live in a tent." The high class citizens of Zion live in a tent![4]

Again, one of the major paradigms of both Testaments is that God comes to "dwell" with man. Jesus came to "dwell in a tent." *The Septuagint* version of the Old Testament translates the Hebrew word *shakan* with two Greek words: *katoikeo* and *skenoo*.

Howbeit the most High dwelleth not in temples made with hands... (See Acts 7:48 and compare with Acts 17:24).

That Christ may dwell in your hearts by faith; that ye, being rooted and grounded in love, (Eph. 3:17).

For in Him (Jesus) *dwelleth all the fulness of the Godhead bodily* (Col. 2:9 and compare with Col. 1:19).

First, *katoikeo* is used far more often than any other. This word (Strong's #2730) means, "to house permanently, reside (literally or figuratively); to dwell fixedly, to settle; to inhabit." It is a compound of *kata* (down) and *oikeo* (to occupy a house, reside, inhabit, remain); "by implication to cohabit."[5]

And the Word (Jesus) *was made flesh, and dwelt* (in a tent) *among us...* (John 1:14).

Therefore are they before the throne of God, and serve Him day and night in His temple: and He that sitteth on the throne shall dwell among them (See Rev. 7:15 and compare with Rev. 12:12; 13:6).

Second, the more direct translation of *shakan* is *skenoo* (Strong's #4637), and it means, "to live in a tent, to tent or encamp, (figuratively) to occupy (as a mansion) or (specifically) to reside (as God did in the Tabernacle of old; a symbol of protection and communion); to fix one's tabernacle, to abide (or live) in a tabernacle (or tent), tabernacle or dwell."

Skenoo is derived from *skenos* (a hut or temporary residence; figuratively the human body as the abode of the spirit); and from *skene* (a tent, a tabernacle made of green boughs, or skins or other materials; habitation); and from *skeous* (a vessel, implement, equipment or apparatus; specifically, a wife as contributing to the usefulness of the husband)." We are the Bride of Christ.

All these Hebrew and Greek words convey the richness of what it means for God to "dwell" in and among His people.

...then shall Jerusalem be holy, and there shall no strangers pass through her any more (Joel 3:17).

"Then" (after the "holy war" of Joel 3:9-11) shall "Jerusalem" (Joel 2:32; 3:1,6,16) be "holy" (sanctified, set apart).

We are confounded, because we have heard reproach: shame hath covered our faces: for strangers are come into the sanctuaries of the Lord's house (see Jer. 51:51 and compare with Lam. 5:2).

Then shall no "strangers" pass "through" (over, by) here "any more" (again). This word means, "a foreigner; strange, profane; specifically, to commit adultery; to be strange, to become estranged; an enemy, another; loathsome (used of breath); a strange woman, a prostitute, a harlot."[6] Every whorish tradition has been judged.

Awake, awake; put on thy strength, O Zion; put on thy beautiful garments, O Jerusalem, the HOLY city: for henceforth there shall no more come into thee the uncircumcised and the unclean (see Isa. 52:1 and compare with 2 Cor.6:14-7:1;10:3-5; Eph. 2:12,19).

There are no strange churches, no strange preachers, no strange worship, no strange thoughts, or no strange gods in Zion! The "strange woman" of the Book of Proverbs, the soul realm, has been transformed into the "virtuous woman" (Prov. 31:10-31). Every strange "nation"— every denomination, every imagination, and every divination (Joel 3:2)—was taken captive in the "holy war" (Joel 3:9-11) and confronted in the "valley of decision" (Joel 3:14).

The Blessings Flow From Zion

And it shall come to pass in that day, that the mountains shall drop down new wine... (Joel 3:18).

This entire verse sets forth an incredibly vivid description of *real* revival, restoration, and reformation! This takes place in "that day," the "day of the Lord" (Joel 1:15; 2:1,11,31; 3:14). The new wine is flowing again.

Son of man, set thy face toward the south, and drop thy word toward the south, and prophesy... (Ezek. 20:46).

...the plowman shall overtake the reaper, and the treader of grapes him that soweth seed; and the mountains shall drop sweet wine... (Amos 9:13).

The "mountains" (Joel 2:2,5) shall "drop down" the "new wine" (Joel 1:5,10). The word for "drop down" means, "to ooze, distil gradually; by implication, to fall in drops; figuratively, to speak by inspiration; to drip, to distill, to prophesy, to preach, to discourse."[7] The mountains shall prophesy! There shall be a fresh outpouring of His joy, for there shall be a fresh Word from the Lord!

...and the hills shall flow with milk... (Joel 3:18).

Therefore they shall come and sing in the height of Zion, and shall flow together to the goodness of the Lord, for wheat, and for wine, and for oil, and for the young of the flock and of the herd: and their soul shall be as a watered garden; and they shall not sorrow any more at all (Jer. 31:12).

In that Day, all the "hills" shall "flow"[8] (carry, walk, go) with "milk." The root word for "hills" means, "convex; a goblet; by analogy, the calyx of a flower; a cup or bowl."[9] This word is used in reference to Joseph's cup (Gen. 44), and the ornamental bowls on the Golden Candlestick in Moses' Tabernacle (Exod. 25:31-34).

Thou shalt also suck the milk of the Gentiles (nations), and shalt suck the breast of kings: and thou shalt know that I the Lord am thy Saviour and thy Redeemer... (Isa. 60:16).

As newborn babes, desire the sincere (undeceitful, unadulterated, guileless, unmixed, pure; with honest intent) *milk of the word, that ye may grow thereby* (see 1 Pet. 2:2 and compare with 1 Cor. 3:2; 9:7; Heb. 5:12-13).

The "milk" in Joel 3:18 is "milk (as the richness of kine); sour milk, cheese; the abundance of the land (metaphorical); white (as milk)." The root means, "to be fat; fat, hence, the richest, choice, best part." This is also rendered as "marrow" (Job 21:24; Ps. 63:5; Prov. 3:8; Isa. 25:6). The Promised Land of Canaan flowed with milk and honey (Exod. 3:8; Deut. 11:9; Song 4:11; 5:1,12).

This abundance of "milk" in the Day of the Lord speaks of all the new believers who will receive Jesus as Savior and Redeemer. This reveals the harvest principle and "flow" of Kingdom evangelism!

...and all the rivers of Judah shall flow with waters... (Joel 3:18).

For the earth shall be filled with the knowledge of the glory of the Lord, as the waters cover the sea (Hab. 2:14).

And it shall be in that day, that living waters shall go out from Jerusalem... (see Zech. 14:8 and compare with Song 4:15; John 4:10-14).

In that Day all the "rivers" (Joel 1:20) of "Judah" (praise) shall "flow" (same word as above) with "waters." This word means, "dual of a primitive noun (but used in a singular sense); water; figuratively, juice; by euphemism, urine, semen."[10] These are waters of *life.*

These "rivers" reveal the pure flow, the moving of God's Word and Spirit. The *prophetic river* is from the belly (John 7:38). The *priestly river* is from the sanctuary (Ezek. 47:1-2), and the *kingly river* is from the throne (Rev. 22:1).

...and a fountain shall come forth of the house of the Lord, and shall water the valley of Shittim (Joel 3:18).

In that day there shall be a fountain[11] opened to the house of David and to the inhabitants of Jerusalem for sin and for uncleanness (Zech. 13:1).

And He said unto me, It is done. I am Alpha and Omega, the beginning and the end. I will give unto him that is athirst of the fountain of the water of life freely (Rev. 21:6).

In that Day, the "fountain" opened at Calvary's Cross shall "come forth of" (go out of, exit) the corporate "House" (dwelling, habitation) of the Lord. This "fountain" is "a spring"; fountain, well (also collectively), figuratively, a source (of satisfaction)." The Hebrew word translated as "eye" also means, "a fountain, as the eye of the landscape."[12]

Jesus Christ is the open Fountain. When He was pierced, there flowed forth blood and water (John 19:34). His blood will cleanse us from all sin (1 John 1:7)! The full effect of His finished work will be manifested in Zion, and then flow out of Zion to the ends of the earth.

He clave the rocks in the wilderness, and gave them drink as out of the great depths (see Ps. 78:15 and compare with Ps. 36:8).

Jesus is the Rock that was smitten (Exod. 17:6; 1 Cor. 10:4). This "fountain" flowing from the House of God will "water" the Valley of Shittim. This word means, "to quaff, (causatively) to irrigate or furnish a potion to; to give to drink, to irrigate, to drink, to water, to cause to drink water (Gen. 2:6,10; 2 Sam. 23:15; 24:25-46).

This living water is going to bring new life to the "valley" (Joel 3:2,12) of "Shittim." This word is *Shittiym* (Strong's #7851), and it means, "acacia wood (used in plural form); the acacia (from its scourging thorns)." Its Hebrew root means "to pierce, to flog or scourge; a goad." Jesus was beaten (Matt. 20:19; 26:67) before He was "pierced" by the thorns and nails at Calvary's bloody hill.

The "valley of Shittim," known for being dry and barren, was a valley (Josh. 2:1; 3:1) which lay a great way off from Jerusalem, between Moab and Israel on the east side of Jordan. This *restoration* shall reach far into the most remote regions of the hearts of men, and unto the "uttermost part" (Ps. 2:8; Acts 1:8) of every nation! Even Moab, the place where people run to when they don't want to change (Jer. 48:11-12), will hear the voice of the Lord, His trumpet from Zion (Ruth. 1:6)!

God is going down to the "gates of hell" (Matt. 16:18), to the "valley of Shittim," to get new building material to finish His House!

The Brazen Altar, the basis for the entire Old Testament system of worship, was made of "shittim" wood, the same wood used in making the Ark of the Covenant, the Table of Shewbread, the Altar of Incense, and boards and the pillars. It took more than one shittah tree to make each of these, revealing the *corporate* nature of the "shittim" in the Mosaic furniture! The living blood and water from His fountain is going to resurrect the corporate anointing!

Wood speaks of humanity. The "shittim wood" is also rendered as "incorruptible wood" in *The Septuagint,* speaking of our King's sinless and deathless humanity (Heb. 2:14; 4:15; 7:26-27). Jesus is the "incorruptible Word" (1 Pet. 1:23). His life is the only perfect life lived on earth. Zion, His mature glorious Church, is a "shittim" wood, a corporate Wood. His crucified ones are a new recreated humanity in Christ.

The World and the Flesh

Egypt shall be a desolation, and Edom shall be a desolate wilderness, for the violence against the children of Judah, because they have shed innocent blood in their land (Joel 3:19).

This verse, in direct contrast to the previous one (compare the different destinies for the wheat and the tares of Matt. 13:24-30), describes how God will deal with the world (Egypt) and the flesh (Edom).

In that Day, "Egypt" shall be a "desolation" (Joel 2:3,20). Egypt is the country in the northeast corner of Africa where the Israelites spent 430 years in servitude. "Egypt" is from the Hebrew *Mitsrayim* (Strong's #4714); compare with *matsowr* (a limit; something hemming in; a mound of besiegers, a siege; distress). Its root *tsuwr* means, "to cramp, confine."

"Egypt" represents the *world* with its bondage to sin.[13] Pharoah, the king and god of Egypt, is a picture of satan, the "prince" and "god" of this world, this transient cosmos (John 12:31; 2 Cor. 4:4).

Moreover, "Edom" shall be a desolate "wilderness" (Joel 1:19-20; 2:3,22). Edom was the name given to Esau after he forfeited the birthright to his brother Jacob. It also was the name of the land inhabited by the descendants of Edom, or Esau. Other Bible designations for Edom are Mount Seir or Idumea. "Edom" is transliterated from the Hebrew *'Edom* (Strong's #123), which means "red; Edom, the elder twin-brother of Jacob; hence the region (Idumea) occupied by him." Its root *'adam* means, "to show blood (in the face), flush or turn rosy."

"Edom" represents the flesh[14] —"Edom" is Adam!

...for the violence against the children of Judah, because they have shed innocent blood in their land (Joel 3:19).

The earth also was corrupt before God, and the earth was filled with violence (in the days before the Flood) (Gen. 6:11).

Violence shall no more be heard in thy land, wasting nor destruction within thy borders; but thou shalt call thy walls Salvation, and thy gates Praise (Isa. 60:18).

Why is it that Egypt and Edom shall become desolate? Because of the "violence" done against the sons of "Judah" (Joel 3:1,6,8,18,20). This word means, "violence; by implication, wrong; unjust gain: cruelty, injustice; maliciousness." It denotes the disruption of the divinely established order of things.[15]

Yea, they sacrificed their sons and their daughters unto devils,

And shed innocent blood, even the blood of their sons and of their daughters, whom they sacrificed unto the idols of Canaan: and the land was polluted with blood (Ps. 106:37-38).

Egypt and Edom have also "shed" (poured out, as in Joel 2:28-29) "innocent" blood. This word means, "innocent; clean, free from, exempt, clear, innocent; free from guilt, from punishment, from obligations; guiltless."[16]

Men and women have sacrificed their children to the ways of the world and the lust of the flesh. The evils of secular humanism in our school systems, domestic or ecclesiastical child abuse, the vile practice of child pornography, and America's national evil of abortion are all examples of shedding "innocent blood." There will be none of these things when Zion rules the earth. Everything that can be shaken or moved will be shaken and removed! All that remains is His unshakeable Kingdom—in Zion (Heb. 12:25-29)!

I Will Cleanse Their Blood

But Judah shall dwell for ever, and Jerusalem from generation to generation (Joel 3:20).

The "Judah" (praise) Company (Joel 3:1,6,8,18,19), the righteous remnant of Zion, are those who have attained the "high calling" (Phil. 3:14). The corporate Overcomer rules and reigns with her Husband and High Priest after the order of Melchisedec, King of Salem or Jerusalem (Gen. 14:18-20; Heb. 5:1-8:6).

The Lord hath sworn, and will not repent, Thou art a priest for ever after the order of Melchizedek (Ps. 110:4).

Who (the Lord Jesus) *is made, not after the law of a carnal commandment, but after the power of an endless life* (Heb. 7:16).

And hast made us unto our God kings and priests: and we shall reign on the earth (See Rev. 5:10 and compare with Rev. 1:6).

His is an everlasting, unending Priesthood! The "royal priest-hood" (1 Pet. 2:9) of "kings and priests" shall "dwell" with Him forever. This word is rendered earlier as "inhabitants" (Joel 1:2, 14; 2:1) and as "sit" (as a judge) in Joel 3:12. It means, "to sit down (specifically as judge; by implication, to dwell, to remain; causatively, to settle, to marry; to dwell, to remain, to abide, to stay."

This "more excellent ministry" (Heb. 8:6) is "from generation to generation." This word means, "a revolution of time, a period, an age or generation; also a dwelling or a habitation." Its root means, "to gyrate (move in a circle), to remain."

The transitory world and the weakness of the flesh, represented by Egypt and Edom in the previous verse, stand in stark contrast to the ministry described here. Thus we see the passing and the permanent, the temporal and the eternal (2 Cor. 4:17-18).

For I will cleanse their blood that I have not cleansed... (Joel 3:21).

For the life (nephesh) *of the flesh is in the blood...* (Lev. 17:11).

In the consummated purpose of Zion, the high calling, God will "cleanse" the Overcomer's blood! This is the root word for "innocent blood" in Joel 3:19, and means, "to be clean or pure; purged."

This final verse of Joel's prophecy rehearses the Kingdom truth about life and immortality. This New Covenant reality was emphasized in Chapter Three of this writing, "One Among a Thousand." Remember, Zion was the final stronghold for David to conquer, and the "last enemy" is death (1 Cor. 15:26)!

The cleansing of the blood has to do with *shared blood.* While blood is considered a symbol for life, it would be better said that blood is a symbol of death, or *life that is poured out!*

The Hebrew word for "life" in Leviticus 17:11 is *nephesh.* Its Greek counterpart is *psuche.* Both words reference the "soul," which is our intellect, our emotions, and our will; this is what we think, what we feel, and what we want or desire (1 Thess. 5:23; Heb. 4:12).

All this lower "life" must be laid down in order to receive the higher life, or the *zoe* life of God (Rom. 5:10). The blood of Adam gives way to the "blood of Christ" (see 1 Cor. 10:16; Eph. 2:13; Heb. 8:14; 1 Pet. 1:19)! The blood or the life of God flows from His "new heart" from within us (Ezek. 18:31; 36:26). We first received this "new heart" in regeneration, the new birth (John 3:7).

There will be a generation of people who will put on life and immortality. God is going to "cleanse [the] blood" of His people. Adam's only real problem is that he has bad blood! But a new creation will be given clean blood. Everything about them—their mind, heart, attitude, will, desire, pleasure, and contentment—will "become new" (2 Cor. 5:17)!

The truth about the blood is greater than we have ever imagined. The "new heart" of the "new man" (Eph. 2:15; 4:24; Col. 3:10) is pumping His new life through us, cleansing us. One day, it is going to break through our skin (Acts 5:15)! Christ *in* you (Col. 1:27) is going to become Christ *on* you! There will be a generation who will break their appointment with the last enemy by His blood! The sons of Zion will be loosed from their appointment with death (Ps. 102:18-21; John 11:25-26; Rom. 2:7).

> *But is now made manifest by the appearing of our Saviour Jesus Christ, who hath abolished death, and hath brought life and immortality to light through the gospel:* (2 Tim. 1:10).

> *And as it is appointed unto men once to die, but after this the judgment* (Heb. 9:27).

This message of life was brought to light through the gospel. *Jesus met the appointment,* tasting death for every man (Heb. 2:9)!

As noted before, we shall be changed "in a moment" (1 Cor. 15:51-57). This is the Greek construction *en atomos.* We shall be changed in the atoms. This shall happen "at" (in, during) the last trump. The last trump is the seventh trump, the clear message of perfection (maturity) being sounded by His prophets. The sting of death is sin, and the strength of sin is the law. No law, no sin. No sin, no death.

Spiritual life is not ethereal and outside of us, or something that we must work hard to obtain. Spiritual life is *within* us, just as blood is in every living thing (John 6:53-57). Again, this is the principle of overcoming in this *shared blood* of His life.

Consider the principle of battle. There are five distinct types of white blood cells. Lyphocytes are white blood cells that preserve the chemical memory of dangerous invaders, all the while "checking in" at their assigned lymph gland every few minutes. These master cells safeguard the chemical aspects that remind the body how to respond to any invader previously encountered (John 16:33; Rev. 12:11). Therefore, a protected person has wise blood!

> *Forasmuch then as the children are partakers of flesh and blood, he also himself likewise took part of the same; that through death he might destroy him that had the power of death, that is, the devil;*
>
> *And deliver them who through fear of death were all their lifetime subject to bondage* (see Heb. 2:14-15 and compare with Heb. 2:10; 4:15).

A serum can be made from the blood. A sickness or disease (such as measles) could be overcome, not by one's own resistance or vitality, but as a result of a battle (like the death of Jesus on the Cross) that had taken place previously within someone else (John 19:30; Col. 2:14; 1 John 3:8)!

Jesus *is* life (John 11:25; Rev. 1:18). The Lord's Supper sums up all three tenses of His once-for-all victory—the Life that *was*, the One who died for us; the Life that *is*, the One who lives in us; and the Life that *will be*, the One who will swallow up every memory of death!

> *And in this mountain* (Zion) *shall the Lord of hosts make unto all people a feast of fat things* (the feast of Tabernacles in fullness)...
>
> *And He will destroy in this mountain the face of the covering cast over all people, and the vail that is spread over all nations.*
>
> *He will swallow up death in victory; and the Lord God will wipe away tears from off all faces; and the rebuke of his people shall he take away from off all the earth: for the Lord hath spoken it* (Isa. 25:6-8).

No other New Testament concept expresses the truth of "Christ in you" (Col. 1:27) better than the blood, His life in you!

> *Be not overcome of evil, but overcome evil with good* (Rom. 12:21).

God responds to evil not by obliterating it, but by making evil itself serve a higher good. God overcomes evil by absorbing it. Death is swallowed up by life. Jesus took death upon Himself and in Himself, forgave it, and then removed it. By His blood Jesus took away sin (John 1:29; Rev. 1:5) and destroyed him who had the power of it. Now His blood within us is at work to fulfill His victory within a people, to bring us into life and immortality! He will "cleanse" our blood!

The Lord Dwells in Zion

...for the Lord dwelleth in Zion (Joel 3:21).

For the Lord hath chosen Zion; He hath desired it (to wish for, to wait longingly, to crave food and drink) *for His habitation. This is My rest for ever: here will I dwell; for I have desired it* (Ps. 132:13-14).

This is My permanent home where I shall live, You said, "for I have always wanted it this way." (Ps. 132:14, TLB).

Joel's prophecy is ended. The "nations"—every denomination, every imagination, every divination—have been judged (Joel 3:2). The Feast of Tabernacles has come. The Lord "dwelleth" (Joel 3:17) in Zion! This is the full meaning of the "high calling" (Phil. 3:14), the destiny of the corporate Overcomer! The Lord now tabernacles Himself in His permanent House of living stones (1 Pet. 2:5). Mount Zion is His resting place of deliverance and holiness (Obad. 1:17).

And saviours shall come up on mount Zion to judge the mount of Esau; and the kingdom shall be the Lord's (See Obad. 1:21 and compare with Isa. 60:20-22; Zech. 14:7).

And the name of the city from that day shall be, the Lord is there (Jehovah-Shammah). (Ezek. 48:35).

And the gates of it shall not be shut at all by day: for there shall be no night there (See Rev. 21:25 and compare with 1 John 1:5).

Joel is the prophet of "the Day of the Lord" (Joel 1:15; 2:1-2,11,31; 3:14). The Day of the Lord comes in fullness when the night is over! The *vindication* in the *valley* has dealt with every strange "nation" (Joel 3:2). In the fullness of that Day, once the night is over and gone, we shall see three glorious things fill the earth.

But ye are a chosen generation, a royal priesthood, an holy nation, a peculiar people; that ye should shew forth the praises of Him who hath called you out of darkness into His marvellous light: (1 Pet. 2:9).

First, there shall be *one Church*, His "holy nation."

And I looked, and, lo, a Lamb stood on the mount Sion, and with Him an hundred forty and four thousand, having His Father's name written in their foreheads (Rev. 14:1).

Second, there shall be *one mind,* His mind (1 Cor. 2:16; Phil. 2:5).

There is one body, and one Spirit, even as ye are called in one hope of your calling;

One Lord, one faith, one baptism,

One God and Father of all, who is above all, and through all, and in you all (Eph. 4:4-6).

Finally, there shall be *one God,* the Lord Jesus Christ, the righteous King of Zion!

No longer will there be any curse. The throne of God and of the Lamb will be in the city (of Zion), *and His servants will serve Him* (in Zion).

They will see His face, and His name will be on their foreheads.

There will be no more night. They will not need the light of a lamp or the light of the sun, for the Lord God will give them light. And they will reign for ever and ever (in Zion) (Rev. 22:3-5, NIV).

ENDNOTES

1. These are the key Scriptures for the Feast of Tabernacles (see Exod. 23:14-16; 34:22-24; Lev. 23:16,33-44; Num. 29:12-40 (the various offerings); Deut. 16:13-17; Deut. 31:10; 1 Kings 8:1-11; 2 Chron. 7:8-11; 8:12-13; Ezra 3:4; Neh. 8:9-18; Ps. 81:1-3; Hos. 12:9; Zech. 14:16-19; and John 7:1-14,37-39).

2. God is the "hope" of His people (see Ps. 14:6; 61:3; 62:7; 62:8; 71:7; 73:28; 91:2,9; 94:22; 104:18; 142:5; and Prov. 14:26).

3. The Lord is the "strength" of the sons of Israel (see Judg. 6:26; Ps. 27:1; 28:8; 31:2,4; 37:39; 43:2; 52:7; 60:7; 108:8; and Prov. 10:29).

4. Compare these verses for God's "dwelling" (see Exod. 24:16; 40:35; Num. 9:17-18; Deut. 12:11; 1 Kings 6:13; 8:12; Neh. 1:9; Ps. 15;1; Isa. 8:18; Ezek. 43:7; and Zech. 2;10-11; 8:8).

5. Note this uses of *katoikeo* (see Matt. 12:45; Luke 11:26; Heb. 11:9; James 4:5; 2 Pet. 3:13; and Rev. 17:2,8).

6. There will be no more "strangers" or "strange" gods in Zion (see Exod. 30:33; Lev. 10:1; Deut. 32:16; Ps. 44:20; 58:3; 81:9; Prov. 7:5; Ezek. 14:5; and Hos. 5:7; 7:9).

7. Note these usages of the word for "drop down" (see Judg. 5:4; Job 29:22; Ps. 68:8; Prov. 5:3; Song 4:11; 5:5,13; Ezek. 20:46; 21:2; Amos 7:16; and Mic. 2:6,11).

8. Note the things that "flow" (see Ps. 147:18; Song 4:16; Isa. 2:2; 48:21; 60:5; 64:1; Jer. 31:12; 51:44; and Mic. 4:1).

9. Note what the Bible says about the "hills" (see Gen. 49:26; Exod. 17:9-10; Ps. 65:12; 72:3; 114:4; Isa. 40:12; 41:15; 55:12; and Mic. 4:1).

10. These Scriptures tell about the "waters" (see Ps. 18:11; 23:2; 29:3; 77:19; 78:16,20; 105:41; 114:8; 147:18; 148:4; Isa. 43:20; 55:1; 58:11; and Ezek. 43:2).

11. This different Hebrew word for "fountain" is used in these Scriptures (see Ps. 36:9; 68:26; Prov. 10:11; 13:14; 14:27; 16:22; 18:4; and Jer. 2:13; 9:1; 17:13).

12. Note these verses about the "fountain" (see Gen. 7:11; Deut. 33:28; 2 Kings 3:19; Ps. 84:6; 87:7; 104:10; 114:8; Prov. 15:6; and Isa. 12:3; 41:18).

13. Egypt represents the world (see Gen. 10:6, 13; 37-50; Exod. 1-12; John 1:29; 1 Chron. 1:8, 11; 1 Cor. 5:5-8; Eph. 2:1-3; and 1 John 2:15-17).

14. Edom represents the flesh (see Gen. 25:29-34; 32:3; 36:1-43; 1 Chron. 1:34-54; Obad. 1:1-21; Rom. 8:1-6; and Gal. 5:13-24).

15. Note these verses that mention "violence" (see 2 Sam. 22:49; Ps. 11:5; 27:12; 140:4; Prov. 3:31; 16:29; Jer. 6:7; 7:23; Amos 3:10; Obad. 1:10; Mic. 6:12; Hab. 1:2-3; and Mal. 2:16).

16. Egypt and Edom shed "innocent blood" (see Exod. 23:7; 1 Sam. 19:25; 2 Kings 24:4; Ps. 10:8; 24:4; Prov. 1:11; 6:17; and Isa. 59:7).

CHAPTER SEVENTEEN

EPILOGUE

Blow the trumpet in Zion; sound the alarm on my holy hill. Let all who live in the land tremble, for the day of the Lord is coming. It is close at hand (Joel 2:1, NIV).

These are awesome, incredible days! God is about to do something so big that He is the only One who has the faith for it. His eyes are running to and fro throughout the earth to find a man or a woman who will do it with Him (2 Chron. 16:9).

Trumpets are blowing and the alarm is sounding throughout every nation. The Word of the Lord through His servants the prophets beckons us to come to the Feast. The Army of God is mustering. The horses can smell the fight that is coming between the sons of Zion and the corporate son of hell.

The Burden of the Lord

What is the burden of the Lord? (Jer. 23:33).

"What is the Lord's answer?" or "What has the Lord spoken?" (Jer. 23:35, NIV).

The "burden" of the Lord is the weight of what He has spoken. This word figuratively means, "an utterance or an oracle." It is also translated as "prophecy" (Prov. 30:1).

The "burden" of my message to you is simple and singular: the Church must repent of all mixture, and return to the Christ-centered paradigm and purity of the gospel of the Kingdom as revealed in the Scriptures by the Spirit!

This is a new Day in God. God's voice has awakened us to realize that the Seventh Day from Adam and the Third Day from Jesus has dawned. The "Day of the Lord," one of the prominent themes of the Book of Joel, is not near—it is here!

I press toward the mark for the prize of the high (upward) *calling of God in Christ Jesus* (Phil. 3:14).

There *is* a "high calling," as introduced in Chapter One! The Feast of Trumpets is calling us to consecrate ourselves in the Feast Day of Atonement. Once we have been cleansed, complete restoration and reformation will soon follow in the Feast of Tabernacles.

Awake, O Zion

Awake, awake, O Zion, clothe yourself with strength. Put on your garments of splendor, O Jerusalem, the holy city. The uncircumcised and defiled will not enter you again.

Shake off your dust; rise up, sit enthroned, O Jerusalem. Free yourself from the chains on your neck, O captive Daughter of Zion (Isa. 52:1-2, NIV).

Chapters Two through Five of this writing carried the theme, "Awake, O Zion"!

Chapter Two encouraged us to awake with *new faith,* even though it's still dark out there! The biblical examples of the four lepers of Samaria, the apostle Peter walking on the water, and Mary Magdalene arising on resurrection morning when it was yet dark, inspired us to rise above the mediocrity of our peers. Only radical disciples who love God more than themselves or the opinions of others will follow on to know the Lord, even though all is not clear, and we don't have all the answers. We have a compass, not a map. The Holy Spirit alone is our Guide, our sole sense of direction.

Chapter Three boldly declared that we are to awake with *new courage,* though we might find ourselves to be "one among a thousand" (Job 33:23). Adam, the old man, is asleep and drunk in the night. Christ, the new Man, is awake and sober in the Day. The "drunkards of Ephraim" (Isa. 28:1), the fading flower of the old order, will not achieve their purpose. Their covenant with death and hell will be broken. We shall not all sleep. Zion's sons will put on incorruption and immortality.

Chapter Four gave us a *new perspective*. Zion is the "church of the firstborn" (Heb. 12:23), and Zion represents the corporate Overcomer within the Church (Rev. 2-3). Zion is a *place*, as revealed throughout the Book of Isaiah. Zion is represented by the Most Holy Place in Moses' Tabernacle, "the secret place of the Most High" (Ps. 91:1).

Chapter Five urged us on to *new relationships*. Zion is also an overcoming *people*, as seen throughout the Book of Psalms. Among many examples, the Bible reveals the sons of Zion to be Joel's army (Joel 2:2-11), the Manchild Company (Rev. 12:1-5), and the 144,000 who stand on Mount Zion with the slain Lamb (Rev. 14:1-5).

An Overview of the Book of Joel

Chapters Six through Eight covered the first section of our exegesis of the Book of Joel (Joel 1:1-20)—Part One is *Desolation*.

Chapter Six presented desolation's *cry* (Joel 1:1-3). We began by introducing Joel, the man and the book. The prophet's cry models the cry of the "whole creation" to be delivered from futility and the bondage of corruption (Rom. 8:22).

Chapter Seven revealed the *cause* of desolation (Joel 1:4-7). The nationwide crisis in Joel's day was brought on by a swarming plague of locusts, compounded by drought and consequent famine. The spiritual counterpart of that hellish horde is *religious tradition*, which has devastated and laid waste the Church for 2,000 years.

Chapter Eight showed the incredible *calamity* of this widespread desolation (Joel 1:8-20). Everyone and everything was impacted and wasted. No one and nothing was exempt. The harvest was ruined, especially the corn, the wine, and the oil.

Chapters Nine through Thirteen covered the second section of the Book of Joel (Joel 2:1-32)—Part Two is *Consecration*.

Chapter Nine set forth consecration's *alarm*, and announced the theme of this writing: "Blow the trumpet in Zion... sound the alarm..." (Joel 2:1). An in-depth study of the Feast of Trumpets

(Num. 10:1-10) persuaded us to hear the sound of the trumpet before it becomes an alarm.

Chapter Ten was all about a consecrated *army* (Joel 2:2-11). The prophet's detailed description of the locust army provides rich insight into our understanding of the corporate Overcomer, Joel's Army. This Firstfruits Company makes the initial consecration to God, and qualifies as His corporate instrument to minister that new-found life to the rest of creation.

Chapter Eleven is the pivotal section of the entire Book of Joel. It showed consecration's *appeal* (Joel 2:12-17)—"sanctify a fast, call a solemn assembly" (Joel 2:15). Trumpets called us to this Feast Day of Atonement (Lev. 16), the time when we afflict our souls and humble ourselves before God (2 Chron. 7:14). The priests, the leaders, are to weep between the porch and the altar.

Chapter Twelve illustrated how this brokenness immediately *affected* the whole society (Joel 2:18-27). What a glorious aftereffect! Everything turned. The Day of the Lord is a day of reversals, wherein the Lord turns the captivity of Zion (Ps. 126:1-2). The pouring out of the former rain and the latter rain will break the famine and restore the harvest. The Lord will restore the years that the locust has eaten (Joel 2:25).

Chapter Thirteen, consecration's *anointing* (Joel 2:28-32), is repeated almost verbatim in Acts 2:14-21. We cannot make this consecration in our own strength. Only the Holy Spirit can reveal the present condition of the Church, enable and empower us to this place of complete surrender, and bring about the reality of revival, restoration, and reformation (Zech. 4:6). His coming means lights out for the old order. God will pour out His Spirit upon all flesh!

Chapters Fourteen through Sixteen comprised the third and final section of the Book of Joel (Joel 3:1-21)—Part Three is *Restoration*.

Chapter Fourteen is restoration's *vindication* (Joel 3:1-8). All the "nations" (Joel 3:2)—every denomination, every imagination, and every divination—are to be dealt with. God brings again the captivity of Judah and Jerusalem, especially the children, as He judges Tyre, Sidon, and Palestine, a picture of all those who dare to come against Zion, the people for His name.

Chapter Fifteen brought everyone and everything to restoration's *valley* (Joel 3:9-15), the Valley of Jehoshaphat, the "valley of decision" (Joel 3:14). Jehovah declared His "holy war" against everything wicked. He invited His "mighty men," His Army, to participate in this judgment.

Chapter Sixteen brings resolution and consummation—Zion's complete *victory* (Joel 3:16-21). Once the "nations" have been judged, along with Egypt (the world) and Edom (the flesh), the new wine, the milk, and the rivers of Judah will flow once again. All of the old will have passed away, and Judah and Jerusalem (Zion) will remain—an unshakeable Kingdom! God will cleanse our blood and we shall live. The Lord dwells in Zion, the chosen place of His eternal habitation!

The Seventh Month

Then Solomon assembled the elders of Israel, and all the heads of the tribes, the chief of the fathers of the children of Israel, unto king Solomon in Jerusalem, that they might bring up the ark of the covenant of the Lord out of the city of David, which is Zion.

And all the men of Israel assembled themselves unto king Solomon at the feast in the month Ethanim, which is the seventh month (1 Kings 8:1-2).

The "seventh month" in Israel's religious calendar, the season for the Feast of Tabernacles, was "Tishri." Only here in 1 Kings 8:2 is it also called "Ethanim."

"Ethanim" is transliterated from *'Eythaniym* (Strong's #388), and it means, "the permanent brooks; enduring." The seventh Jewish month, corresponding to our modern October to November, was so named because permanent streams still flowed. It is derived from *'eythan* (Strong's #386), which means, "to continue; permanence, permanent; perpetual, constant, perennial, ever-flowing; specifically, a chieftain." The latter is translated as, "hard, mighty, rough, strength, strong."

But let judgment run down as waters, and righteousness as a mighty (ever-flowing, continual) *stream* (Amos 5:24).

The primary idea here is that of *endurance!* We are to "abide" (stay, remain) in Christ (John 15:1-11).[1]

We must be willing to embrace the truths of the seventh month, and then endure or continue throughout that season. We must hear the blowing of the trumpets (on the first day), stay on and humble ourselves in the Feast Day of Atonement (the tenth day), and then persist for the entire Feast of Tabernacles.

The fruit of our endurance will be His enduring or abiding presence that never ends! The Lord will dwell in Zion!

And ye shall be hated of all men for My name's sake: but he that endureth to the end shall be saved (Matt. 10:22).

Labour not for the meat which perisheth, but for that meat which endureth unto (into) *everlasting life, which the Son of man shall give unto you: for him hath God the Father sealed* (John 6:27).

There are three kinds of people in the Church. They reveal three reactions or responses to the gospel of the Kingdom and the principles of present truth as set forth in this writing.

First, some never hear the trumpet's alarm because they don't believe in real prophets. They stopped at the Feast of Passover in the first month, or the Feast of Pentecost in the third month. The "any-minute," pre-tribulation rapture theory, along with all the other trappings of dispensationalism, has robbed them of their inheritance as the Seed of Abraham and the Seed of David (compare Jeroboam's false Feast of Tabernacles in 1 Kings 12:26-33).

Second, some hear the joyful sound and respond, but later faint on the way to Zion. As with Naomi (Ruth 1:11-15), they disqualify themselves because of bitterness, blaming God and others for their own unwise choices. Essentially self-centered, these folks have focused on their suffering, and not His grace. They have moved out of rest, and have stopped flowing in and with God. Behind their every excuse is a lack of desire.

Third, overcomers hear and respond to Zion's call, and endure to the end. Their fruit remains. Like the second group, they experience incredible tests and trials, but cast all their care upon the Lord. In spite of overwhelming opposition, we are still flowing!

Nothing has diminished the river of God into or out of our lives and ministries.

How about you, friend? How about you, preacher? Have you made it to the seventh month? Can you hear the trumpet blowing in Zion? Can you hear me? If so, are you still flowing, still praising Him, or are you mad at God and everybody else?

Do you have a personal passion for the real gospel of the Kingdom? Are you relentlessly pursuing truth? Are you still in love with Jesus, the King of Zion? Will you follow Him all the way (Rev. 14:4)?

Enlarge My Borders

To all those who have made it to the seventh month, and who have endured, be encouraged to press all the way up to Zion.

And Jabez was more honourable than his brethren: and his mother called his name Jabez, saying, Because I bare him with sorrow.

And Jabez called on the God of Israel, saying, Oh that Thou wouldest bless me indeed, and enlarge my coast, and that Thine hand might be with me, and that Thou wouldest keep me from evil, that it may not grieve me! And God granted him that which he requested (1 Chron. 4:9-10).

The first nine chapters of First Chronicles are not easy reading. They mundanely give name after name in the genealogies of Judah. I call them the Old Testament "begat-itudes."

Right in the middle of this long, drawn-out list (he lived, he died; he lived, he died), like a great tree arising from the earth, one name stands forth, immediately different from the rest—"and Jabez was more honourable than his brethren."

Why is this man, a divine interjection into the man-made order, unlike all the rest who simply lived and died?

First, there *is* a "high calling." Jabez was more "honourable" than his peers. This Hebrew word for "glory" reveals the "weighty" or "heavy" glory of the high calling and the burdensome price to pay for it! (Phil. 3:12-14; Rev. 14:1-5).

Jabez was born in "sorrow" (pain, labor). His very name means, "to grieve, sorrowful; causing pain or travail." This reveals the principle of sonship as seen in Jesus, "the Man of sorrows" (Isa. 53:3); and in His overcoming brethren who are conformed to His image (Rev. 12:1-5). Those who know the greatest sorrow and travail of soul shall also know the greatest joy (John 16:21; Heb. 1:9; 12:1-2).

Jabez was born in obscurity. We know nothing of Jabez's history or family. He was known only in the eyes of God, one of God's "are nots" (1 Cor. 1:26-29).

Jabez, like Joel, cried out with passion, calling on the name of the Lord. The word "oh" reveals the intensity and anguish of his soul.[2]

Jabez' passion was God-ward, directed alone to Him. Like Jesus, Jabez only wanted what God desired or willed (see John 4:34; 5:30; 6:38; 8:29; 15:10; 17:4).

Jabez' request matched his calling—"Enlarge my coasts (borders)!" His was a passion for enlargement. The word "enlarge" in 1 Chronicles 4:10 means, "increase; be (or become) great, many, much, numerous; to multiply (used of people, animals, or things); to make large; to make much to do; to do much."

Jabez understood God's "hand" of discipline, the importance of restraint, correction, and adjustment (Ps. 145:15-16; Eph. 4:11; 1 Pet. 5:6).

Jabez prayed to be delivered from the "evil" of mediocrity. This word means, "to spoil (literally, by breaking to pieces); bad, unpleasant, evil (giving pain, unhappiness, misery), distress, injury, calamity." He did not want to be "grieved" (to carve, fabricate, fashion, shape or form; hence, to worry, vex, torture, pain or anger). Jabez refused to be marked or scarred with an ordinary frame of mind. He knew that there was something more for him in God!

And God granted him (to bring, or cause to come in, to gather, to bring to pass) *that which he requested* (1 Chron. 4:10).

Take heart, you sons of Zion. God will answer our prayer! Though things look bleak to the natural eye, Heaven knows that "the whole earth *is* full of His glory" (Isa. 6:3).

We have heard the voice of the *shophar* and have taken our place in Jehovah's Army.

We have experienced the brokenness and humiliation of the "solemn assembly" (Joel 2:15). We have afflicted our souls.

The time to favor Zion has come. Take your seat beside your King. We who have heard the trumpet sound have now *become* His voice in the earth. *Blow the trumpet in Zion! Sound the alarm throughout His holy mountain!*

ENDNOTES

1. We are to "abide" in Christ. Note these uses of the Greek word *meno*, which means, "to stay in a given place, state, relation, or expectancy" (see Matt. 26:38; John 15:4-7,9-10,16; Rom. 9:11; 1 Cor. 3:14; 13:13; 2 Cor. 3:11; 2 Tim. 3:14; Heb. 13:1; 1 John 2:14,27; 4:12-16; and 2 John 1:9).

2. Note these other cries of "Oh" (see 1 Chron. 11:17; Job 6:8; Ps.14:7; 107:8; and Isa. 64:1).

APPENDIX

−A−

Prophecy given to Dr. Kelley Varner by Pastor William Hinn on the evening of February 20, 2004:

NOTE: This word from the Lord was uttered in the Friday evening service at Rivers of Life Church, Macclesfield, North Carolina, with host pastors Donald and Joann Harrell. It is noteworthy that among all the men and women who gathered at that meeting that I was the only one who received a personal word of prophecy from Pastor Hinn.

PRAYER: "...Lord, in Jesus' mighty Name, let the year 2004 be a year of restoration, be a year of harvest. Church, agree with me. Lord, in the Name of Jesus, let it be the year that brings back that which is right in Your sight. We've had so many times and so many seasons pass us by with so many people running through. So many times that we thought we did it right, only to end up back where we started all over again. Stripping after stripping, purging after purging. Change what You must change in us to break us out of the cycle. Do what You must do, until there comes a freshness with that which we say is what You do.

"Lord, in the mighty Name of Jesus, as You raised Lazarus on the fourth day, let this year of 2004 be the year of our resurrection. Come on, Church, agree that we are not dependent on who will approve of us, or disapprove of us. We are not dependent upon somebody opening the door, or of somebody giving us the money. We are not dependent upon someone doing something for us. Lord, let us be dependent on the authority that You placed in our mouth, that in the Name of Jesus, no powers of Heaven, no powers of hell, shall be able to stand, Lord, except by the Word that proceeds out of our mouth. For there is nothing greater than the power of Your authority. You've shown us no greater demonstration of Your power than you did in the resurrection. All the creation of all creation, all the creation of Heaven and Earth, and the stars of Heaven, do not compare to the power of resurrection. Everything that we see has been created by Your Word, for that which You raise no man can kill..."

PROPHECY: "Father, I pray for my brother, Kelley, this Your friend and my friend; this faithful servant, this man that has toiled and labored in the fields for many years; this man that knows the heights and the lows, this man that understands and has learned how to abound and how to be abased, that this shall be the year...

"I declare to you in the Name of Jesus, servant of God, this shall be the year of your resurrection. This shall be the year where all that which opposed you shall not be able to stand with you. And I have removed from your midst all that which has wounded you. I have even removed that which has robbed from you!

"But I declare unto you that there shall be a generation that shall come and stand by your side and under your own wings. There shall be even children in comparison to that which is old. They shall be the young, and they shall be the child-like, but they shall hear what the old could not hear, and they shall obey the way that they could never obey.

"And I declare to you that the four winds of Heaven shall begin to blow upon your House, and your words shall reach the north, and the south, and the east, and the west, and even unto the nations it shall go, and you shall no longer be dependent on who will come and who will accept and who will receive, but your words shall not fall to the ground, and it shall reach the ears of them that I have prepared them for.

"And the name Kelley Varner shall not be an old name of an old book of an old generation, but today it shall be unto the young, unto the youth, and it shall cause your heart to leap with great joy. And even many that have walked away shall stand in awe and see what I will accomplish. That which I have begun, says the Lord, I will finish. That which is Mine no one can take from Me, and that which I have approved no one can disannul.

"That which I have placed in you shall continue to spring out, and that which I have formed within your spirit shall be multiplied. Your children's children shall declare the glory of God, and you shall stand and see it with your own eyes.

"No, you will not die. You will live! They tried to kill you, but they can't because I have killed you already, and I am raising you up. And they shall know the authority that is in you by the resurrection power that is in you.

"This is the year of your resurrection, man of God. I know it's been long. I know the years have been hard, but I declare to you, 'Stand still, and see the salvation of the Lord.'

"What you are about to see you have never seen, in Jesus' mighty Name!"

CAROLINA LEADERSHIP INST.
(CLI)
(A Third Day Finishing School)

CAROLINA LEADERSHIP INSTITUTE is a vision and concept of an apostolic burden and mandate to impart the "word of the Kingdom" to the Carolinas and the nations.

> Acts 19:8-10 NIV
>
> *Paul entered the synagogue and spoke boldly there for three months, arguing persuasively about the kingdom of God.*
>
> *But some of them became obstinate; they refused to believe and publicly maligned the way. So Paul left them. He took the disciples with him and had discussions daily in the lecture hall of Tyrannus.*
>
> *This went on for two years, so that all the Jews and Greeks who lived in the province of Asia heard the word of the Lord.*

Our short-term goal is to impart a biblical foundation for understanding and expressing Kingdom principles through periodic weekend seminars called "Kingdom Institutes." The participants for these initial "Institutes" will be drawn from five fold ministries and other church leaders throughout the Eastern Carolina region.

Our long-term goal is to establish a School of the Bible through which a residential and on-line course of study would equip individuals for Kingdom ministry. This more traditional approach to Bible training would reach out to individuals who are answering a vocational call to ministry and those who seek to be more equipped for ministry in their local church setting.

Contact information:
CAROLINA LEADERSHIP INSTITUTE
Wendall S. Ward, Jr.
P.O. Box 1599
Richlands, NC 28574
Phone 910.324.5026
E-mail: CLI2002@earthlink.net

TAPE CATALOG

To receive a full listing of Pastor Varner's books and tapes (audio and video), or information about our Tape of the Month and Seminars and Conferences, write or call for our current catalog:

PRAISE TABERNACLE
P.O. Box 785
Richlands, NC 28574-0785

Phone: 910-324-5026 or 324-5027
FAX: 910-324-1048

E-mail: praiztab1@earthlink.net
OR kvarner2@earthlink.net

Internet: www.kelleyvarner.org (Order on-line), or
www.ptmrichlands.org

E-MAIL NEWSLETTER

Subscribe to Pastor Varner's weekly E-mail newsletter, "The Praise Report," a resource for leaders, at www.kelleyvarner.org

TAPE OF THE MONTH

Two cassette tapes (including sermon notes) by Pastor Varner and other ministries are available each month on a monthly or annual offering basis. Write or call to join this growing family of listeners.

CONFERENCES AND SEMINARS

A variety of regional and national gatherings happen throughout the year here at Praise Tabernacle and the Crystal Coast Conference Center. Pastor Varner and the apostolic ministry team at Praise Tabernacle are also available for ministry in your church and local area.

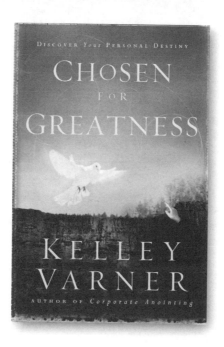

MOSES, THE MASTER, AND THE MANCHILD

The seed is buried in the bed of humanity. It grew out of Moses. It blossomed in the Son and it is to be revealed in the Manchild-the mature, victorious Church of the end of the age. You are about to be given prophetic keys that unlock the mysteries of the end times. Discover how Moses, our Lord Jesus, and the mighty victorious Church of the last days paint a picture of hope, power, and glory for God's people. You will be left breathless as this prophetic writer cuts through the confusion and fear surrounding the times in which we live. Be prepared to see and understand the end of the age like never before. Be prepared to discover your role during the most incredible time in history to be alive.

ISBN 0-7684-2121-7

Available at your local Christian bookstore.